D1271956

DE PROPRIETATIBUS LITTERARUM

edenda curat

C. H. VAN SCHOONEVELD

Indiana University

Series Maior, 19

REPRESENTATIVE SHORT STORY CYCLES OF THE TWENTIETH CENTURY

Studies in a Literary Genre

by

FORREST L. INGRAM
Loyola University, New Orleans

1971
MOUTON
THE HAGUE · PARIS

LIBRARY OF CONGRESS CATALOG CARD NUMBER: 75-159465

Printed in The Netherlands by Mouton & Co., Printers, The Hague.

To my mother and father

A Sportsman's Sketches
may well be the greatest book
of short stories
ever written.
Nobody,
at the time it was written,
knew
quite how great it was,
or
what influence it was to have
in the creation
of
a new art form.

Frank O'Connor,
The Lonely Voice

ACKNOWLEDGEMENTS

Few if any insights into literature arise in a vacuum. The valid insights in this study certainly did not. Therefore, I would like to acknowledge generally, at the head of this study, my debt to countless scholars who, through their serious examinations of individual works, have made historically possible this present synthesis and my discovery of the short story cycle genre.

On a more personal level, I want to thank publicly those professors who, during my undergraduate years, made literature "come alive" for me, and who, through their concern for exact analysis and thorough research, have nurtured in me a similar spirit: first of all, to Fr. Edward J. Romagosa, S.J., the inspiring teacher who first called to my attention the critical importance of literary genres; to Professors William Sessions, Auguste C. Coyle, S.J., and the late Edward B. Moody, S.J. (all of Spring Hill College) who led me to a deeper penetration of literature; and finally, to Professors Charles Boyle, Daniel P. Deneau, and J. Franklin Murray, S.J., who, as teachers, advisers, and friends, encouraged me to pursue further studies in comparative literature.

For the financial assistance to enable me to continue my studies, I am thankful to the Department of Health, Education, and Welfare, who (through the University of Southern California) granted me a three-year fellowship under the National Defense Education Act, Title IV. I am also grateful to the Woodrow Wilson Foundation for offering me a fellowship and for accepting me as an Honorary Woodrow Wilson Fellow.

To the Program of Comparative Literature at the University of Southern California, I owe a special debt of gratitude both for recommending that I be granted the NDEA Title IV fellowship and for providing learned and congenial professors, in dialogue with whom I have grown not only in knowledge, but also in appreciation of literature. Among the professors in the comparative literature program to whom I am particularly grateful are Professors David H. Malone (Chairman), Norma Lorre Goodrich, René Bellé, Gerald Gillespie, James Bailey, Hildegard Platzer (Collins) Brownfield, Edward Phinney, Eleazer Lecky, Arthur Knodel, Harold von Hofe, and Paul Hadley.

Very special thanks are due to Professor Malone, the director of my dissertation, for long hours spent in consultation, blue-penciling, rereading drafts, and suggesting further revisions; to Professor N. L. Goodrich, who first encouraged me in my choice of a topic, and whose detailed criticism of my work has made it possible significantly to reduce errors, infelicitous wording, and obscurities in my final draft; and to Professor Harold von Hofe, whose comments, especially on the Kafka chapter, have been most helpful.

Many of the insights and clarifications which appear in my study originated in dialogue with my fellow graduate students at the University of Southern California. I am especially grateful to them for their friendship, critical acumen, and love of literature. In their presence, I was always aware that the study of literature is a community enterprise.

I am further grateful to Professors Malcolm Cowley, Warren French, and Robert Fitzgerald for kindly answering my letters, for encouraging me in the study I had undertaken, and for offering me their further assistance.

Finally, I would like to thank Miss Barbara Frank for her research assistance; Mrs. Maxine Royds for long hours of labor at the typewriter; and Fr. Arthur Rutledge, S.J., of Loyola University, for handling many details for me while I was living in Europe.

Without the assistance of these men and women, this initial study of the SHORT STORY CYCLE would not now be finished. For their help, suggestions, encouragement, friendships, criticism, and corrections, I am deeply grateful. The errors and weaknesses in this study I acknowledge as fully my own.

TABLE OF CONTENTS

I

INTRODUCTION: THEORY AND PERSPECTIVE

A story cycle is a set of stories so linked to one another that the reader's experience of each one is modified by his experience of the others. Whether in prose or verse or both, story cycles have emerged from the center of the literary ferment of their times. They flowed from the creative ingenuity of such internationally esteemed authors as Homer, Ovid, Boccaccio, Chaucer, Pushkin, Daudet, Turgenev, Browning, Keller, Joyce, Hemingway, Faulkner, and Camus. Story cycles present, *en masse*, a formidable body of impressive and immensely entertaining literature. Nevertheless, literary critics and theorists, in their general treatments of fiction – its forms, craft, techniques, structure, norms, rhetoric, art, development, and history – show little or no interest in the story cycle as a genre. As yet, no attempt has been made to examine systematically the characteristics or range of the story cycle, to understand its dynamics and structure, or to trace its mutations from author to author and century to century.[1]

While each story in a cycle may be relatively simple, the dynamics of the cycle itself often poses a major challenge to the critic. Like the moving parts of a mobile, the interconnected parts of some story cycles seem to shift their positions with relation to the other parts, as the cycle moves forward in its typical pattern of recurrent development. Shifting internal relationships, of course, continually alter the originally perceived pattern of the whole cycle. A cycle's form is elusive. Its patterns must be studied in detail and as the cycle progresses from first story to last.

Modern genre theory, according to René Wellek and Austin Warren,

> is, clearly, descriptive. It doesn't limit the number of possible kinds and doesn't prescribe rules to authors. It supposes that traditional kinds may be "mixed" and produce a new kind.... It sees that genres can be built up on the basis of

[1] A beginning has been made in an unpublished dissertation by Friedrich Weltz, "Vier amerikanische Erzählungszyklen" (Universität München, 1953). Though my study was almost completed by the time this work arrived into my hands, I have tried to incorporate Weltz's findings into my treatment. (See bibliography.)

inclusiveness or "richness" as well as that of "purity" (genre by accretion as well as by reduction) ... it is interested in finding the common denominator of a kind, its shared literary devices and literary purposes.[2]

Every literary genre boasts a number of works which theorists consider to be central to that genre's tradition. If we pictured the panorama of short story cycles as a spectrum, the limit of one extreme of the spectrum would be the "mere" collection of unconnected stories, while the limit of the other extreme would be the novel.

I have chosen for extended analysis three cycles which show the range, versatility, and characteristics of the twentieth-century short story cycle. Kafka's *Ein Hungerkünstler* stands near one extreme of the spectrum. Most critics discuss it as a mere *Sammlung*. Yet *Ein Hungerkünstler* displays "both a consistency of theme and a development from one story to the next"[3] that compel us to place it within the short story cycle genre. Competent critics such as Hyatt Waggoner[4] and Cleanth Brooks[5] have described Faulkner's *The Unvanquished* as a novel. Yet Faulkner conceived it as a series of stories, and the book's structure adequately substantiates his view. Each of the book's major divisions is a relatively independent, self-contained short story. Faulkner's cycle may be used to delineate the other extreme of the spectrum.

Although Anderson's *Winesburg, Ohio* has baffled and exasperated several of its critics, only a rash few try to locate it within the novel genre. None has failed to perceive in it a certain unity of character, theme, setting, and symbolism. Anderson himself broadcast his achievement as a triumph to be imitated by the younger generation of writers. As an ardent admirer of Turgenev's *A Sportsman's Sketches* and as an original genius in his own right, he transmitted as well as helped to form the cyclic tradition in America. Further, since his handling of setting, action, theme, time, character, and symbol all show the typical pattern of story cycles, that is, of recurrence and development as an integrated movement, his *Winesburg* best represents the center of the short story cycle spectrum.

2 René Wellek and Austin Warren, *Theory of Literature* (New York, 1956), p. 225.

3 Jean A. Morrison, "Kafka as Hungerkünstler" (unpublished dissertation, Tulane University, 1963), p. 97.

4 H. H. Waggoner, *William Faulkner: From Jefferson to the World* (Lexington, Kentucky, 1959).

5 Cleanth Brooks, *William Faulkner, The Yoknapatawpha Country* (New Haven and London, 1963).

A. DEFINITIONS AND DIVISIONS

Critics of cyclic literature frequently shape their definitions of CYCLE to suit their particular purposes. Helen M. Mustard, for instance, writing a critical history of *The Lyric Cycle in German Literature*,[6] chooses a broad meaning for her term "lyric cycle". A lyric cycle, she says, is "a group of poems indicated by their author as belonging together". Later in her study, she modifies her use of the term so that it means "a group of poems linked to a central concept and to each other in such a way as to maintain a balance between the individuality of the poem and the necessities of the larger unit". P. M. Kramer,[7] on the other hand, applies the term "cycle" to story collections but then only to such tightly organized works as Gottfried Keller's *Das Sinngedicht*, in which the "action of the story returns to its starting point after having progressed circuitously through several stages".

My purposes approximate those of Helen Mustard more than those of P. M. Kramer. I have begun my investigations, therefore, with an inclusive rather than an exclusive definition. By gradually paring away nonessential characteristics from essential ones, by comparing and contrasting, dividing and subdividing, I seek to arrive at a profile of the story-cycle genre in the twentieth century.

A STORY CYCLE, then, is a set of stories linked to each other in such a way as to maintain a balance between the individuality of each of the stories and the necessities of the larger unit.[8]

Such a "set" (series or group) of stories could be collected or uncol-

[6] (Morningside Heights, N.Y., 1946), p. 1.

[7] (New York, 1939), p. 5. See also Joachim Müller, "Das zyklische Prinzip in der Lyrik", *Germanisch-Romanische Monatsschrift*, XX (1932), 1-20.

[8] In this general definition, stories could be in prose or verse, by one author or more, collected or uncollected. They could be tales, anecdotes, fables, Märchen, epic episodes, gestes, or formal short stories. They could even be novels. TALES are simple narratives in prose or verse, without complicated plot or tight-knit structures, amenable to digressions, and usually with an emphasis on the action-element. ANECDOTES are short narratives detailing particulars of an interesting episode or event, often in the life of a well-known historical or fictional person. FABLES are brief tales, either in prose or verse, told to point a moral, usually by instructive comparison. MÄRCHEN are folk tales dealing with the marvelous. GESTES are tales of war or adventure. THE FORMAL SHORT STORY is a condensed fictional narrative in prose, having a definite formal development. Wallace Stegner in "Teaching the Short Story" (Davis, California, 1965), writes that "there may be a number of kinds of short stories, but all demand an intense concision and economy, and all must somehow achieve a satisfying sense of finality. Beyond that I don't think we should define or prescribe" (p. 11). I agree with Professor Stegner. When I use the term "short story" in my text, I refer to the general meaning of "formal short story" as elucidated above.

lected. Salinger's Glass family stories and Fitzgerald's Basil Duke Lee stories,[9] though linked by repetition of characters, have never been collected into a single volume. I have chosen to exclude from my discussion this kind of cycle (a twentieth-century counterpart to the ancient epic cycle) because it does not raise the question of specific aesthetic pattern, and so cannot help us to discover to what kind of structure the term "cycle" applies.

Sets of stories may be "collected" by an editor or by an editor-author or by a single author. While the collections of linked stories by a single author stand a greater chance of displaying traits of cyclic COMPOSITION than collections by editors or editor-authors, single authorship of the individual pieces should not be a final criterion separating a short story cycle from either a "mere" collection of stories or a novel. For the purposes of investigating twentieth-century short story cycles, however, I have chosen only sets of stories which the respective authors have indicated belong in one volume.

Editors who collect stories into a single volume base their choice of entries on a variety of criteria. There are collections of humorous stories, war stories, horror stories, detective stories and so forth. A collection based, for example, only on such a nebulous unifying element as the fact that the authors represented were all recipients of the Nobel Prize for Literature can hardly boast a sufficient unity to merit inclusion in a study of story cycles. Zola's *Les Soirées de Médan* (1880)[10] and the interconnected series by various hands entitled *The New Decameron* (1919-

9 I want to thank Professor Malcolm Cowley for pointing out Fitzgerald's Basil Duke Lee stories as an example of an "interesting cycle never published as a separate book". Cowley recognizes that the cycle of stories is "a form between the novel and the mere collection of stories". He sees that the magazines' demands for series of stories about the same characters or the same background was a strong influence on the appearance of such story series as Poe's Dupin stories, *The Country of the Pointed Firs*, Cable's *Old Creole Days*, Kate Chopin's *Bayou Folk*, Crane's Whilomville stories, the Scattergood Baines stories, the Octavus Roy Cohen stories, *Get Rich Quick Wallingford*, *Potash and Perlmutter*, Booth Tarkington's *Penrod*, and many others. Cowley says that Faulkner took advantage of the opportunities this form offered in *The Unvanquished*, *Go Down, Moses*, *The Hamlet* ("which is more a cycle of stories than a novel"), *Knight's Gambit*, and *Big Woods* (Letter to me, June 23, 1966).

10 A collection of naturalistic short stories with a military setting. The collection was engineered by Zola, and the stories in it were written by five authors who were his disciples at that time. Zola's own story, it was agreed, would come first and set the scene for the others. The stories as they appeared were Émile Zola, "L'Attaque au moulin"; Guy de Maupassant, "Boule-de-suif"; J. K. Huysmans, "Sac au dos"; Henry Céard, "La Saignée"; Léon Hennique, "L'Affaire du grand 7"; and Paul Alexis, "Après la bataille". I am grateful to Professor N. L. Goodrich for pointing out this volume to me.

1925)[11] do, however, deserve closer inspection as story cycles.

Editor-authors take already existing materials and rewrite them into a connected series of stories. In fact, story cycles probably originated this way. Homer's *Odyssey*, Ovid's *Metamorphoses*, Boccaccio's *Decameron*, Chaucer's *The Canterbury Tales*, the Indian *Panchatantra*, the Arabian *A Thousand and One Nights*, and Malory's *Morte d'Arthur* all share this fundamental similarity. The fact that the original stories arose from folk imagination, from the collective effort of many people, gave each a separate identity, a uniqueness, and an independence which then was subsumed and integrated into a whole, by a single author who modified and retold the stories as he fitted them into his own design. Within this general tradition, some twentieth-century writers (such as Faulkner and Joyce) at times reworked and retold in a new setting stories from the ancient past or from their own previous writings.

Twentieth-century short story cycles, though composed by a single author, pattern themselves on the story cycles of the past. They struggle to maintain a balanced tension between the demands of each short story and the patterning of the whole cycle. Anderson's "new looseness of form", though as old as the *Odyssey*, has adapted itself to include the tightest of twentieth-century prose-fiction forms: the short story.

Linked stories may have been COMPOSED as a continuous whole, or ARRANGED into a series, or COMPLETED to form a set.[12] A composed cycle is one which the author had conceived as a whole from the time he wrote its first story. As story follows story in the series, the author allows himself to be governed by the demands of some master plan, or at least by a unifying directional impulse. Keller's *Das Sinngedicht*, as Kramer has shown, follows this pattern. Composed cycles normally tend to be more highly unified than the arranged or completed variety; one thinks of

11 *The New Decameron* (Oxford, 1919-1925); Vol. I, "Prologue and First Day", 1919; Vol. II, "The Second Day", 1920; Vol. III, "The Third Day" (containing stories by Compton Mackenzie, J. D. Beresford, Desmond Coke, D. H. Lawrence, Michael Sadleir, Storm Jameson, Robert Keable, V. Sackville Wert, and Bill Nobbs), 1922; Vol. IV, "The Fourth Day", ed. Blair (containing stories by J. D. Beresford, Storm Jameson, Robert Keable, D. H. Lawrence, Michael Sadleir, Horace Horsnell, Edgell Rickword, L. A. G. Strong, and Blair), 1925. The basic "frame story" is a continental tour, directed by Hector Turpin, Esq., of "Turpin's Temperamental Tours". When the ship on which they are to depart breaks down and is delayed for two hours, Hector poses to his tourees that they imitate the fictive characters in Boccaccio's *Decameron*, and entertain one another with stories.

12 "Composed Cycles" and "Arranged Cycles" are terms borrowed from Helen W. Mustard's *The Lyric Cycle in German Literature*. Her terminology is helpful but not complete. I myself have added the third division.

Steinbeck's *Tortilla Flat* and Lagerlöf's *The Story of Gösta Berling*. On the other hand, Steinbeck's *The Pastures of Heaven*, though created according to a master plan, seems "looser" in its form than such a "completed" cycle as Faulkner's *The Unvanquished*. From the beginning, Anderson vaguely conceived his *Winesburg* as a unified whole. But his general plan included no detailed outline of his stories. He had to rearrange and "complete" his cycle before he could publish it as a unit.

An arranged cycle consists of stories which an author or editor-author has brought together to illuminate or comment upon one another by juxtaposition or association. The criteria for such "arrangements" are varied: repetition of a single theme (Flannery O'Connor's *Everything That Rises Must Converge*),[13] recurrence of a single character or set of characters (Erskine Caldwell's *Georgia Boy*), or even a grouping of representatives of a single generation (Fitzgerald's *All the Sad Young Men* and *Tales of the Jazz Age*). For obvious reasons, arranged cycles are usually the loosest cycle forms.

The three short story cycles I have chosen to treat in detail are all "completed cycles". By completed cycles I mean sets of linked stories which are neither strictly composed nor merely arranged. They may have begun as independent dissociated stories. But soon their author became conscious of unifying strands which he may have, even subconsciously, woven into the action of the stories. Consciously, then, he completed the unifying task which he may have subconsciously begun.

The process of completion may consist merely in adding stories which collect, develop, intensify, and extend the thematic patterns of the earlier stories in the series (*Ein Hungerkünstler*); or it may include extensive revisions of earlier stories in the cycle (*The Unvanquished*); or, finally, it may also entail regrouping and rearranging (*Winesburg, Ohio*). *Winesburg* began as a "composed" cycle with a loose plan. Anderson had to "complete" it, to round it off, before publishing it as a cycle. Other important examples of "completed" cycles are Joyce's *Dubliners* and Steinbeck's *The Red Pony*.

[13] (New York, 1965). Some of the stories appeared between 1956 and 1962 in *Kenyon Review*, *New World Writing*, *Partisan Review*, *Esquire*, and *Harper's Bazaar*. Professor Robert Fitzgerald, in a letter to me (June 30, 1966), assures me that Flannery O'Connor had planned the order of the stories in this collection and had intended it for publication in that order. Exception must be made for the last two stories, "Parker's Back" and "Judgement Day", which were the last two stories she ever wrote. Professor Fitzgerald writes that the "order of the final two stories was determined by her publisher and myself". I feel that the collection would form a more homogeneous unit if it had ended with "Revelation" ("what she heard were the voices of the souls climbing upward into het starry field and shouting hallelujah" [p. 218]).

The final phrase of our introductory definition asks that there be preserved "a balance between the individuality of each of the stories and the necessities of the larger unit". In such books as Faulkner's *The Hamlet*, one feels that the necessities of the larger unit may have triumphed over the individuality of the independent stories. In *Go Down, Moses* (except for the revised form of "The Bear") the individuality of most of the stories almost demolishes the cohesion of the larger unit.

Central to the dynamics of the short story cycle is the tension between the one and the many. When do the many cease being merely many and congeal into one? Conversely, when does a "one" become so discrete and differentiated that it dissolves into a "many"? Every story cycle displays a double tendency of asserting the individuality of its components on the one hand and of highlighting, on the other, the bonds of unity which make the many into a single whole.

In the twentieth century, the devices by which the "many" become components of the pattern of the "one" are more subtle, generally, than the devices used in past ages. Rarely today does one find so obvious a device of "framing" as in Boccaccio's *Decameron*. When it does occur, as in Bradbury's *The Illustrated Man*, one finds often enough that the framing device is the ONLY source of unity in a collection of otherwise disparate stories.

The dynamics of the twentieth-century short story cycle require a modification of our initial definition of story cycles. I will define a *short story cycle* as *a book of short stories so linked to each other by their author that the reader's successive experience on various levels of the pattern of the whole significantly modifies his experience of each of its component parts*. The new elements in our revised definition require elucidation.

For the limited purposes of my discussion, I will not be dealing with just any set of stories (Glass family stories, Basil Duke Lee stories), but only those story-groups which have been given an order, a pattern, by their author: therefore, a book. Further, I have chosen to limit my study arbitrarily only to books of short stories in the modern acceptation of that term.[14] Generally, a short story is a condensed fictional narrative

14 See n. 8. See also: Norman Friedman, "What Makes A Short Story Short?" *Modern Fiction Studies*, IV (Summer, 1958) 103-117. All of the stories I have treated in this book have been designated by major critics as "short stories" (in the general acceptation of that term as I have outlined it above). Though some critics have called Anderson's stories "tales", Joyce's "epiphanies", Camus's "nouvelles", and Kafka's "Erzählungen", I see nothing to be gained at this juncture by trying to ferret out the differentiating norms behind these various terms. My emphasis has been primarily on cyclic structure rather than on the definitions and divisions of the smaller forms which enter into the cyclic composition.

in prose, having a definite formal development. The form includes such brief presentations as Isaac Babel's "Crossing into Poland" and such longer narratives as Joyce's "The Dead".

The crucial phrase in the revised definition is "the pattern of the whole", which the reader experiences "successively" and "on various levels". This pattern structures the "many" into an integral "one", and in so doing "significantly modifies" the reader's experience of each story in the pattern. Here we are at the heart of what Helen Mustard has called the "cyclic principle". Cycles are made by establishing "such relationships among smaller entities as to create a larger whole" without at the same time destroying the identity of the smaller entities.[15]

I have borrowed the term PATTERN from E. M. Forster,[16] who in turn borrowed it from painting. I do not limit my use of that term, as he did, to the static pattern of external structure but extend it to include the dynamic patterns of internal structure. An examination of the static pattern of a short story cycle reveals a series of self-contained fictional prose-units (short stories) bound into a single volume at the author's direction. Static structure may include a framing device, or an indication of divisions by chapter-numbers or titles, or it may show an increase in length as the series progresses (*Ein Hungerkünstler*) or an alternation of stories and "interchapters" (*In Our Time*).

More important by far for determining the special kind of unity a short story cycle has are the dynamic patterns of RECURRENCE and DEVELOPMENT. The patterns of recurrence may be symmetrical (note the balance on the level of narrational technique in *Ein Hungerkünstler*, and the symmetry in thematic presentation of *The Red Pony*); or asymmetrical (see below my discussion of the "associational technique" in *Winesburg, Ohio*). The patterns of development may be linear (such as the chronologically sequential development of action in *The Unvanquished*); or multi-directional, such as thematic and symbolic expansion, or deepening and broadening of meaning in *Ein Hungerkünstler*, *L'Exil et le royaume*, and many other cycles.

Recurrence and development usually operate concurrently like the motion of a wheel. The rim of the wheel represents recurrent elements in a cycle which rotate around a thematic center. As these elements (motifs,

15 Mustard, *The Lyric Cycle in German Literature*, p. 75.

16 *Aspects of the Novel* (New York, 1927), pp. 213-242. Forster also uses the term "rhythm" to mean "repetition with variation". When I use the word "rhythm", I do not mean only REGULAR recurrence of some element, but also IRREGULAR recurrence. In music, "rhythm" applies as much to Gregorian chant as to 4/4 time.

symbols, characters, words) repeat themselves, turn in on themselves, recur, the whole wheel moves forward. The motion of a wheel is a single process. In a single process, too, the thematic core of a cycle expands and deepens as the elements of the cycle repeat themselves in varied contexts.

The dynamic pattern of recurrent development (which I will call "typically cyclic") affects the themes, leitmotifs, settings, characters, and structures of individual stories. As these elements expand their context and deepen their poetic significance, they tend to form, together, a composite myth. Kafka's narratives have been called "experimental myths", Faulkner's Yoknapatawpha County a "mythic kingdom", and Anderson's *Winesburg*, the making of a myth.[17] Realistic detail does not disrupt symbolic intent. Rather, it enhances it. Joyce's Dublin, Steinbeck's Pastures of Heaven, Camus's Algeria, Paris, and Brazil (*L'Exil et le royaume*) are all lands replete with symbolic landscape, meticulously described, but displaying details which primarily reinforce one or more dimensions of the thematic or mythic movement of the cycle. In *Dubliners*, for example, a mythic Dublin emerges through Joyce's patterning of the paralysis motif; through the symbolism of setting, movement, and color; through recurrent ecclesiastical and patriotic imagery; through repeated associations with the *Odyssey*; and through example after example of moral lassitude. *Dubliners*' complex mythi-thematic core, clothed as it is in the rich garments of Joyce's symbology and phraseology, justifies our including the volume in a treatment of short story cycles. The same may be said of *L'Exil et le royaume*. The thematic core of *Ein Hungerkünstler*, like that of *Dubliners*, is a complex interweave of antinomous attitudes toward life. Later, I will show in detail how that multi-leveled thematic center draws Kafka's four stories together and by so doing constitutes them a cycle.

Recurrent development not only operates on the level of theme, but diffuses its dynamism throughout the cycle. In the chapter on *Winesburg*, I will show in detail how the motifs of departure, adventure, dreaming, and hungering develop as they recur in story after story of the cycle; how the recurrent symbolism of setting and gesture unifies the cycle at the same time it individualizes each story; how, through typically cyclic patterns, an entire (mythic) community emerges in the mind of the cycle's narrator; and finally, how George Willard, through his reappearances in varied contexts, comes to embody the frustrated desire of Winesburg's inhabitants to break out of their perpetual adolescence and grostesquerie.

[17] The significance of such terminology is discussed in its proper place in the chapters devoted to Kafka, Faulkner, and Anderson.

In short story cycles, characters do not usually develop in the kind of single continuous process one finds most often in novels. If a character appears in more than one story of the cycle (as in *Winesburg*, *The Unvanquished*, *Gösta Berling*, *Tortilla Flat*, *Red Pony*, *My Name is Aram*, *In Our Time*), he rarely if ever occupies the center of the action in all the stories. In cycles, "minor" characters collectively receive as much, if not more, attention than do the "major" protagonists.

Character development in a cycle, when it occurs, also follows a typically cyclic pattern. "Major" protagonists become "realized" through recurrence, repetition with variation, association, and so on. But characters which in a novel would be "minor" figures are often, in a cycle, the center of interest in some particular story. Even then, they are often delineated through comparison with and contrast to the other characters in the cycle, some of whom may actively influence their growth or present condition, others of whom merely serve to deepen the reader's insight by juxtaposition. During those precious moments when the protagonist of a single story occupies the spotlight, he demands our full attention. His story can never be a digression from some kind of "main plot" of the cycle. At any given moment, the action of the cycle is centered in the action of the story which is at that moment being experienced.

Numerous and varied connective strands draw the co-protagonists of any story cycle into a single community. Some co-protagonists possess only the tenuous bond of belonging to the same generation (*All the Sad Young Men*), or to the same sex (*A Gallery of Women*), or to the same family (*Go Down, Moses*). Some are united in the connective memory of a single fictionalized narrator-participant (*The Unvanquished*, *My Name Is Aram*, *Georgia Boy*); some are members of the same (mythic) town (*Dubliners*, *Winesburg*), or live in the same general locale. Some have a similar hazy relationship with the same man (*The Pastures of Heaven*), or share the same destiny (*The Bridge of San Luis Rey*). However this community may be achieved, it usually can be said to constitute the central character of a cycle. Even *Ein Hungerkünstler* has its community of "outsiders", and *L'Exil et le royaume* its community of solitary searchers for solidarity.

Since short story cycles do not usually have a single multiple-stranded action which must taper off through climax and denouement as do most traditional novels, its typical concluding section or sections round off the themes, symbolism, and whatever patterned action the cycle possesses. The rounding off process could simply complete the design announced (subtly) in a prologue. Usually, however, it attempts to draw together in a final story or series of stories the themes and motifs, symbols, and (sometimes) characters which have been developing throughout. All three cycles I treat in detail conclude in this way.

One "rounding off" device employed frequently in cycles of the ancient past was the use of a frame. When the frame was filled, the cycle was complete. The *Rahmenerzählung* is a story which collects other stories within its frame. A *Rahmenerzählung* constitutes a cycle, however, only when the stories collected in the frame are joined together by the dynamic patterns of recurrence and development. The frame itself is merely a device which is one part of the static structure of a complex fictional narrative. It is a literary device, not a genre. One finds the device employed in novels (*Der Schimmelreiter*), in individual short stories (William Sansom's "Through the Quinquina Glass"), in poems ("Rime of the Ancient Mariner"), in collections of narrative poems (*The Ring and the Book*), and even in "mere" collections of stories (*The Illustrated Man*). The *Rahmenerzählung*-device (known in English as the "frame-story") is not, then, the same as a story cycle.[18] A final "rounding off" device, similar to the framing device just discussed, is the use of a prologue and/or an epilogue. Turgenev in *A Sportsman's Sketches* employs an epilogue, Anderson in *Winesburg* uses a story which most commentators interpret as a prologue, Hemingway in *In Our Time* uses both (he calls his epilogue "L'Envoi"). Steinbeck in *The Pastures of Heaven* also employs both.

Time patterns in a story cycle show all the vagaries of other forms of fiction. One always must distinguish the sequence of the events-which-are-related from the sequence of the relation itself. Rarely in twentieth-century storytelling do the two coincide. The attitude of writers of short story cycles about the time relationship among stories in the cycle seems to be one of unconcern. They are more interested in the rhythmic pattern of the telling than in the chronological consistency of the events themselves. Often, too, no temporal relationship at all exists among the various stories of a cycle (*Ein Hungerkünstler*, *L'Exil et le royaume*), but frequently enough one notes some kind of mythic advance in time (*Winesburg, Ohio*, *In Our Time*), or some general, though often inconsistent, reference to historical time (*The Unvanquished*). Even when events in all

[18] There are many varieties of the *Rahmenerzählung*. The frame may encircle only one story or it may embrace a thousand as it does in *A Thousand and One Nights*. All the stories in the frame may be on the same narrative level (as in *The Decameron*) or stories which are framed may themselves serve as frames for other stories (the "Chinese box technique" of *The Panchatantra*). The frame-story may be merely an artificial frame, or it may excite interest in its own right (*The Canterbury Tales*). Other distinctions could be made if this were a treatise on the *Rahmenerzählung*.

the stories of a cycle take place in the same general locale, no temporal relationship (*Dubliners*) or a meager one (*The Pastures of Heaven*) may be indicated. Chief concern is for psychological time, symbolic times of seasons, times which recur, and mythic times of legendary events.

B. SUGGESTIONS FOR AN HISTORICAL PERSPECTIVE

In the above discussion, I have differentiated three kinds of short story cycles: composed, arranged, and completed. For its genesis, each requires in a different degree what P. M. Kramer has called the "cyclical habit of mind". The cyclical habit of mind is merely the tendency to compose, arrange, or complete sets of individual units so that they form a new whole through patterns of recurrence and development.

The cyclical habit of mind emerges with greater or less frequency in different epochs and in different cultures. It seems to have some connection with "mythic consciousness", but little connection with primitivism. The men who finally reshaped and wrote the *Panchatantra* and the *Odyssey* respectively were in many ways as sophisticated as today's authors who so assiduously re-work public and private myths in an attitude of irony. Neither Boccaccio nor Chaucer were primitives. One need not read far in the composed compilations of the Tristan cycles, or the Grail cycles, or other Arthurian cycles to become aware of a delicacy in the handling of symbolism, a subtleness in presenting scenes. Motifs, themes, and phraseology of earlier chapters echo in the ones that follow. Situations recur, gestures are repeated until they become signs of character, emblems broadcast character. No one seems to care whether or not discrepancies seep into the legend or whether the succession of events described is chronologically possible. Authors interest themselves in "mythic pattern", in recurrent development such as one finds in the parallel events of Gawain and Parzival in Wolfram von Esenbach's famous book. One thinks too of Roland's triple ascent of the little knoll to peer out on the advancing Saracens.

Time does not exist in a cycle for the sake of hurrying through a single series of events, but rather for going over the same kind of action again, for repeating the situation while varying its components, for deepening one's appreciation of the significance of an action. Typical devices in the cycles of the ancient past and of the Middle Ages were comment through parallels, enlargement through juxtaposition, and definition by contrast. The hero is made to appear more heroic than he is by contrasting him with a villain; Roland's stature increases by his association with Charlemagne; while the Green Knight hunts game in the woods, his wife tempts Gawain at home.

The writers of today often seem intent on building mythic kingdoms of some sort. Faulkner has his Yoknapatawpha County, Steinbeck his Pastures of Heaven, Camus his kingdom of solidarity, Joyce his city of paralysis, and Anderson his Winesburg. Heroes, usually diminished in stature, roam the imaginary streets and plains of these kingdoms. Like heroes of past ages, they, too, are often defined by comparison and contrast, measured by juxtaposition, and judged by how they react to recurrent situations. Bayard Sartoris crystallizes his heroic stance by opposing Ringo, Drusilla, George Wyatt, and other Southerners who urge him to kill Redmond. The process of George Willard's growth can be charted against his reactions to the wide variety of male and female figures he encounters in Winesburg – from Louise Trunnion to Helen White, from Wing Biddlebaum to Enoch Robinson.

Admittedly, the "cyclical habit of mind" does not adequately explain why short story cycles have been so popular in the twentieth century. A further partial reason may be the immense popularity of the short story form itself. Since Poe, Turgenev, Gogol, Hawthorne, Maupassant, and Chekhov pared their narratives down to tightly constructed artistic units, writers have considered the shaping of a solid short story a challenge equal to any that longer literary forms may offer. And when writers of this century saw what a Turgenev could do in *A Sportsman's Sketches* – how he preserved the integrity of the more condensed form while incorporating his stories into a single overall design – they could not be adverse to trying the form themselves.

Malcolm Cowley proposes a further reason for the interest in story cycles in this century. Literary magazines liked to publish series of stories dealing with the same characters or the same locale. Writers of genius, Cowley says, realized the fuller possibilities of the cycle form and began conceiving their narratives to fit such a pattern. In other words, the existence of popular story-series tended to encourage in writers like Faulkner and Steinbeck that "cylical habit of mind" of which we spoke of earlier – the habit of drawing smaller units into the integral wholeness of a superstructure.

II

CRITICAL APPROACHES TO TWENTIETH-CENTURY SHORT STORY CYCLES

From the 1940's to the present, an increasing number of articles have elucidated the structural and thematic patterns which weld the individual stories of a collection into a cycle. No one, however, has publicly recognized the existence of a unique literary genre or synthesized the insights of disparate scholars into a comprehensive treatment of the outer (static) and inner (dynamic) patterns and laws of short story cycles. A brief history of the growth of critical insight into the structural dynamics of Joyce's *Dubliners*, Camus's *L'Exil et le royaume*, and Steinbeck's *The Pastures of Heaven* will help to place my study within a tradition of criticism. At the same time, it will open up to the public eye some of the treasures of the short story cycle genre, and prepare the reader for the more detailed discussions of cyclic patterns to be treated in the following chapters.

A. JAMES JOYCE: *DUBLINERS*

In 1905, James Joyce sent twelve stories to Grant Richards for publication. The publisher's reader of the manuscript noted the "order and symmetrical connection between the stories making them one book".[1] Three more stories ("Two Gallants", "A Little Cloud", and "The Dead") were added to the volume before Grant Richards finally published it in June, 1914.[2] Thirty years passed before critics began to recognize the

[1] The reader was probably Filson Young. See Marvin Magalaner and Richard M. Kain, *Joyce: The Man, the Work, the Reputation* (London, 1957), p. 53. Joyce himself had written to his publisher: "My intention was to write a chapter of the moral history of my country and I chose Dublin for the scene because that city seemed to me the centre of paralysis. I have tried to present it to the indifferent public under four of its aspects: childhood, adolescence, maturity and public life. The stories are arranged in this order." (Herbert Gorman, *James Joyce* [New York, 1939], p. 150). In his letters, he says: "I have written my book with considerable care" and speaks of the elements which "rivet the book together", though he does not detail them.

[2] The *Dubliners* manuscript was submitted to Grant Richards for the first time in November, 1905. It consisted of twelve stories. "Two Gallants" was mailed to Richards early in 1906, but Richards finally decided not to publish the book. Joyce signed a

various levels on which *Dubliners*, now fifteen stories, cohered to form a single book.

In 1944, Levin and Shattack[3] lamented the fact that for "three decades now *Dubliners*...has been for most readers merely one of Joyce's 'easier' books...a collection of discrete sketches" (p. 26). They argued that *Dubliners* "has an architectural unity in a secret technique...*Dubliners* is based upon Homer's *Odyssey*" (p. 76). Working from the book's static patterning, these ingenious men uncovered hidden analogies in the *Dubliners* to the episodes of the *Odyssey*. The first three stories ("The Sisters" through "Araby") are analogues of Homer's Books I-IV (and part of Book XV): the adventures of Telemachus. The next four stories ("Eveline" through "The Boarding House") analogize Homer's Books V-VIII (and part of Book XIII): Odysseus' adventures at Ogygia and Phaeacia. "A Little Cloud" through "A Painful Case" (the next four stories) treat materials deriving from Homer's Books IX-XII: Odysseus' recapitulation of his ten years of wandering. But here, Levin and Shattack admit, the analogies begin to break down: Book IX is omitted entirely and Book XII is treated only incidentally.

The four last stories ("Ivy Day in the Committee Room" through "The Dead") begin to use materials of the second half of the *Odyssey*, but break off before completing a perfect pattern. Joyce had intended, Levin and Shattack say, to write a second series of *Dubliners*. "The Dead" was "perhaps intended partly as an artistic substitute for the second series never to be born: it is a faithful analogue of Odysseus' last and greatest adventures, his slaying of the wooers and his reunion with Penelope (Books XX through XXIII)" (p. 77).

To support their claim, Levin and Shattack summon Joyce's lifelong interest in the *Odyssey*, beginning with his schoolboy essay in praise of Ulysses ("My Favorite Hero"),[4] his correspondence with publishers,[5] his

---

contract with Mausel and Company in 1909; they postponed its publication in 1910, reneged on their contract and broke the type in 1912, burning 1,000 copies of *Dubliners*. The manuscript had been rejected by Elkin Mathews twice (1907 and 1913) and by John Long (1908) before Richards finally agreed to publish the book (fifteen stories now) in 1914.

[3] Richard Levin and Charles Shattack, "First Flight to Ithaca – A New Reading of Joyce's 'Dubliners'", *Accent*, IV (Winter, 1944), 75-99. In 1941, Harry Levin had already noted Joyce's expressed intentions of arranging his book (twelve stories) under the four aspects of childhood, adolescence, maturity, and public life (see *James Joyce: A Critical Introduction* [Norfolk, Connecticut, 1941], p. 30).

[4] See Gorman, *James Joyce*, p. 45.

[5] Marvin Magalaner and Richard Kain take exception to Levin and Shattack's interpretation of Joyce's correspondence with his publisher. Though they admit that Joyce's

insistence that all the stories be published in the order which he had specified; and his remark to one of his language students: "When I wrote *Dubliners*, I was tempted to give it the title of 'Ulysses at Dublin' but I changed my mind."[6]

Joyce does not, they go on to stress, merely parody the *Odyssey*, but constructs his own unique work of art with analogues to the *Odyssey*. "Therefore it must not be expected that every detail in *Dubliners* derives from Homer, or that every Homeric detail is rendered by Joyce...." (p. 78). Moreover, Joyce tends to translate Homeric present vivid action either into past or future time, or to reduce it to mere wish, threat, or ambiguous imagery. So the counterparts to Homer in *Dubliners* are more likely to be in the area of symbol and abortive deeds than on the level of positive exterior action. Levin and Shattack conclude that "the whole book... gains in dignity and weight from the recognition of its structural continuity; it is something more than a collection of discrete sketches" (p. 99).

Because of their balanced attitude toward their thesis, this article may not be sluffed off as a mere cerebral exercise which is as unconvincing as it is ingenious. Nevertheless, certain questions arise concerning the apparent tightness of structure in *Dubliners*. Why, for instance, must the order of "Two Gallants" and "After the Race" be inverted before they can be fitted into the sequence of events in the *Odyssey*? Why does the analogizing process begin to break down in stories 8 through 11? If the *Odyssey* is the basis of Joyce's static STRUCTURE, why does he allow his correspondences IN STRUCTURE to hang together loosely and to be incomplete? Few critics would deny that Odyssey motifs can be found in all of Joyce's work. But even this detailed study of Levin's and Shattack's does not totally convince their readers that the prime source of unity in *Dubliners* is a static structure analogous to that of the *Odyssey*.

Dubliners, like Turgenev's *A Sportsman's Sketches*, produces "the overall effect of a corrupt, dying, despairing country whose inhabitants are trapped in a system of their own making" (p. 64), they do not agree that Joyce's pieces fit so tightly together as Levin and Shattack believe. Magalaner and Kain quote from Joyce's correspondence with Grant Richards: "I have agreed to omit the troublesome word in *Two Gallants*. To omit the story from the book would really be disastrous. It is one of the most important stories in the book. I would rather sacrifice *five* of the other stories (which I could name) than this one." Magalaner and Kain believe Joyce really meant he would take out five stories in order to be allowed to insert this one, and so he could not have been arguing from structural compulsion, as Levin and Shattack thought. Joyce's quote, it seems to me, could be interpreted favorably for either party. It could be a bluff (and I think it probably was), or it could be a sincere offer. One quote from Joyce, however, cannot substitute for a close study of the relationships of the stories in *Dubliners*.

[6] Quoted in Levin and Shattack, p. 77.

If "First Flight to Ithaca" attempted to define through analogy the static structure of *Dubliners,* Brewster Ghiselin's "The Unity of Joyce's 'Dubliners'"[7] tries to ascertain its symbolic structure. "When the outlines of the symbolic pattern have been grasped", he argues,

> the whole unifying development will be discernible as a sequence of events in a moral drama, an action of the human spirit struggling for survival under peculiar conditions of deprivation, enclosed and disabled by a degenerate environment that provides none of the primary necessities of spiritual life. (p. 76)

Dubliners, Ghiselin concludes, is "both a group of short stories and a novel, the separate histories of its protagonists composing one essential history, that of the soul of a people..." (p. 77).

Ghiselin points out a number of symbolic patterns which have fed the critical insights of later commentators. Dublin, as the "centre of paralysis", holds its debilitated subjects in its magnetic grasp. Escape "is envisaged in traveling eastward from the city, across the seas to the freedom of the open world" (p. 77). The citizens of Joyce's Dublin are haunted by "dreams of escape", which rarely if ever are realized. Instead of effective action, the pages of *Dubliners* abound in tropes dealing with enclosure and arrest of motion. The "nets" which inhibit Dubliners from "flying away to another country" are not only external ones – environment, attitudes of one's associates – but internal ones – deficiencies of impulse and power. Most debilitating of all diseases is moral paralysis. Ghiselin finds, then, in *Dubliners,*

> a fundamental structure of movements and stases, a system of significant motions, countermotions, and arrests, involving every story, making one consecutive narrative of surge and subsidence of life in Dublin. (p. 78)

The eastward movement, Ghiselin says, signifies a struggle toward spiritual rebirth, rejuvenation. So interpreted, it allies closely with what he calls "the unifying action" of *Dubliners,* which, in general, is

> a movement of the human soul, in desire of life, through various conditions of Christian virtue and stages of deadly sin, toward or away from the font and the altar and all the gifts of the two chief sacraments provided for its salvation, toward or away from God. (p. 80)

The unifying action of *Dubliners,* then, is a "spiritual action". In the

7 Brewster Ghiselin, "The Unity of Joyce's 'Dubliners'", *Accent,* XVI (Spring, 1956), 75-87; (Summer, 1956), 196-213.

course of the fifteen stories, the motivation, goals, and means of reaching the goals of this action are all elucidated.

Each of the stories, Ghiselin says, deals with some virtue or sin, and "the entire sequence represents the whole course of moral deterioration ending in the death of the soul" (p. 80). Joyce expresses the incompatibility of salvation with life-in-Dublin in a "systematic display, one by one in these stories", of the theological and cardinal virtues suppressed, of the seven deadly sins triumphant, and finally, of spiritual death. A schematization of Ghiselin's correspondences shows that Joyce, if indeed this were his plan, did not list all the virtues and sins in their conventional order:

The Sisters: faith suppressed
An Encounter: hope suppressed
Araby: love suppressed

Eveline: lack of fortitude

After the Race: pride triumphant
Two Gallants: covetousness triumphant
The Boarding House: lust triumphant
A Little Cloud: envy trimphant
Counterparts: anger triumphant
Clay: gluttony triumphant
A Painful Case: sloth triumphant

Ivy Day in the Committee Room: justice subverted
A Mother: temperance subverted
Grace: prudence subverted

The Dead: the completion of spiritual disintegration; death itself.

Ghiselin notes that the important spiritual and sacramental images in *Dubliners* concern rebirth and nourishment of the spiritual life: water, wine, bread. Also one finds the symbols of the sea, the altar, color, music, clothing, and various images of enclosure. In Part II of his article, Ghiselin shows how each of these symbols operates to bring forward "the single action of *Dubliners* in the separate actions of the principal figures" (p. 196). One can argue with the specific applications of symbolic significance which Ghiselin makes, but that the texture of *Dubliners* demands a systematization of Joyce's symbolic patterns can hardly be doubted. Ghiselin's particular pattern of "deadly sins", however, seems somewhat arbitrary. Most of the stories, as Tindall shows,[8] deal centrally with more than one of the virtues. Further, "A Painful Case" seems much more exemplary of a failure to love than of the triumph of sloth, and Ghiselin's calling "Clay" an example of gluttony triumphant seems dictated more by the demands of his scheme than by the dynamics of the story. Finally, one is hard put to see how "A Boarding House" reveals the triumphant influence of lust.

Still, Ghiselin's insights into sacramental symbolism and the significance of directional movement and stasis are solid contributions to one's understanding of the dynamic patterns of *Dubliners*. Whereas eastward movement in the early stories indicates a desire to escape to some Oriental or continental land of freedom, in the later stories westward movement promises only death. Circular movement (Lenehan, Gabriel Conroy) suggests hopeless acceptance of one's paralysis.

To the growing tendency to treat *Dubliners* as an artistic whole, Tindall contributes his insistence on unification through theme. What holds the stories together and makes them a book, he says, "is a theme or common idea. Hinted on the first page of *Dubliners* and displayed in the last story, this theme is 'paralysis' or living death" (p. 3). Paralysis in Dublin is not merely moral, as other commentators had noted, but intellectual and spiritual as well. Through his manipulation of image clusters (the two principal ones being [a] light and fire, and [b] cold and snow) as well as through diminished heroic action, systematization of eastward-westward-circular movement, and the other patterns Joyce has woven into his fabric, *Dubliners* systematically unravels the implications of this theme through childhood to maturity, broadening its scope from private life to public.

As a further principle of cohesion, Tindall proposes that *Dubliners* presents Joyce's reasons for self-inflicted exile and its justification. "Not only a picture of what he had escaped, the book is a picture of what, had he remained, he might have become" (p. 6). Again, Tindall compares the structure of *Dubliners* to that of Joyce's *Chamber Music* – a 36-poem lyric cycle which had been completed shortly before Joyce began *Dubliners*. Other unifying techniques Tindall notes are: Joyce's use of season symbolism (Christmas, New Year, Epiphany, etc.), Biblical symbolism (e.g., *Michael* Furey and *Gabriel* Conroy in "The Dead"), the technique of the

8 William York Tindall, *A Reader's Guide to James Joyce* (New York, 1959).

"epiphany",[9] interconnections of characters,[10] and even the technique which I have called, in my chapter on Anderson, the "associational technique".[11]

Finally, Tindall notices certain similarities between the final story in the volume and the first story. Harry Levin had remarked some years earlier that "death is one of the few things that happen to *Dubliners*; it is the subject of the first and last stories in the volume" (p. 35). Tindall finds that "The Dead" acts as both "the summary and climax of *Dubliners*" (p. 42) and as "a preface to *A Portrait*, *Exiles*, and *Ulysses*" (p. 49). Gabriel's aunts in "The Dead" parallel Father Flynn's sisters in "The Sisters", and so the end of the cycle reverts to a situation reminiscent of its beginning. Through an explication of the symbolic meanings in "The Dead", the essentially symbolic texture of the other stories becomes less obscure. Finally, as his first major presentation of that conflict of pride with love, of ego with humanity, which so obsessed him, "The Dead" heralds the intensification of symbolic techniques one finds in Joyce's later works.

James R. Baker in his "Ibsen, Joyce, and the Living-Dead"[12] has sought in Ibsen's plays the clue to a design in *Dubliners*. In one sense, his article has nothing fundamentally new to offer: *Dubliners*, he says, "is an exposé of the paralysis of spirit which binds the urban bourgeois" (p. 64). Still, he argues that the analogue of *Dubliners*' dynamic and static structure is not the *Odyssey* or any other scheme presented by previous critics. Rather, "the basic themes, the structural design, and the symbolism of the stories parallel Ibsen's work in the group of plays beginning with *A Doll's House* and ending with *When We Dead Awaken*" (p. 64). According to Baker's singular theory

> the real unity of *Dubliners* derives from the condensed symbolism of Ibsen's last

[9] "We know that Joyce, apparently regarding his collection of twenty-two fragments as a kind of storehouse of material, adapted several for his later works. What better way of conceiving *Dubliners* than as an elaborate extension of these radiant fragments, a more formidable work of the same design." (Tindall, pp. 11-12).

[10] The same first-person narrator relates the first three stories. Also, Kernan of "Grace" knows Crofton of "Ivy Day", and Lenehan of "Two Gallants" knows Holohan of "A Mother". See Tindall, p. 41.

[11] For instance, the "Hail Mary", in "Counterparts", Tindall says, "could also serve as a kind of preface to Maria in the next story" (p. 29); again, "As we have been prepared for a meaning of 'Clay' by a reference in 'A Little Cloud', so we have been prepared for Maria's song from *The Bohemian Girl* by a reference in 'Eveline'" (p. 30).

[12] In William T. Moynihan, (ed.), *Joyce's The Dead* (Boston, 1965), pp. 64-70. Reprinted from *A James Joyce Miscellany: Third Series*, ed. Marvin Magalaner (Carbondale, 1962).

play [*When We Dead Awaken*]. The technique of epiphany [Tindall] is only a means to that end, the pattern of eastward and westward movement [Ghiselin] only an adjunct to the Ibsenesque juxtaposition of life in death, and the Homeric counterparts [Levin and Shattack] (if they exist at all) are occasional analogies which function within the larger scheme provided by the dramatist's example. (p. 66)

Joyce's admiration and understanding of Ibsen's dramas, says Baker, are sufficient evidence that he *could* have had this plan. Baker insists that the similarities in treatment of the fundamental trope (the living-dead) in Ibsen's last play and in *Dubliners* force one to conclude that Joyce actually *did* structure his stories after Ibsen.

Other works which have attempted to see some pattern in *Dubliners* range from reasonable exposés of the paralytic process and the paralysis images which abound in the volume,[13] to clever, exasperating, and fundamentally unconvincing articles which trace obscure clues through a labyrinth of inverted symbology leading nowhere.[14]

Levin and Shattack, Ghiselin, and Tindall, however, have uncovered a sufficient amount of convincing data to establish *Dubliners* as one of the most significant short story cycles of this half-century. Like *Ein Hungerkünstler*, its unity rests primarily on its concommitant development of themes and motifs. These are crystallized and elaborated in the final story, which is longer than the others and more public in scope. As in other cycles, Joyce's final story concentrates dominant motifs, and structures more clearly central symbols so that, in retrospect, earlier stories of the cycle are illumined.

Further, it seems to me that in establishing his Dublin as a "centre of paralysis" Joyce has created a mythic kingdom, a microcosm, not unlike Winesburg, Ohio, or the Pastures of Heaven. His Dublin is a city of moral, spiritual, and intellectual paralytics, a living Spoon River cemetery-society, a community of hollow men who inhabit a symbolic wasteland landscape. The dynamic patterns and rhythms of a short story cycle need not be as architecturally symmetrical as Levin and Shattack, Ghiselin, or Gerhard Friedrich seem to require. Joyce planned his work with considerable care. But that does not mean necessarily that he planned it to be symmetrical or geometrical. Whether or not we are willing to accept any or all of the various static patternings that have been proposed, we

13 Florence L. Walzl, "Pattern of Paralysis in Joyce's *Dubliners*", *College English*, XXII (January, 1961), 221-228.

14 Gerhard Friedrich, "The Gnomonic Clue to James Joyce's *Dubliners*", *Modern Language Notes*, LXXII (June, 1957), 421-424.

cannot close our eyes to the dynamic patterns of themes, motifs, and symbols which course through the book. These patterns repeat themselves, develop, broaden their scope, and lead ultimately to other vistas of significance. The Homeric references; the motifs of direction, of sacramental rejuvenation, of paralysis, of kinesis and stasis, and of living death; the presentations of moral, intellectual, and spiritual degeneration and deterioration – all of these are so patterned as to warrant the kind of detailed study which the dynamics of a short story cycle require.

B. ALBERT CAMUS: *L'EXIL ET LE ROYAUME*

A brief review of the main lines of the criticism of *Dubliners* has revealed how successive scholars have gradually come to perceive some of the intricate aesthetic patterns of Joyce's cycle. Their studies speak specifically about *Dubliners*, but their questions concerning Joyce's patterning of theme and symbol could have served as an investigative framework for approaching the story cycle of Albert Camus.

Camus's *L'Exil et le royaume* (1957)[15] announces, through its title, that it is no mere bundle of unconnected stories. Gaëton Picon, in his review of the volume for *Le Mercure de France*[16] notices that "*Exile and the Kingdom* contains a definite movement" (p. 155), a rhythm which approximates "the very pulse of existence – which unfolds, then shuts up tight; reveals itself in a flash of light, then veils itself in obscurity; waxes and then wanes" (p. 156). If the theme of the book may be stated in most general terms as the relationship of "exile" to "kingdom" on several planes of human experience, the critic's problem will be to discover how this theme develops from story to story.

"The exile and the kingdom", Picon writes, "are two aspects of the same breath and heartbeat. The kingdom is in the exile, the exile is a path toward the kingdom – in fact, exile could actually be the kingdom"

15 (Paris: Libraire Gallimard, 1957). My quotations are all from this edition. Camus had begun writing the stories in 1952. "La Femme adultère" appeared in Algiers in 1954 in a limited edition, illustrated by P. Clarin. "Le Renégat" was published in *La Nouvelle Revue Française* under the title of "L'Esprit confus" in June, 1956. "La Pierre qui pousse" was never published separately, but (like Joyce's "The Dead", Anderson's "Departure", Faulkner's "An Odor of Verbena", and Kafka's "Josefine") was published originally with the cycle it concludes.

16 (May, 1957), pp. 127-131. Reprinted in Germaine Brée, (ed.), *Camus: A Collection of Critical Essays* (Englewood Cliffs, New Jersey, 1962), pp. 152-156. Translated by Josephine Valenza.

(p. 155). Though Picon goes on to point out how three of these stories exemplify the conflict between some kind of exile and some kind of kingdom,[17] he does not treat in detail the total movement of the cycle.

Philip Thody[18] shares Picon's view that all these stories deal with the struggle of exiled people to discover their kingdom. "The order in which the short stories are presented", he goes on to say, "has been carefully thought out by Camus" (p. 89). But Thody does not detail the reasons behind the order Camus did, in fact, choose, except to say that "the leisurely irony of *Jonah* [sic]...provides a slackening of tension before the final story gathers together the ideas of exile and of belonging, and expresses them in a final synthesis" (p. 89). Again, as in Kafka, Faulkner, Anderson, and Joyce, the final story of a cycle rounds off and completes the thematic movement which has gathered momentum in the earlier stories.

Carina Gadourek's study of *L'Exil et le royaume*[19] argues that exile consists in a duality of personality, a disruption of one's inner self, and that the kingdom consists in becoming whole again. Exile arises when a man feels himself suddenly a stranger in a dark universe. To enter the kingdom, a man must associate his present surroundings with his home. "Une des conditions essentielles pour faire cesser l'exil...semble être l'arrêt du temps qui permet l'invasion des souvenirs ou de l'espoir" (pp. 202-203). All of the characters in *L'Exil*, Gadourek argues, re-achieve some measure of self-unification, attain their kingdom – although *le renégat* must do it through his death.

Gadourek was the first scholar, to my knowledge, to propose that some specific dynamic pattern influenced the order that Camus gave to his stories. Each story marks a stage in the progress from exile toward the kingdom.

Janine retrouve ce qu'elle est, mais reste dans son exil conjugal. L'Esprit confus est prêt à fonder en rêve la cité de la miséricorde. Les ouvriers dans Les Muets refont la communauté du travail entre eux, mais ne parviennent pas à y inclure le patron. Daru crée une sorte de solidarité entre "l'ennemi" et lui, sans que

[17] "The Artist at Work": Jonas is in exile among his own circle of friends and family. He finds his true home in the solitude of his work. His cage is a mock kingdom. "The Silent Men": exile is the hostility of society; kingdom is their silent revolt. "The Adulterous Woman": exile is her marital and daily life, the desert expanse her kingdom.

[18] *Albert Camus: A Study of His Work* (New York, 1957), pp. 81-93.

[19] *Les Innocents et les coupables* (The Hague, 1963), pp. 202-223. "Les personnages de toutes les nouvelles sont des êtres 'doubles' qui se savent tels ou en qui naît pleine conscience de leur dualité. Ils savent qu'ils ont perdu ou exilé, une part d'eux-mêmes et que le royaume consite à la ré-intéger, à devenir 'entiers'." (p. 202)

l'autre parti comprenne vraiment. Jonas, guéri, peut essayer à l'avenir de concilier la fidélité à lui-même et celle à autri. D'Arrast atteint à ce sommet. (p. 223)

Adele King[20] sees duality not in the protagonists of the stories, but in nature itself: the world is the place of man's exile, but it is also his only kingdom. In the final story, King says, Camus tries to create a myth of the condition of modern man. By carrying the rock, D'Arrast strikes a blow against racial, cultural, and economic barriers which separate men. But D'Arrast's struggle is directed against the gods and against fate, and so this kingdom must be "a temporary construction within the exile" (p. 102).

The most extensive study of the cycle I have read is that of Frank D. Wetherill in his unpublished dissertation, "Albert Camus and the Kingdom of Nature".[21] *Exile*, he says, is equivalent to isolation from nature, mankind, and generally both. *Kingdom* is solidarity within the world of nature, mankind, or both. "This duality forms the basis of each story in which one of these two opposing forces dominates" (p. 434).[22]

Wetherill analyzes in some detail the symbolism of the landscape in which Camus' protagonists find themselves. Each of the characters enters a world completely foreign to him. The first four stories take place in arid Algeria, the fifth in an artist colony in Montmartre (Paris), and the last in the jungles of Brazil. Wetherill seems especially interested in the symbolic relationship of landscape to inscape (if I may borrow Hopkins' term). A stifling atmosphere, he notes, always heralds a negative landscape, a domain of exile. All of the characters in *L'Exil* at some time or another find difficulty in breathing.

Though Wetherill's analysis of the individual symbols of each of the stories is quite illuminating, he does not sufficiently recognize the development of the cycle's symbolic texture from story to story. Janine's "adulterous" communion on the parapet is not with the arid desert but with the expanse of night and the dark sky through which the stars seem to have ceased coursing. In the hiatus of suspended time, Janine feels that she has escaped the long anguish of living and dying. In the following story ("Le Renégat") the renegade faces the desert sun; the sun-god speaks to him

20 *Albert Camus* (New York, 1964), pp. 97-102.

21 University of Southern California, 1964.

22 "La Femme adultère": Janine accepts solidarity with the natural world and isolation within society. "Le Renégat": the Renegade suffers from a complete exile in every respect. "Les Muets": Yvars suffers from a partial exile. "L'Hôte": Daru is isolated by his physical position and his inability to communicate with his guest. "Jonas": Jonas' isolation from society results (as in "Le Renégat") in a tragic loss of lucidity. "La Pierre qui pousse": D'Arrast achieves social solidarity (*cf.* pp. 434-435).

through a hole in the white-hot metal sky, which seems to the renegade a mouth as voluble as his own – a mouth which vomits rivers of flame over the burning desert.

The next story moves from desert to the sea. Yvars avoids looking at the sea as he rides past it in the morning. The sea (like the stars and the desert) is timeless and immutable, but Yvars grows old. The sea is full of promise, and so "Yvars continuait d'aimer la mer, mais seulement à la fin du jour quand les eaux de la baie fonçaient un peu" (p. 81). In the night, Yvars feels a harmony with the universe. But "les matins où il regagnait son travail, au contraire, il n'aimait plus regarder la mer" (p. 81). The final sentence of the story recalls Joyce's "Eveline", in that lands beyond the sea offer rejuvenation, new life, the promise of perpetual youth: "Il aurait voulu être jeune, et que Fernande le fût encore, et ils seraient partis, de l'autre côté de la mer" (p. 102).

"L'Hôte" is situated "sur l'immense étendue du haut plateau désert" (p. 105). The terrain is covered with snow. Before the story ends, however, the sun begins to melt the snow and drink up the puddles of water. Later still, "le soleil était maintenant assez haut dans le ciel et commençait de lui dévorer le front" (p. 129). Tropes from all the stories converge in the final paragraph. From his plateau pinnacle, Daru stands with his back to the blackboard sketches [Jonas] of rivers [La pierre qui pousse] and looks out over "le ciel [La Femme adultère], le plateau [L'Hôte] et, au-delà, les terres invisibles [Le Renégat] qui s'étendaient jusqu'à la mer [Les Muets]. Dans ce vaste pays qu'il avait tant aimé, il était seul" (p. 130). Daru, who had made his place of exile into a kingdom, now finds it has again become a place of exile.

Gilbert Jonas in the following story has reduced the vast expanses of the sky and the sea to "his star" and to his tiny enclosure (which Wetherill and others compare to the belly of the whale in *The Book of Jonas*). In the early portions of the story, Jonas pays tribute to his lucky star in a way that resembles that which religious people pay to their god. But after success comes his way, Jonas "leva les yeux vers le ciel sans étoiles, et alla tirer les rideaux" (p. 166). Jonas soon began to work less, to accomplish less, even when he was not surrounded by admirers. He spent his moments of solitude looking at the sky. "A cette époque, il peignait des ciels" (p. 170). Despite the fact that his pictures were not selling, Jonas felt a monumental opus rising within him: "l'étoile sortirait lavée à neuf, étincelante, de ces brouillards obscurs" (p. 172). But Jonas sees his star rising in the dark only at the termination of his career. The single word Jonas had written in the center of his final canvas expresses in its ambiguity the intimate yet paradoxical relationship between exile and kingdom: no one can tell whether the word should read "solitaire" or "solidaire".

A river runs through the final story of the series. The river is a force, a sinuous, muscular force which flows powerfully out toward the sea and the night. The sky itself "semblait encore liquide. Dans son eau transparente et sombre, bas sur l'horizon, des étoiles commençaient de s'allumer" (p. 219). But the stars seem at once to flicker out, as if the last lights were trickling from the sky. Even time in this story seems liquid to D'Arrast. D'Arrast has come to arrest time, to build a dam in the steadily flowing river, to set a stone in the flux of life – a stone which, like the miraculous stone of Iguape, will grow, will become a bridge between men, cultures, times. In the beginning of the story, the sound of the waters disgusts and discourages D'Arrast; at the end, it fills him with unutterable happiness. The strange jungle river had become, through D'Arrast's symbolic act of carrying the stone to the hearth of new friends, his river; time was now his time; this culture was no longer "exile and solitude" but his hearth and home, his kingdom.

The symbolism of landscape and setting provides only one of the connective links which unite these stories into a cycle. One needs to examine the dynamic interplay of "exile" and "kingdom" on every level: these terms designate inner attitudes as well as physical or sociological realities. One may be exiled or alienated from oneself as well as from nature or society. One may be a "stranger" by choice as well as by accident.

The central theme of the cycle (oversimplified, to be sure) may be expressed in the paradoxical terms Camus himself chose for the ending of "Jonas". Man desires to "exist", to become himself, to create, to commune in silence with his own spirit. At the same time, he seeks union with the spirit of nature, solidarity with mankind. To become "solidaire", he must for a while be "solitaire". It is the old war between the one and the many. There will always be conflicts between maintaining one's individuality and fusing oneself with mankind; between the demands of isolation and self-sufficient reflection on the one hand, and immersion in society, reflective interchange with men on the other. Neither the one nor the other suffices in itself to satisfy man.

This theme develops through Camus' artistic presentation of situation, setting, characterization, action, dialogue, motifs, and symbols. Before one can understand completely the dynamics of the cycle, one must investigate similarities of characters; repetitions (with variation) of such motifs as time and memory; recurrence (with development) of such symbols as rocks, sand, water (rain, river, and sea), snow and cold, sun and light, heat, silence as a means of communication, birds and the cry of birds, breathing and the inability to breathe, enclosures and open expanses. One should note, for instance, how the dry cracking rocks of "La Femme adultère" and "Le Renégat" lose their brittleness as the cycle concludes to become the growing stone of "La Pierre qui pousse".[23] Camus speaks of adultery only twice in the book: in "La Femme adultère" Janine communes with the night; in "Jonas" the artist's mother is divorced on the grounds of adultery – that is, she spends too much time serving the poor and the suffering. These and other dynamic patterns in the collection must be investigated before Camus' cycle of stories can be adequately appreciated.

C. JOHN STEINBECK: *THE PASTURES OF HEAVEN*

The dynamic patterns of Steinbeck's *The Pastures of Heaven*[24] have challenged critical investigation for over thirty years. In May 1931, Steinbeck had written to his agents that he was working on a book which showed a diffusion of evil through a normal, unmalicious family, the M----s. "The manuscript", he said, "is made up of stories each one complete in itself, having its rise, climax, and ending. Each story deals with a family or individual. They are tied together only by the common locality and by the contact with the M----s."[25] Critics have observed, however, that Steinbeck's book did not turn out precisely as planned. He had intended, for instance, to devote one chapter to the valley itself, then nine or ten chapters to nine or ten families who lived there before the M----s should finally arrive upon the scene. In the completed volume, the Munroes in every chapter affect the fortunes of each of the co-protagonists, and links other than "common locality" and "contact with the M----s" bind the volume into a cycle.

In 1953, Friedrich Weltz treated the volume in his unpublished disser-

23 Wetherill suggests that the stones of the desert in "La Femme adultère" approximate, symbolically, fallen stars which have lost their fire (*cf.* p. 443). Janine's kingdom had not been what she expected it to be. She found cold instead of heat, rocks instead of soft flowing sand and palm trees. She sees "seulement la pierre, la pierre partout, dans le ciel où regnait encore, crissante et froide, la seule poussière de pierre, comme sur le sol où poussaient seulement, entre les pierres, des graminées" (p. 18). When she finally communes with night on the parapet, she hears the rocks cracking in the embrace of the cold night.

24 (New York: Brewer, Warren and Putnam, 1932). My quotations, however, are from the Bantam edition, 1956.

25 In Peter Lisca, *The Wide World of John Steinbeck* (New Brunswick, New Jersey, 1958), p. 57.

tation (München), "Vier amerikanische Erzählungszyklen".[26] He did not delve into such possible thematic patterns as the contrast between dream and reality,[27] the realization of life through illusion,[28] or the suppression of the individual by society.[29] Rather, he pointed out how each story, structured around a single individual or family (co-protagonist), both retained its individuality and became part of the pattern of the whole book. Realistic details serve primarily as background for thematic action. Bert Munroe, for instance, comes to Pastures of Heaven "because he was tired of battling with a force which invariably defeated him". But where does he settle? On "Battle Farm", which the inhabitants of the valley consider to be haunted and cursed. The mythic action of the book is summarized in a statement T. B. Allen makes to Bert: "Maybe your curse and the farm's curse have mated and gone into a gopher hole like a pair of rattlesnakes. Maybe there'll be a lot of baby curses crawling around the Pastures the first thing we know" (p. 15).

Hildegard Schumann[30] calls Steinbeck's book a *Kurzgeschichtenroman* whose stories are held together "durch eine Rahmenerzählung". Though she draws parallels between Steinbeck's technique and that of *A Thousand and One Nights*, *The Decameron*, and *The Canterbury Tales*, she admits that the work in form and content most closely resembles Anderson's *Winesburg, Ohio*. Peter Lisca departs from previous Steinbeck critical tradition by refusing to call the book a novel since "the several stories are too autonomous structurally and aesthetically".[31] Further, he sees no reason why one story in the series should precede or follow another.

Warren French's chapter on *The Pastures of Heaven*[32] offers significant new insights into the dynamic pattern of the book. French notes, for instance, that the "consistently ironic tone of the narrative" draws the stories together more effectively than does their common setting. The framing prologue and epilogue stress the irony in the very name "Pastures of Heaven". The prologue reveals that the Spanish corporal who discovered and named the valley died there, locked in a barn while wasting away with a pox contracted from an Indian woman. The epilogue presents bus

[26] Weltz, pp. 46-47.

[27] See Frederick I. Carpenter, "John Steinbeck, American Dreamer", *Southwest Review*, XXI (Summer, 1941), 458-459.

[28] See Blake Nevius, "Steinbeck: One Aspect", *The Pacific Spectator*, III (Summer, 1949), 302.

[29] *Cf.* Albert Gérard, *A la recontre de John Steinbeck* (Liège, Belgium, 1947), pp. 34-35.

[30] *Zum Problem des kritischen Realismus bei John Steinbeck* (Haille, 1958), pp. 26-44.

[31] Peter Lisca, p. 49.

[32] In his *John Steinbeck* (New York, 1961), pp. 39-46.

tourists who look down on the valley and wish they could share the tranquil life it seems to promise.

Though the Munroes provide the "physical connecting link between the stories", the book (French says) is not so much about them as about their effect upon others. Each chapter deals with one of the "baby curses" spawned when Bert's curse and the Farm's curse mated. French says that Steinbeck does not share Munroe's view of the nature of the curse. Rather, he provides in each story a clue to a natural explanation of the Munroes' evil influence: their own insensitivity to others and their complacency in the face of the disasters which they cause in others. French goes on to show how the misfortune of each of those families who come in contact with the Munroes results from the Munroes' "misjudging some aspect of a situation or by thoughtlessly saying or doing the wrong thing – the thing that will destroy the world another person has either carefully constructed for himself or come painfully to accept" (pp. 42-43).

The Munroes are not always culpable, however. Pat Humbert had eavesdropped and Tularecito was partially insane – their own character had more to do with their fates than did their incidental contact with one of the Munroes. In some stories, a Munroe will mean well, but judge wrongly. In others, he will be insensitive, self-justifying, or flippantly disrespectful. Mrs. Munroe, for instance, judges that Robbie Maltby's health "is more important than his feelings", and Bert tells Ray Banks that if he had any imagination, he could not enjoy prison executions.

Though French's insights are valuable and significant,[33] I think he goes a little too far in condemning the Munroes. "Because they are self-righteous in their wrongness", he says, "they are culpable of destroying the happiness of those they come in contact with – culpable not in the insensitive eyes of the law, but in the sensitive eyes of the compassionate artist" (p. 43). What I feel is lacking in French's otherwise perceptive account is the insight that the book centers not only on the effect the Munroes have on other people, but on the other people who sometime or another have some contact with the Munroes. Each of the protagonists of the stories is a co-protagonist of the cycle. The dynamics of the cycle,

[33] French also notes that the stories proceed chronologically if one's criterion of placement is the time the stories end. I think one should be aware also that the events of the prologue occur before any other action in the cycle and the events of the epilogue (presumably) happen after the action of the other stories has been completed. The next to last story in the volume – Richard Whiteside's building of his dynastic house and the story of its collapse – serves a function similar to that of the "Godliness" stories in *Winesburg*.

then, must be studied as much through *their* actions and attitudes as through the attitudes and actions of the Munroes.

Joseph Fontenrose[34] notes a continuous linking pattern used throughout the book. In each chapter, he says, "the principal character had founded his tranquil life in the valley upon an unhealthy adjustment, an evasion of reality, an illusion, or an unrealizable dream; and a deed of a Munroe forced him to face the truth, if but for a moment" (p. 25). The stories, he says, are linked "in a series of ironic contrasts" – [II-III]: Bert Munroe, having failed in business, became a prosperous farmer in Pastures of Heaven; Shark Wicks, having failed as a farmer, leaves Pastures of Heaven to seek success in business. [III-IV]: Tularecito (ugly, stupid, but talented), contrasts with Alice Wicks (beautiful, stupid, untalented). [IV-V]: Hilda Van Deventer saw halucinations without wanting them; Tularecito searched for gnomes without finding them. [V-VI]: Helen Van Deventer who lost her husband just before Hilda was born, was unsuccessful in raising her insane child; Junius Maltby, who lost his wife when Robbie was born, raised a normal child without trying. [VI-VII]: Junius Maltby, lazy but moral, left Pastures for an honorable occupation in the city; the Lopez sisters, industrious but "immoral", left Pastures for a dishonorable occupation in the city. [VII-VIII]: The Lopez sisters left Pastures having given up their illusions; Molly Morgan left in order to maintain her illusions. [VIII-IX]: Molly gave up a position she liked because she did not want to identify herself with a suffering man; Raymond Banks gave up a custom he liked because he had identified himself with suffering men. [IX-X]: Ray Banks turned away from death; Pat Humbert turned away from life. [X-XI]: Pat Humbert built a Vermont house for Mae Munroe, but abandoned it when she married someone else; Richard Whiteside built a house before he had any particular woman in mind, but continued to live there even after hopes of abundant progeny had been dashed. A final irony which Fontenrose does not point out is that Bill Whiteside marries the same Mae Munroe for whom Pat Humbert had remodeled his house. She had been destined to become mistress of the mansion Richard Whiteside had constructed. Instead, she encourages Bill to leave Pastures and to go away to Monterey.

Fontenrose offers a final significant insight into the mythic substratum of the book. He shows how each of the stories – and especially the history of Richard Whiteside's founding of a dynasty in The Pastures of Heaven – has its roots in folklore and mythology. But, he notes "Steinbeck trans-

[34] *John Steinbeck: An Introduction and Interpretation* (New York, 1963), pp. 20-29.

lates myth and legend into twentieth-century realism, showing what paradise, curses, oracles, ghosts, knights, Robin Hoods, and gnomes amount to in everyday terms" (p. 29). Still, though myth is used ironically in *The Pastures of Heaven,* it serves also "to sublimate reality", to uncover levels of significance in the lives of ordinary people.

D. A SYSTEMATIC APPROACH TO SHORT STORY CYCLES

The several criticisms I have summarized above show how successive critics have gradually uncovered many of the static and dynamic patterns of three specific short story cycles.[35] Each succeeding scholar built on and expanded the insights of those who had broken the ground before him. The first attempts to define the unity of one of these puzzling books usually concentrate on some static pattern – a geometric relationship of parts, a blueprint or master plan which an author (allegedly) followed in detail. Later studies penetrate beneath surface relationships to the dynamic patterns of the book – the movement and direction its stories take, associational rhythms, thematic variations, ironic contrasts of characters or symbols.

Very few of the critics have seemed fully to realize what kind of work they were analyzing. If they thought of it as a novel, they only embarrassed themselves when they looked for a "main plot" or "central strand of action". If they assumed it was a "mere collection of stories", they almost forced themselves not to notice the intricate dynamic patterns which the volume possessed.

My fundamental assumptions in this study agree with those expressed by the formalist critic who wrote:

> That literary criticism is a description and an evaluation of its object.
>
> That the primary concern of criticism is with the problem of unity – the kind of whole which the literary work forms or fails to form, and the relation of the various parts to each other in building up this whole.[36]

Only through a detailed investigation of form can a critic hope to penetrate every dimension of meaning which the aesthetic object possesses.

Criticism of a form which has eluded so many scholars requires an

[35] These are not, of course, the only story cycles which have been examined by critics up to now. See bibliography for treatments of Isaac Babel's *Red Cavalry*, Hemingway's *In Our Time*, Steinbeck's *The Red Pony*, and Welty's *The Golden Apples*.

[36] Cleanth Brooks, Jr., "The Formalist Critic", *Kenyon Review*, XIII (1951), 1-6.

exact analytic methodology. That methodology should be comprehensive enough to apply to all cases of the genre and supple enough to adjust itself to that unique example of the genre which a critic may be trying to comprehend.

As a first step toward understanding the dynamics of a story cycle, nothing can substitute for several initial readings of the work. During the course of these readings, patterns and rhythms, directions and movements, parallels and contrasts will begin to suggest to the critic that the dynamics of this collection of stories are the dynamics of a cycle. At this point, however, one's analysis is just beginning.

Each story of the collection must be studied in detail. Where does it take place? When? From what point of view is the story told? Is the narrator reliable or unreliable? Is he a participant or an observer? How does he narrate? What does he narrate? Who are his central figures? What themes and motifs course through the story? What symbolic words, gestures, objects, acts? Where does the center of interest in the story lie? How do its various elements contribute to that center, and form with it an intergral whole?

After each of the stories has been examined, the critic of a short story cycle will begin to notice in detail what relationships exist among the stories. Are they all set in the same locale or during the same epoch? Are they all related by the same narrator? Or is there some other pattern which controls the author's choice of setting, time, and narrator? Are the stories put together in some obvious geometric pattern? Does the author use a framing device? A prologue or epilogue? Some other introductory or rounding-off device?

Does a single character occupy a central position in the cycle? Or does each story have its own co-protagonist? Do all the co-protagonists together form some kind of community? Do they appear juxtaposed in parallel or contrastive pairs? What relationship does the co-protagonist of the final story have with the central figure of the initial story? Do some some characters appear in several stories? Do they develop? Does any patterning of kinds of characters suggest a reason why one story in the cycle should lead to another? Are the characters presented "realistically"? Do they serve purposes of allegory, symbolism, legend, or myth?

Is a single event treated in all the stories? A single kind of event (war, marriage, hunting, death)? In the pattern of the stories, do different attitudes toward this event or kind of event emerge?

Does the pattern of all the themes of the separate stories constitute a new theme for the cycle? Does the pattern of the whole cycle throw any light on the meaning of any of the individual stories? Do minor themes and motifs of some stories assume major importance in others? Does any theme or set of themes develop systematically as the cycle moves from story to story?

Do tropes, symbols, phrases, rhetorical patterns recur? If so, for what poetic reasons? Does any symbol or set of symbols assume, as the cycle progresses, mythic or archetypal proportions? How does the later development of a symbol affect earlier stories in which it appears?

Is the center of interest in all the stories the same? If so, how does the author pattern the stories in order to broaden his perspective on that single center of interest? If the center of interest shifts from story to story, does it do so in any recognizable pattern? Does the fact that the center of interest shifts in a certain pattern indicate that the entire cycle has a center of interest quite different from that of each of its component parts?

Not all of the above methodological questions, of course, are relevant to every cycle of stories. Initial perceptive readings of any volume of stories should signal to the critic which of the above questions are relevant and what other questions must be asked if the work of art he is examining is to be grasped as an artistic whole. For only by asking relavant questions can a reader hope to perceive, in an epiphany of critical understanding, how, without contradiction, the many are one and the one many. Only then will the *claritas* of the whole be perceived as a function of the *integritas* and *consonantia* of its parts.

III

FRANZ KAFKA: *EIN HUNGERKÜNSTLER*

Franz Kafka's final gift to the literary world, his volume *Ein Hungerkünstler*,[1] is no mere haphazard bundle of stories thrown together from earlier scraps and fragments of prose. Nor is it an attempt to peddle four tales on the merits of one, its title story. True enough, Kafka wrote these *Geschichten* over a period of four years;[2] and he published the title story in *Die neue Rundschau* in October, 1922.[3] But he also consciously selected these particular stories for inclusion in a single volume. He worked feverishly to correct the proofs on his death-bed, insisted on the present order of the stories, and became angry with his publishers for not carrying out certain details of his instructions exactly.[4]

So, despite the fact that some motifs, themes, and symbols which one can find in many of Kafka's works recur as part of the texture of these last published stories, and granted too that his narrative techniques do not depart much from his generally recognized, unique mode of storytelling; still, one may and must ask: is the collection as a whole an aesthetic unit?

1 The only book-length works which Kafka prepared for publication during his lifetime were the prose collections: *Betrachtung* (Leipzig, 1912); *Ein Landarzt* (München/Leipzig, 1919); and *Ein Hungerkünstler. Vier Geschichten* (Berlin: "Die Schmiede", 1924).

2 See Malcolm Pasley and Klaus Wagenbach, "Versuch einer Datierung sämtlicher Texte Franz Kafkas", *Deutsche Vierteljahrsschrift*, XXXVIII (Juli, 1964), 149-167. They give the following dates for the composition of the stories: "Erstes Leid", Spätherbst 1921/Frühjahr 1922; "Ein Hungerkünstler", Frühjahr 1922; "Eine kleine Frau", Oktober 1923; and "Josefine...", März 1924.

3 XXXIII (Oktober 1922), 983-992. Three major divisions are indicated at the beginning of the second and third sections by breaks in the text, and by doubling the size of the initial capital letter of the new paragraph. The second section begins: "So lebte er mit regelmäßigen kleinen Ruhepausen..." and the third: "Doch vergingen wieder viele Tage..." (pp. 987, 991).

4 See Max Brod, *Franz Kafka: a Biography* (New York, 1947), p. 211. See Franz Baumer, *Franz Kafka* (Berlin, 1960), p. 90. In his *Nachwort* to the *Erzählungen*, in which the stories of *Ein Hungerkünstler* are reprinted, Brod writes: "Ich habe die einzelnen Prosastücke in derselben Reihenfolge und Zusammenstellung belassen, in der sie Franz Kafka selbst in den gennanten Büchern veröffentlich hat. Insoweit diese Bücher Sammlungen bilden, kann in der Aneinanderreihung der Teile kein Zufall erblickt werden. Auch haben die Bücher als Einheiten ihre Wirkung geübt und gehören daher in dieser Form der Geistesgeschichte an." (Reprinted in *Erzählungen* [Berlin, 1965], pp. 320-321. Originally published, 1946.)

Are the stories which Kafka bound together in this one volume also structurally unified by a single aesthetic pattern? Is our reading of each of the stories a totally isolated experience, or is it significantly modified by our reading that story as a part of a larger structural unit? I do not here speak about mere recurrence of themes, archetypes, or rhetorical constructions, but about a unique patterning of theme, structures, and rhetoric observable in a single volume of stories.

A. PREVIOUS CRITICISM

The first sustained attempt to work out the unity of this collection appeared some thirty-two years after "Die Schmiede" press published the stories under Kafka's instructions. Norbert Furst, in 1965,[5] working from the clue that three of the stories mention *Kunst*, proposed that the entire collection dealt with art, each story taking a different perspective. The subtitles of his study indicate the general orientation of his interpretation: "'Josefine die Sängerin' oder Kunst und Volk", "'Ein Hungerkünstler' oder Kunst und Publikum", "'Eine kleine Frau' oder Frau Kunst und Kafka", and "'Erstes Leid' oder Kunst an sich". Furst's basic mistake was his confusion of form: since he believed he was criticizing allegories in the traditional sense, he felt he had to "reconstruct, though with coarse hands, a scaffolding of abstract structure".[6]

Four years later, Hermann Pongs[7] offered no significantly new insights. His analysis follows Furst's interpretation and is guilty of its *Hauptschwäche*, based on a misunderstanding of form. Both men offer perceptive critical remarks, but neither had learned to deal with the "entirely

[5] *Die offenen Geheimtüren Franz Kafkas* (Heidelberg, 1956), pp. 72-80. Furst's method is to work backward. In his forword, he writes: "Jede Parabel ist am durchsichtigsten an ihrem Ende. Kafkas ganzes Werk wird durchsichtiger gegen das Ende. Deshalb muß man ihn von hinten her interpretieren, wenn man ihn auch von vorne lesen muß." (p. 8). He applies this technique to *Ein Hungerkünstler*, but must admit at the end of his presentation that Kafka's *Vieldeutigkeit* has been too much for him: "Alles kann alles bedeuten, – das ist nicht Fortschritt, das ist Verfall einer Kunst. Das ist die Schwäche dieses Symbol-Realismus, das ist die Hauptschwäche unserer Interpretationen."(pp. 79-80). For briefer references to interconnections among the stories, see Herbert Tauber, *Franz Kafka: Eine Deutung seiner Werke* (Zurich, 1941), p. 180; Charles Neider, *The Frozen Sea* (New York, 1948), p. 82; Walter Sokel, *Franz Kafka: Tragik und Ironie* (München, 1964), p. 471. Also see Brod's remark quoted above in note four.

[6] "...wieder mit den groben Händen begrifflicher Konstruktion ein Gerüst darum zimmern müssen" (p. 73, my translation).

[7] *Franz Kafka: Dichter des Labyrinths* (Heidelberg, 1960). He treats *Ein Hungerkünstler* in his chapter entitled "Negative Urbilder", pages 86-93.

new phenomenon which Kafka's prose represents".[8]

Although Heinz Politzer does not explicitly treat the collection as a unit, and seems doubtful about any such attempt, his analysis of the *ur*-bachelor in the *Tagebücher* and of other bachelors in the early works widens one's horizons beyond narrow biographical and allegorical interpretative views. The artist of the later works, Politzer says, parallels the bachelor of the earlier works. Both are representatives of man as "outsider". Politzer writes: "The bachelor was the first mask Kafka put on to stylize his mode of expression and to raise his monologues beyond the level of a private confession".[9] He continues:

> The paradox of his existence makes the *ur*-bachelor of 1910 the model of Kafka's principal figures. He "stands once and for all outside our people, outside our humanity", like Josephine the Singer. "He is continually starved" (*DI*, 2, 6), a description which anticipates the figure of the Hunger Artist.... The bachelor has less hold on life "than the trapeze artist in a variety show, who still has a net hung up for him below". (p. 45)

The most detailed analysis of the volume *Ein Hungerkünstler* is that of Heinz Hillmann in *Franz Kafka: Dichtungstheorie und Dichtungsgestalt*.[10] Unfortunately, Hillmann accepts the general lines of Furst's interpretation, though he repudiates Furst's and Pong's total equation of the little woman of the second story with "Frau Kunst" or the Muse. Nor does he seem aware of Politzer's insight that the artist-figure is merely a mask for the more fundamental phenomenon of modern man: the outsider. If we prescind from the fact that Hillmann's formulation of the central "meaning" of the story is fundamentally inadequate, since it is biased by a desire to superimpose an artist-in-society interpretation on the stories, we may still find many helpful insights in Hillmann's discussion.

Even within the framework of his interpretation, Hillmann recognizes, for instance, that the artist in the stories struggles not only with art and society, but also with truth, freedom, and life itself. The crowds, which Hillmann groups together as "non-artists", manifest in a variety of ways a fundamental "will-to-live", while those he groups as "artists" follow a tragic path into sorrow, loneliness, bachelorhood, and annihilation.

Hillmann also perceives a dynamic structure of theme and technique in

[8] Günther Anders, *Franz Kafka*, trans. A. Steer and A. K. Thorlby (London, 1960), p. 43. The original may be found in *Kafka: Pro und Contra* (München, 1951), p. 40.

[9] *Franz Kafka: Parable and Paradox* (Ithaca, New York, 1962), p. 36. The *ur*-bachelor passage may be found in *Tagebücher*, ed. Max Brod (New York, 1949), I, 17-24.

[10] (Bonn, 1964), pp. 68-112. See especially pp. 107-112.

the story cycle. Motifs develop, he says, through a shifting of perspectives, a broadening of horizons, a heightening of dominant characteristics, and a buttressing of them with less commanding features. His analysis fails, not because he was blind to relationships which actually exist in the collection, but because his inner impulse toward clarity actually clouded his vision and drove him beyond the data of the stories to an abstract meaning quite apart from the imaginative structure itself. He himself realized that his study was incomplete. One must, he said, gather together all the themes of the collection if he hopes to present a complete picture of Kafka's imaginative meaning.[11]

This study will offer no substitute allegorical interpretation for that of Furst, Pongs, and Hillmann. As Emrich,[12] Collins,[13] and others[14] insist, Kafka was not writing allegories in the traditional sense. Indeed, he repudiated allegorical presentations as mere fragments of truth which tend to contradict themselves by assuming the role of total truth. They falsify the richness of both life and art by attempting to simplify their complexity.

My intent in the following pages is to point out the developing complexities of *Ein Hungerkünstler*, not to reduce it to a false simplicity; to trace the patterns in the weave, not to unwind the fabric. Also, I hope to show that this collection is representative of one kind of short story cycle: that is, that the reader's experience of each of the stories is significantly modified by his experience of the other stories in the cycle, since their patterning reveals the simultaneous development of several interconnected themes.

If Kafka's prose is an "entirely new phenomenon" (Anders) and if it introduces "eine neue Epoche der Dichtung" (Emrich), it is essential to pause on the threshhold of our analysis to ask: what kind of new creature

11 "...erst wenn wir sämtliche Aussagen der Sammlung zusammennehmen, ergibt sich das Totum aller Aspekte. Nicht eine der Erzählungen sagt die ganze Wirklichkeit... sondern erst alle zusammen ergeben ein adäquates Bild" (p. 112).

12 Wilhelm Emrich, *Franz Kafka* (Bonn, 1958), p. 81. "Seine Dichtung ist weder allegorisch noch symbolisch. Sie besitzt vielmehr einen Gleichnischarakter, für den die seitherige Äesthetik und Poetik noch keinen Namen bereitgestellt had, weil eine derartige Gleichniswelt vor ihm noch nicht in Erscheinung getreten ist. Kafkas Gleichnis- und Bilderwelt leitet eine neue Epoche der Dichtung ein."

13 Hildegard Platzer Collins, *A Study of the Relationships Between Technique and Theme in the Shorter Works of Kafka* (Dissertation: University of Southern California, 1962) p. 64.

14 See Dieter Hasselblatt, *Zauber und Logik. Ein Kafka-Studie* (Köln, 1964), p. 183. Heinz Politzer, *Franz Kafka: Parable and Paradox*, p. 8; Benno von Wiese, *Die Deutsche Novelle*, Vol. II (Dusseldorf, 1960), pp. 330-331.

are we dealing with? In 1939, Philip Rahv proposed the term "experimental myth". Unfortunately, the term has been either discarded or ignored in the hassel over "allegory", "symbol", "parable", and other half-helpful, half-confusing terms.[15] Kafka's narratives, Rahv says,

> are speculations translated into the language of the imagination; they are myths whose judicious, mock-scientific tonality at once dissociates them from the myth as an historical product.... Experimental in tendency, they are not so much findings about reality as methods of exploring it. One might call them experimental myths.[16]

The distinct advantage of such a term as EXPERIMENTAL MYTH is its "open-endedness": one feels no pressure to search for a tight meaning-structure to superimpose on the detailed imaginative structure. The myth expresses its own inner significance. It speaks directly to each man's consciousness. Kafka's personal literary myths do not spring from primitive folk-beliefs directly, but they do make use of epic motifs, primitive symbols, and pseudo-heroic rhetoric in the hope of expressing for today's lackluster world the inexpressible mysteries at the heart of life – mysteries Kafka felt could be experienced by everyone, but could not be abstractly stated. "Ich suche immerfort etwas Nicht-Mitteilbares mitzuteilen", Kafka wrote to Milena, "etwas Unerklärbares zu erklären".[17] One does not choose allegory to communicate obscurities. One chooses a complex form to express a complex of meanings.

Kafka's miniature myths have something of the epical, the heroic about them – their inflated diction,[18] for instance, or their presentation of an

[15] As one might expect, critics disagree widely on what genre, tone, intentions, influences, problems, devices, motifs, themes, techniques, and points of view are to be discovered in and beneath the works of Kafka. Thomas Mann calls him a "dreamer" and his compositions "dreamlike". Austin Warren says he is "a metaphysical poet in symbolist narrative". Edwin Muir says his chief problem is that of "finding one's true vocation". Oskar Baum calls it the "struggle to become a part of the community". Friedrich Beißner says, "the unsuccessful arrival or the failure to reach the goal" is Kafka's recurrent theme.

The most recent full-length studies of Kafka emphasize continuity of theme, motif, myths and archetypes, structural patterns, and narrative techniques. See especially Hermann Pongs, *Franz Kafka, Dichter des Labyrinths*; Heinz Politzer, *Franz Kafka: Parable and Paradox*; Kurt Weinburg, *Kafkas Dichtungen. Die Travestien des Mythos* (Bern/München, 1963); Christoph Bezzel, *Natur bei Kafka* (Nurnberg, 1964); Walter H. Sokel, *Franz Kafka. Tragik und Ironie*; and Dieter Hasselblatt, *Zauber und Logik.*

[16] "The Hero as Lonely Man", *Kenyon Review*, I (Winter, 1939), p. 62.

[17] *Briefe an Milena* (New York, 1952), p. 249.

[18] See Michel Dentan, *Humour et création littéraire dans l'oeuvre de Kafka* (Paris, 1961).

isolated hero in the midst of his quest. His heroes, however, live in diminished, nonheroic surroundings. The inflated diction and intensification of quest often center around trivia, and even then the outcome leads to compromise or defeat, rarely to victory.

Hypothesis casts its frail shadow over every thought and action and interpretation of action. The texture of these myths is overlaid with judicious self-conscious reflection. Their images derive not from a wellspring of unguarded archetypes, but from the laboratory atmosphere of experimental self-consciousness. Mix assurance with error in the test-tube of the brain; mix identity with community, the spirit of quest with the chemistry of habitual behavior, the desire to communicate with the impossibility to communicate – Kafka's experimental myths seem to be imaginative formulations of the complex interreactions of such antinomies.

If the expression "experimental myths" approximates the inner dynamic structure of many of Kafka's works, *Geschichten* or *Kurzgeschichten*[19] may serve to designate the general literary form of the four stories in the collection under consideration. Hillmann distinguishes among *Betrachtung*, *Parabel*, and *Geschichte*. The *Geschichte*, which he also calls *parabolische Erzählung*, allows for "die Verschränkung der Realen und der vergleichsweisen Ebene". "Diese Erzählung", he continues,

> unterscheidet sich aber in einem ganz wesentlichen Moment von der Betrachtung und der Parabel. Sie kennt nämlich nicht wie diese eine einzige in sich abgeschlossene Situation, sondern sie ist bestimmt durch die Abfolge von Situation, also durch Bewegung und Handlungsablauf. (pp. 170-171)

Kafka himself gave the subtitle "Geschichte" to his story "Das Urteil". More important, he subtitled his collection *Ein Hungerkünstler: Vier Geschichten*. These, I submit, are short stories in the general twentieth-century acceptation of that term: tightly constructed, relatively brief prose fictions whose movements highlight meaningful situations rather than evolve through extended connected action from a leisurely examination of event, character, and environment.[20]

19 See Hermann Pongs, p. 86.

20 Other criteria of classification, of course, would yield different terminology. But this would not conflict with a classification of genre according to the criteria I proposed in the first chapter. Classifications based on other criteria might place these stories in the "absurdist" or "surrealistic" schools. They might be called fantasies, *Forschungen*, expressionistic stories, German literature, Jewish writings, and so forth. Hillmann subclassifies "Josefine..." as *Bericht* using the criterion of point-of-view.

B. STRUCTURE OF STORY AND CYCLE

The collection *Ein Hungerkünstler*, then, forms a cycle of four short stories which fill fifty pages of Max Brod's edition of *Erzählungen*.[21] The stories in the order given by Kafka and maintained by Brod are: "Erstes Leid"[22] (four pages, five paragraphs; translation "First Sorrow"); "Eine kleine Frau"[23] (ten pages, nine paragraphs; translation "A Little

[21] (Berlin: Fischer Verlag, 1965). All of my quotations are taken from this edition. Page references are included in the text immediately after a quotation.

[22] Written 1921-1922. In 1961, the MSS of the four stories were deposited (along with the bulk of Kafka's *Nachlaß*) in the Bodleian Library (Oxford) by their previous owner, Mrs. Marianna Steiner. See J. M. S. Pasley, "Franz Kafka's MSS: Description and Select Inedita", *Modern Language Review*, LVII (January 1962), 53-59. "Erstes Leid" was first published with the collection in 1924.

Capsulization of criticism. Herbert Tauber, *Franz Kafka*, pp. 180-181 [The trapeze artist represents the extreme of detachment from the difficult aspects of earthly life. When forced to change places, he has to recall his connection with the "untern Sphären".]. Charles Neider, *The Frozen Sea*, p. 83 ["'First Sorrow'...exploits the ridiculousness of the extremist as well as his sadness in solitude."]. Hans S. Reiss, *Franz Kafka* (Heidelberg, 1952), pp. 105-106 [Story concerns the sorrows that threaten each person who is uncertain about his *Grundlagen* of existence.]. Norbert Furst, *Die offenen Geheimtüren*, p. 78. Heinz Politzer, *Franz Kafka*, p. 303 ["The inner movement of this little piece...is contrapuntal in a highly ironical fashion. It turns out that the manager – and not the artist – is the real victim of this 'first sorrow', and that as far as the artist is concerned, the 'first sorrow' may easily prove to be his last."]. Kurt Weinburg, *Kafkas Dichtungen*, p. 50 [Calls the trapeze artist a god-figure.]. Hildegard Platzer Collins, *A Study of the Relationships Between Technique and Theme...*, pp. 293-294 [Trapeze artist is in love with his alienation. In desiring a second bar, he wishes to create a complete existence in the air. "Kafka's judgment upon those who seek to escape through this form of relinquishment is that they are the most complete of egoists; they seek to have all judgments against them suspended, to achieve both freedom from all prohibitions and honor for having observed all of them."].

[23] Written October 1923. The four leaves of large quarto (280 × 205 mm) light-blue paper on which the MS appears is of the same cut and color as the "Josefine" MS. "Eine kleine Frau" was first published with the collection *Ein Hungerkünstler* in 1924.

Capsulization of criticism. Herbert Tauber, *Franz Kafka*, 179-180 ["Die 'kleine Frau' ist die Projektion einer innern Unruhe."]. Kate Flores, "Biographical Note" in *The Kafka Problem*, ed. Angel Flores (New York, 1946), p. 18 [The little woman is Frau Hermann.]. Jean Carrive, Note to his translation of "Die [sic] kleine Frau", *Le Cheval de Troie* (Paris, 1948), pp. 808-809 [The little woman is Kafka's conscience; the man, Kafka's representative before his conscience.]. Max Brod, *Franz Kafka, A Biography*, p. 197 ["The 'little woman-judge' who lives her life in constant anger with her own 'ego', which is really a stranger to her, is none other than their (Kafka's and Dora Dymant's) landlady. She must have put a lot of difficulties in the way of the young couple."]. Charles Neider, *The Frozen Sea*, p. 83 [Its motifs are "introversion, despair, fear, loneliness, acute self-analysis, sick scrupulosity."]. Johannes Pfeiffer, "Franz Kafka: 'Eine kleine Frau'", in *Wege zur Erzählkunst* (Hamburg, 1953), pp. 108-115 [Nicht eingesehen.]. Norbert Furst, *Die offenen Geheimtüren*, pp. 76-77 ["...sie ist die 'Muse'."]. H. P. Collins, *A Study...*, pp. 261-263 ["One is guilty for not marrying, and displays that guilt by seeking to marry. This paradox is the occasion for the story 'Eine Kleine

Woman"); "Ein Hungerkünstler"[24] (thirteen and a half pages, ten paragraphs; translation "A Hunger Artist"); and "Josefine die Sängerin, oder Das Volk der Mäuse"[25] (twenty-two and a half pages, thirty-four paragraphs; translation "Josephine the Singer, or The Mouse Folk").

Each story begins with a description of a fundamentally calm situation, a positive presentation under which only slight negative hints lurk; immediately, then, some disturbing change, either in the situation itself

Frau',... There is no actual personal relationship between them; she regards him not as an individual but as man. He offends her by the fact of his existence, both because he does not approach her and because he might by his male nature presume to do so.... The protagonist causes her to suffer by the fact of his existence; whether he has no choice in the matter does not eliminate the guilt. She need not feel it but she does, and – more important – he feels her suffering and sees it as a judgment. Thus, the guilt of the individual becomes analyzed in a parable based on the absurdity of it."]. Heinz Politzer, *Franz Kafka*, p. 303 [The story is a thumbnail sketch of Kafka's landlady in Berlin. "It is the only one among the four stories contained in *A Hunger Artist* which does not sound the artist theme explicitly, although it is connected to the rest of the volume by the flexibility of its cadences and the ease of its tone."].

24 Written by Spring 1922. See Meno Spann, "Die beiden Zettel Kafkas", *Monatshefte*, XLVII (1955), 321-328. Also, Malcolm Pasley and Klaus Wagenbach, "Datierung...", pp. 149-167. First published in *Die neue Rundschau*, XXXIII (Oktober 1922), 983-992. This story is said to be Kafka's favorite among his later works.

Capsulization of criticism. Harry Steinhauer, *Die Deutsche Novelle* (New York, 1936), pp. 190-193 ["The hunger artist is the saint, who has subdued his selfish instincts and joyfully denies himself all worldly pleaures, devoting his life to the service of God... He symbolizes the spirit of true religion."]. Harry Slochower, "Franz Kafka – Pre-Fascist Exile", in *A Franz Kafka Miscellany* (New York, 1940), p. 29. Herbert Tauber, *Franz Kafka*, pp. 181-182 [The basic irony of the story is that the hunger artist is no artist. "Das Hungern ist ihm Bedürfnis, er leidet an chronischer Appetitlosigkeit." When the Impresario and the sick man get together, a special situation emerges: "Negative Kräfte erhalten durch eine schauspielerische Verkehrung einen positiven Anschein."]. Claude-Edmonde Magny, "The Objective Depiction of Absurdity", in *The Kafka Problem*, pp. 75-96 [Fasting is a fate, not a vocation.]. Paul Goodman, *Kafka's Prayer* (New York, 1947), p. 232 ["Hunger-Art, the abstention from trying to be happy in the conditions of hopelessness...."]. R. W. Stallman, "A Hunger-Artist", in *Franz Kafka Today*, ed. Angel Flores (Madison, Wisconsin, 1958), pp. 61-70 ["'A Hunger-Artist' epitomizes Kafka's theme of the corruption of interhuman relationships." "...it is possible to read the meanings of 'A Hunger-Artist' on at least three different levels; there is never a time when we can say that any of its elements means precisely and exactly this."]. Günther Anders, *Franz Kafka*, p. 38 ["He does not feel shut *in* but shut *out*. His purpose is not to break out but to break in – into the world. And the symbol of this negative imprisonment is a barred cage, for the world from which he is shut out is visible to him."]. William C. Rubinstein, "A Hunger Artist", *Monatshefte*, XLIV (January 1952), 13-19 ["This short story is one of Kafka's final statements on the condition of art in general and on his art in particular."]. Walter Muschg, *Tragische Literaturgeschichte* (Bern, 1953), pp. 545ff [Nicht eingesehen.]. Colin Wilson, *The Outsider* (London/Boston, 1956), p. 118 ["Kafka's story 'The Fasting Showman' is the climax of his work, his clearest statement of the Outsider's position."]. Norbert Furst, *Die offenen Geheimtüren*, pp. 74-76. Claude Vigée, "Les artistes de la faim", *Table Ronde* (Avril 1957), 43-64 ["L'Artiste de la Faim, dans le schéma mental de Kafka, est

or in the narrator's recollection of it, destroys the placidity of the opening section. Finally, the narrative advances to a partial climax, an imagined revelation or a projected crisis; and then sinks back into an insecure state of apparent calm.

The positive description of a person or a situation in each case emphasizes normality or typicality and casts a protective glaze over the fundamental strangeness of that which is accepted as everyday. Implied narrative

---

l'équivalent renversé de la paternité, l'image négative d'une fertilité convoitée mais interdite."]. Felix Weltsch, *Religion und Humor im Leben und Werk Franz Kafkas* (Berlin, 1957), pp. 79-83 [Treats four lines of meanings through the story.]. Meno Spann, "Franz Kafka's Leopard", *The Germanic Review*, XXXIV (April 1959), 85-104 [For Kafka, the story is an expression of regret for an unfulfilled life. The story is "an intimate revelation of Kafka's *Lebensgefühl.*" Kafka shows a sincere admiration for the leopard's "authentic existence even in captivity".]. H. M. Waidson, "The Starvation-Artist and the Leopard", *The Germanic Review*, XXXV (December 1960), 262-269 ["The starvation-artist unites in himself man's aspirations both in realms of art and of religion; the leopard represents the predatory urge of a life-force that is hostile to these spheres...."]. Benno von Wiese, *Die Deutsche Novelle* (Düsseldorf, 1960), Vol. II, pp. 325-342 ["Die Zweideutigkeit des Hungerkünstlers beginnt mit dem Zuschaustellen seiner Kunst. Sein Verhältnis zum Publikum ist ein ununterbrochenes wechselseitiges Mißverständnis." "Für den Hungerkünstler ist die Welt im Zustand der Verfremdung, für die Welt ist es der Hungerkünstler. Indem Kafka beides wechselseitig spiegelt, spricht er seine parabolische Wahrheit aus." "Wenn die geistige Existenz des Hungerkünstlers negative beschrieben werden mußte, ...so bedeutet die vitale des Panthers eine positive Illusion der Freiheit."]. Arthur E. Waterman, "Kafka's The [sic!] Hunger Artist", *CEA Critic*, XXIII (1961), 9 ["In short, 'The (sic!) Hunger Artist' is a dream rendered in the universal language of the dream."]. Michel Dentan, *Humour et création littéraire...*, pp. 143-168 [The hunger artist's art is only "le signe de son impuissance à vivre. La panthère seule a droit aux regards des visiteurs."]. Heinz Politzer, *Franz Kafka*, 318-319 ["...the 'Hunger Artist' conveys to the reader the unresolved ambiguity of Kafka's attitude toward the relationship between artist and art and 'Josephine' is intended to make a similarly noncommittal statement about the interaction of artist and society."]; p. 308 ["This art is fatal since it can only be perfected by the Artist's death."]. Harry Steinhauer, "Hungering Artist or Artist in Hungering", *Criticism*, IV (1962), 28-43 [Says previous criticism is unanimously wrong in saying that the hunger artist is the artist in the modern world. Concentrates on the symbolic function of the children. Relates the title to Raabe's *Hungerpastor*, which deals with a clergyman whose life is devoted to the pursuit of positive ideals. "What Kafka tells us in *A Hunger Artist* is that even he who has found the way and lives by hungering has a rough time of it in our world.... Perhaps all that Kafka is saying is: even if we can conceive of a man who is all spirit and no flesh...we shall find that his career is one of frustration; for no one ever really cared about him and today we care even less."]. H. P. Collins, *A Study...*, p. 139 ["The powerful brutes that occur in Kafka's stories are invariably representatives of external force...they always exist as awesome figures to the protagonist."]. Ingeborg Henel, "Ein Hungerkünstler", *Deutsche Vierteljahrsschrift*, XXXVIII (1964), 230-247 [The central theme is the "Widerspruchlichkeit des Lebens". In man, Kafka displays two contrary movements: "Die erste drängt ihn aus seinen Ursprung über das Leben hinaus, die andere stößt ihn in seinen Ursprung zurück." The hunger artist represents one of these movements, the leopard the other. "Das

judgments in these descriptive sketches redound to the credit of the unusual individual around whom they center. For instance, everyone "forgives" the trapeze artist the minor disturbances he causes by being always aloft "weil er ein außerordentlicher, unersetzlicher Künstler war" (p. 24). The prim little woman, though she wears nothing extraordinary and is possessed of a perfectly normal hand, is "leicht beweglich" – a quality which the narrator later says might have influenced his alleged love affair, had

Publikum, das weder die Fähigkeit zum Hungern noch die Vitalität des Tieres in sich hat, bewegt sich zwischen diesen beiden Extremen. Seine Sensationslust treibt es erst zu dem Käfig des Hungerkünstlers, später zu den Ställen der Raubtiere."].

[25] Though some critics have placed this story's composition as early as 1922, Pasley and Wagenbach date it March, 1924. Emrich calls it Kafka's "swansong". Most probably, it was the last piece Kafka wrote. The MS fills nine and a half leaves of large quarto (280 × 205) lightblue, square paper, of the same kind and cut as that used for "Eine kleine Frau".

Capsulization of criticism. Brod, *Franz Kafka, A Biography*, p. 95 ["'To be alone brings nothing but punishment' – this sentence from the diary is a *leitmotiv* that...finds its strongest positive expression just in the last piece he wrote, in the story called 'Josephine the Songstress – or The Mice Nation'."]; pp. 192-193 ["The negative aspect of the Jewish problem, the indefensibility of the Jewish position, is also demonstrated in the story, 'Josephine the Songstress – or The Mice Nation', the last finished work of Kafka's, and one which he himself destined for the printing press."]. Tauber, p. 183-4 ["Kafka hat in dem Volk der Mäuse sein besonders geartetes Bild des jüdischen Volkes gezeichnet und zugleich seinem persönlichen jüdischen Gemeinschaftsgefühl Ausdruck gegeben." The story, he says, "bringt gegenüber der Ironie der übrigen Teile des Sammelbandes etwas Positives".]. Goodman, pp. 257-258. Neider, pp. 82-83 ["A masochistic touch is Kafka's choice of a mouse to represent the artist."]. Friedrich Beißner, *Der Erzähler Franz Kafka* (Stuttgart, 1952), p. 41 [Disagrees with Anders who says Josephine stands unambiguously for the Jewish religion as an episode in the history of the Jewish people. Agrees more with Walter Muschg's idea that in this story Kafka carries the "Lebensform des Künstlers" to its absurd limits.]. P. P. J. van Caspel, "Josefine und Jeremias", *Neophilologus*, XXXVII, iv (1953), 241-245 [Josephine represents the Jewish prophets, especially Jeremias.]. Furst, pp. 73-74 [Kafka allegorizes his own art and art in general.]. Weltsch, p. 83 [Calls "Josephine" one of the most wonderful representations of the theme "Volk und Kunst" that world literature knows.]. Carl R. Woodring, "Josephine the Singer, or the Mouse Folk", in *Franz Kafka Today*, ed. Angel Flores and Homer Swander (Madison, 1958), 71-75 [Josephine is a leading actress of a Jewish theatrical troupe, or a cantor in the Jewish synagogue, but at the same time, an artist and a representative of the universal artist. "...in 'Josephine' a singer is masterfully symbolized by a singer; here an artist is an artist is an artist." "Kafka's symbols have as specific referents only themselves.... Josephine is Josephine, skillfully blurred."]. Emrich, pp. 167-172 [Treats "Josephine" in his section dealing with *Tiererzählungen.* Though he entitles his subsection on "Josphine": "Rechtfertigung und Kritik der Kunst", at the end of the story he says: "Sie ist nicht nur Bild der 'Kunst', sondern übersteigt die Kunst in eine universelle freie 'Existenz' hinein, in der sich alle wiedererkennen." Also: "Die gerecht Abwägung zwischen Sängerin und Volk ist in der Tat das Thema der Erzählung." The people were right not to grant Josephine's demands. To do otherwise would bring about chaos.]. Dentan, pp. 143-151 [Kafka is denouncing the sham artist, but also doing much more. Calls the story a "récit". He makes special note of the questions and contradictions, the suspiciousness

her good qualities not been perniciously directed toward his discomfort. The professional faster receives enthusiastic support from the crowds of spectators who press around his cage. And the narrator of "Josephine" describes her affectionately as "unsere Sängerin", pointing out what a prodigy she is, since she alone of all the mouse people appreciates music and is able to communicate it.

Each of these positive descriptions, however, carries within it the seeds

---

of the narrator. He speaks especially of the narrator's inflation of diction. "Plus l'auteur affecte une attitude de tranquille assurance dans sa démarche, plus on se prend à douter de la gravité de cette démarche...." He notes the ease of misinterpreting the story: "Le chant de Joséphine est un image à laquelle on est porté à attribuer immédiatement un sens: il représente l'art, la fonction de l'art. Tel est le premier mouvement du lecteur, et ce premier mouvement est décu. La signification de l'image offrait une fausse évidence." Later he says (p. 164): "Il est question sans cesse de graves problèmes et d'objects élevés: les besoins de l'âme, la nostalgie du bonheur, les misères de la vie, le problème de l'art et de son apport spirituel, le statut de l'artiste dans la société, le but et lespossibilitiés de l'existence, le problème de l'enfance, etc."]. Politzer, pp. 309-316 ["Like the Hunger Artist's fasting, Josephine's piping is only the exaggeration of a very common experience." Josephine is "the highly professional performer of an art which is at best an illusion, at worst nothing". The lack of "interest by the Mouse Folk in their own history casts considerable doubt on their affinity with the Jews, who are extremely conscious of history...." "The report of the narrator...can be read as an attempt on the part of Kafka to establish the amount of truth which a community can still discover and communicate about itself."]. Collins, pp. 223-231 ["The relationship of Josephine to the community is the basic theme of the story, of course, and I would suggest that as such she represents the whole body of cultural beliefs and traditions of the community. That the community itself is not simply the Jews, but mankind as it is related to the forces of the universe, is fairly decisive from Kafka's constant use of vermin in this way.... To the extent that one may include both art and religious prophecy in the traditions of the human community, both of these interpretations represent partial truth." "...in 'Josefine' there is no searching protagonist; the story is that of the community in the form of its doubts, reservations, and indecisiveness regarding Josefine." "The latest word on Josefine is that she has disappeared – indicative, perhaps, of the twentieth-century loss of cultural tradition. Church, Art, Law – all have been cited as losing their hold over the 'nation'...."]. Sokel, pp. 523-531 [Mentions that Josephine is the first of Kafka's heroes to be called "*Held*", and she is so named by her alleged opponent. "Ihre Kunst macht sie zum Helden", says Sokel. Among the characteristics of Josephine, Sokel notes: *Kindheit*, *Eitelkeit*, *Ichsucht*, *Machttrieb*, and *Ehrgeiz*. "Und daher ist unter allen Kafka-Helden Josefine die einzige, die errecht, was alle anderen vergeblich anstreben. Sie gewinnt Macht über die Macht." Sokel, more than any other critic, emphasizes the reality of Josephine's heroic position in society: "Zum ersten Mal erhebt Kafka in *Josefine* seinen Helden als Einsel-Ich und Künstler zum fraglosen Erlöser der Welt und der Macht. Es ist das Kind, das hier den Vater, der Einzelne, der die Gesamtheit, die Kunst, die das Leben erlöst, ja die das Leben erst verbürgt." Before, the saving-function of the hero in Kafka was always questionable. Sokel believes Josephine UNAMBIGUOUSLY saves the community: "Erst in *Josefine* wird der Ich-Held ganz eindeutig Erlöser...."].

of its own disintegration. The acrobat's home in the dome isolates him from "menschlichen Verkehr" and limits the possibilities of growth. The little woman, though she is "leicht beweglich", still "übertreibt freilich diese Beweglichkeit". In "A Hunger Artist" some of the adults who crowd around the man in the cage, look upon him as a joke who happens to be in fashion. And Josephine carries her alleged gift of song in a clay jar, for mice are fundamentally unmusical and could never be expected to appreciate real singing.

The second major portion of each of the stories bursts the glazed bubble of false securities which surround those hidden, fundamentally destructive elements of the first. An unavoidable change of place, or an unfortunate shift of public interest, attacks the roots of false security in stories one and three.[26] In stories two and four, the first-person narrators, beginning with the phrase (identical in both): "ich habe oft darüber nachgedacht" (pp. 245 and 269), frantically, yet with a mask of calm, examine the disguised destructive elements of the first section from a variety of viewpoints.

The central sections of those two stories are built around a set of questions, posed consciously by the narrators. In the ten pages of "Eine kleine Frau", fourteen structural questions (direct and indirect) are posed, none of them is answered with affirmative non-modal replies, some are not answered at all, some are answered conjecturally ("mag sein..."), and some negatively[27]. The narrator in "Josephine" spends the greater part of his narrative over two central questions about Josephine's music and its relation to the people. Primarily he asks (and repeats the question): "Ist es denn überhaupt Gesang? Ist es nicht vielleicht doch nur ein Pfeifen?" (p. 269). And later:

> Was treibt das Volk dazu, sich für Josefine so zu bemühen? Ein Frage, nicht leichter zu beantworten als die nach Josefinens Gesang, mit der sie ja auch zusammenhängt. (p. 275)

More than ten paragraphs from this second section are devoted to possible explanations. The penultimate paragraph of "Josephine" raises four more unanswerable questions – all connected with the two on which the major portion of the story had been based. Posed in quick succession, they receive as answer only a general conjecture.

[26] For the sake of simplification, I will often use the numbers one ("First Sorrow"), two ("A Little Woman"), three ("A Hunger Artist") and four ("Josephine....") to indicate the stories as they occur in a pattern.

[27] See Hillmann, pp. 127 ff.

The final portions of stories one and three (both third-person omniscient narratives) employ dialogue in dramatized scenes. The acrobat in his luggage rack whispers his dream of two trapeze bars to the Impresario. The conversation mounts unreasonably from request to demand to outburst, till at last the acrobat's tears flow down the concerned Impresario's cheeks. At last, a vague expression of ultimate concern flows from the disturbed acrobat: "'Nur diese eine Stange in den Händen – wie kann ich denn leben!'" (p. 244). After the manager has soothed the trembling acrobat into a "scheinbar ruhigen Schlaf", a flood of questions which indicate that true childlike peace can never again protect the acrobat from "existenzbedrohende" questions, flows, one assumes, through the manager's mind. In "A Hunger Artist" the question-answer dialogue between the *Aufseher* and the starving man in the cage appears to the *Aufseher* as the final outpourings of a confused and muddled brain. The world-shaking revelation, which seems so important to the hunger artist, holds no interest for the crowds. They thrill, rather, to see a sprightly leopard fill the once drab cage.

The first person narratives (stories two and four) conclude with summaries, not scenes, of the interior states of the narrators (in "Josephine", the narrator speaks in behalf of *das Volk*). Each is primarily concerned with re-evaluating his relationship with the central subject – in both cases a woman. Both conclude with a reaffirmation of interior calm: the one, of himself only; the other, of all the *Volk* of whom he is a responsible member.

Each story, then, represents both a dialectic moving out from, and a cyclic motion returning again to the original starting point. The hidden, disturbing elements of the first section of each story are brought gradually to the center of attention in the second part; finally a conclusion ("scene" in one and three, "summary" in two and four) is presented which is both a development of, and a return to the original situation. At the end of "First Sorrow", the acrobat falls asleep, but leaves the Impresario wakeful and disturbed. The return to a childhood of sleep and dreams, apparently so peaceful, leaves the acrobat in as unstable a situation, and on as precarious a balance, as his habitual life on the trapeze. The very character of the acrobat's life must lead him deeper and deeper into existential *Angst*.

"A Hunger Artist" ends with the death of the emaciated showman and the display of a vigorous young leopard. As the "vergnügungssüchtige Menge" had crowded around the cage of the man who fasted because he could do nothing else, now they press around the cage of a beast who eats heartily because he can do nothing else. In the similarity of end and beginning, one sees an obvious irony of reversal.

At the end of "A Little Woman" the narrator assures himself that he will keep "diese kleine Sache verdeckt" and continue to live "ungestört von der Welt" as calmly as before. But his words serve only as a cloak for his own anxiety. As an "interested" narrator, all he says is highly suspect. He protests too much. He is merely trying to keep his anxiety from destroying him. The perceptive reader will understand that the story's end is merely a return to the unstable equilibrium of its beginning, and that the entire process of over-intense reflection can easily be precipitated again by the slightest push from outside.

The cyclic character of "Josephine" is less obvious, because it not only draws together previously treated themes from the earlier stories but also terminates the collection and points beyond it. Nevertheless, it, too, leaves open a thematic return to the initial situation. Josephine's case is universalized by the narrator and set up as typical of the dialectic of the people versus one of their own. Despite the fatherly and protective characteristics the people show, they are also capable of becoming coldly judicious. The narrator remarks:

> Es handelt sich eben auch bei der Abweisung, ähnlich wie bei der Forderung, nicht um die Sache selbst, sondern darum, daß sich das Volk gegen einen Volksgenossen derart undurchdringlich abschließen kann und um so undurchdringlicher, als es sonst für eben diesen Genossen väterlich und mehr als väterlich, demütig sorgt.

While the people as a whole can manage to be indifferent to Josephine's demands, the very fact that this *Volk* is capable of turning an impenetrable front to one of their own must necessarily disturb each individual of the group.

On another level, this narrator is no less suspect than the narrator of "A Little Woman". He speaks frequently in the first person plural, both as a representative of the people as a whole and as a member of that special group of *Gegner* whom he portrays as possessing the most detached and adult view of the entire struggle. The narrator's anxieties about the struggles of life and about Josephine's role in alleviating the anxieties by her song, emerge gradually from beneath the cool, lengthy, and detailed questioning, reflection, and balancing of judgments which occupy the central and by far the most extensive part of the story. The narrator fears

Josephine really does help to save the people somehow, but refuses to admit that this could be a possibility. Instead, he repeats that this army of mice, though continually under threat of attack and death by the ever-watchful enemy, will, despite the *Hingang* of Josephine, continue on its way, "ruhig, ohne sichtbare Enttäuschung, herrisch, eine in sich ruhende Masse" (p. 290).

"Eine gewisse Schlauheit", he has said in the first paragraph of the story, is the chief characteristic of these people, and their greatest wish is tranquil peace. So one would expect that through *Schlauheit* (manifested as intense rationalization) they would seek peace – calmness in the face of dangers, control of existential *Angst*. At bottom, though anxiety in each story is controlled, it is never conquered. Each story is a return to its beginning. Each ending is the posing of a new disturbing situation. As before, this new situation may explode at any moment into a disruptive nervousness which impedes action and threatens life itself.

While each of the stories shows in itself this double (cyclic and dialectical) movement, the collection as a whole progresses linearly toward greater universality of scene and action, represented by the ever-increasing role of the general populace in that action. The first story deals primarily with a trapeze artist's vague fears, which he tries in vain to communicate to his manager through the ever more intense and irrational urging of already granted demands. The central action is limited to these two characters. The *Umwelt* of the variety theater and the audience at the show are peripheral, unconcerned onlookers. The second story also centers about two people, both of whom are deeply disturbed by one another, though allegedly there exists no external connection between them. Here, however, the narrator attempts to explain the affair to a friend; and the little woman's family involves itself in her failing health; also, there are the "Nachrichtenüberbringer" (p. 248) who are on the point of discovering that the narrator is the cause of the woman's ill health; and finally, on the fringe of the affair, nosy onlookers are trying to smell out a love relationship (energetically denied by the narrator) which they believe (or will believe) must exist between the two central figures.

Within the confines of this story, however, *die Welt* never comes forward to pose those embarrassing and unanswerable questions about which the narrator shudders even to think. Nor does the little woman succeed in expanding her private rancor into public rancor by slyly bringing the situation before the eyes of the *Öffentlichkeit*. Both her *Ärger* and the narrator's *Nervosität* remain, for different reasons, under cover.

The opening paragraph of "A Hunger Artist" introduces a radical expansion of context: the starvation artist, who allows himself to be honored for that which he knows to be essentially unworthy of esteem – his inability to eat – displays his increasing *Magerkeit* before the enthusiastic crowd. Unlike the narrator of "A Little Woman", the fasting showman hides nothing from his admirers. He tells them clearly that he finds it easy to fast; he sits up nights with certain *Wachgruppen* (telling them stories of his *Wanderleben*), to assure them he has nothing edible in the cage. Still the public suspects him of cheating, of bribing the official watchers, or of having discovered some secret trick that makes fasting easy. Once the public involves itself in the hunger artist's life, it controls it completely – that is precisely what the narrator of the second story was trying to avoid. The public, indeed, assumes the role of protagonist and relegates the showman to a side stall in a circus.

In this third story, the extent of the public's involvement, its seeping into and penetrating the texture of the hunger artist's life, is characterized by the gradual penetration, in every page of text, of a wide variety of collective, relational, and functional names for the whole public or some sector of it: (1) inclusive names: *das Publikum, die Leute, die Welt, die ganze Stadt, die Massen, die Menge, Zuschauern, Tausende, das Interesse, Teilnahme, Zeugen, man, jeder, niemand*; (2) relational names: *Kinder, Erwachsenen, gesunder Männer, Familienvater*; (3) functional and official names intimately connected with the hunger artist's performance: *Wächter (vom Publikum erwählte), Fleischhauer, Ärzte, Damen, Orchestra, Fachleute, Impresario, Personal, Diener, Aufseher, Direktion*; (4) names of those peripherally connected with the performance: *Abonnenten, Bestimmter, Mußigganger, Eingeweihten, Wachgruppen*, and *Gemütiger*.

This flood of witnesses, functionaries, officials, engaged spectators, and general public appear most often as subjects of active verbs, of which the hunger artist is often the direct or indirect object.[28] His inner quest and his more fundamental existence-threatening debility have become their personal domain. If they should transfer their interest to some other object – and this is the major action of the story, stated clearly in the opening sentence[29] – the hunger artist's proclivity for starving would (as later happened) draw him down into death.

[28] Whenever the hunger artist functions syntactically as the subject of a sentence, the verb he governs is either passive or intransitive. An important exception to this (there are several others) is the action of answering questions.

[29] "In den letzten Jahrzehnten ist das Interesse an Hungerkünstler sehr zurückgegangen" (p. 255).

His death, however, does not carry the primary thematic weight of the story any more than does Josephine's winning or losing her struggle for recognition by *das Volk* in the fourth story. Rather, the structure of the story indicates a universal and repeatable possibility of a popular shift of interest at any time and for the least discernible reasons from any object or situation to any other. The causes of the change of interest are unknown; its duration is uncertain; but its effects for some members of society are unavoidably ruinous.

Kafka's most frequent characterization of the people as *das Publikum* in this third story indicates an impersonal relationship between the hunger artist and his public. The first sentence of "Josephine", however, immediately establishes a more familiar, more personal connection between Josephine and her "people": "Unsere Sängerin heißt Josephine". Josephine is the only character in the collection to be given an individual name, even though it is joined in the title, almost like a Greek epithet, with her function in society: "Josefine die Sängerin". Still, she is "unsere Sängerin", at once the most highly individualized and the most representative embodiment of the entire people.[30]

Nevertheless, the fact that she is the single exception among the entire race of mice, the only one who both appreciates music and knows how to impart it, places her in direct opposition to that same *Volk* of which she is a member: a tribe of workers who know little or nothing about music, whose lives are full of dangers and whose sole weapon against defeat and death is their cunning.

Several levels of society are differentiated in "Josephine": the *Gegner* and the *Schmeichler*, the *Kinder* and *Erwachsenen*, and an occasional *Störerin* who pipes up during one of Josephine's performances. But all of these groups blend into one – *das Volk* – during Josephine's song. There can be no opposition, the narrator says, when one sits before her. Her song carries in its light half-whistled strains something of the perpetual childishness of the race as well as something of its premature old age. All levels of *das Volk*, when they hear about Josephine's absence, engage

30 The title, conferred by Kafka on his death bed, was, "Josefine die Sängerin, oder Das Volk der Mäuse". See Brod, p. 211; see also *Erzählungen*, p. 278: "Dieses Pfeifen... kommt fast wie ein Botschaft des Volkes zu dem Einzelnen; das dunne Pfeifen Josefinens mitten in den schweren Entscheidungen ist fast wie die armsselige Existenz unseres Volkes mitten im Tumult der feindlichen Welt." In Josephine's music there is something special: "Etwas von der armen kurzen Kindheit ist darin, etwas von verlorenem, die wieder aufzufindendem Glück, aber auch etwas von tätigen heutigen Leben ist darin, von seiner kleinen, unbegreiflichen und dennoch bestehenden und nicht zu ertötenden Munterkeit" (p. 282).

frantically in the massive search to find her: for they have lost something of themselves.

"Josephine" embodies a universalized struggle between identity and community, individual and society, inner call and social function. At the same time, it indicates a possible synthesis of those sets of thematic antinomies. In the final paragraph, the narrator speculates about Josephine (in terminology reminiscent both of a saint's legend and of folk epic) that she has "perhaps" been redeemed in being forgotten. Josephine will join in oblivion the "zahllosen Menge der Helden unseres Volkes" (p. 291). In this forgotten community of exceptional people her gift and her achievement will be both appreciated as *außerordentlich* and accepted as *gewöhnlich*.

C. THEMATIC DIALECTICAL ANTINOMIES

The least common thematic denominator embodied imaginatively in Kafka's four stories is the unstable balance precariously maintained between sets of opposites or antinomies: in other words, the fundamental ambivalences of human living. Individually and as a whole, the stories struggle to control thematic tensions which are set up between: anxiousness and calm; the exceptional and the ordinary; isolation and communication; the individual and society; freedom and the law; perpetual youth and premature old age; the temporary and the permanent. The "essential ambiguity" which several critics have noted in Kafka results from his refusal to opt unconditionally for one side of any of these sets of antinomies. He trenchantly refuses to simplify life in his stories.

Each of these stories forms a complex multiweave tapestry which seems to take different shapes before one's eyes the longer he scrutinizes it. New patterns, new tensions between meanings emerge. Any serious treatment of Kafka's stories must find a way to deal with these tensions and shiftings of perspective.

The underlying dynamico-thematic pattern of the stories, then, is that of oscillation between two poles of the above sets of antinomies. This oscillation weaves ambiguity into the fabric of the work, and by so doing, expresses a fundamental ambivalence in human living. In so far as this alternating, hesitating movement also describes a pattern of thematic development, it assumes the characteristics of a dialectic: the antinomies serve as non-absolute theses and antitheses which emerge into partial syntheses.

These thematic antinomies interpenetrate one another on every level. A man's anxiety, for instance, may be cause or effect or symptom of his inability to communicate, his isolation from society, his failure to attain his hoped-for goal, or his lack of inner freedom. For the sake of intelligibility, however, I will speak of each set of antinomies and their dialectic as critically separable (though not in fact separated) from the "unity of meaning"[31] of the single aesthetic structure: the collection.

Since Kafka's narratives are unique, I shall give a more precise, and perhaps a new meaning to an old critical term. I shall use the word THEME to mean a set of meaning-units; or the set of those situations, words, attitudes, actions, and emotional responses which, as meaning-units, express some aspect of the dynamic relationship between any pair of the above dialectical antinomies. Often in these stories, Kafka indicates his alteration of fictionalized attitude by inserting at pivotal positions key theme-carrying words and phrases of first one pole of the antinomy then the other. At the end of the work appear words and phrases which indicate a partial resolution or a substitute compromise of the viewpoints expressed by each side of the antinomy.

A number of themes parallel one another or envelop one another as the cycle moves from its brief beginning to its more involved conclusion. I shall trace only the three most important of those themes: (1) the theme of anxiety temporarily controlled; pivotal words *ruhig*, *unruhig*, *scheinbar ruhig*; (2) the theme of the exceptional as ordinary, or of compromise in striving; pivotal words *außerordentlich*, *gewöhnlich*, and a variety of synthesizing or compromising responses; (3) the theme of failure to communicate, which progresses through development of situation or of action rather than through pivotally placed words and phrases.

Other themes intermingle with these – such as the themes of man in society, of freedom under the law, of vocation within one's social function, of the childish grown-up, and of the passing of time. Intertwined together, they form a rich weave expressive of the ambivalences of human living.

D. THEME OF ANXIETY TEMPORARILY CONTROLLED

With that general outline of the cyclic and dialectical structures of each of the stories and the linear, universalizing, progressive structure of the cycle

31 See Beissner, in *Kafka*, ed. Gray, p. 19.

in mind, we turn now to a closer examination of the thematic developments which operate within those structures and form their texture. The first and by far the most pervasive of these is the theme (in the sense defined above) of anxiety temporarily controlled. The root of anxiety lies most deeply in the struggle for a secure and/or meaningful existence. The rapid approach of death – that door which opens into a dark world of uncertainties, that axe which smashes into meaningless splinters the life one has been feverishly constructing with such ingenuity and meticulous care over such a long time – ultimately is the chief cause of anxiety.

The proximate causes or occasions of anxiety are myriad:[32] one's innermost security seems threatened because one lacks relationship, or is questing towards some goal, or merely striving to live a full life, or looking forward to final annihilation and total oblivion, or living in a state of economic insecurity or separation from community life; or one is baffled by his own sexuality, or is muddled by his environment, exposed to the world after being overprotected by his parents. One becomes interiorly aware of the passing of time, of apparently arbitrary shifts of fortune, chance occurrences, the apparent meaninglessness of past, present, and future. One feels misunderstood, unable to communicate; feels locked in, limited, or constantly watched, and so forth.

1. "*First Sorrow*"

Many proximate causes or occasions of anxiety form part of the design of *Ein Hungerkünstler* and inhere in the fundamental situation of each of the stories. The trapeze artist, for instance, certainly lacks relationship: "sein menschlicher Verkehr war eingeschränkt" (p. 242) up in the dome of the variety theater. Occasionally he may chat with a *Turnerkollege* or exchange a passing word with the roof repairman or the man who inspects the fire-extinguishing system. (There is no indication that he speaks to the *Diener* who bring his food up to him, nor that he converses with any of the other theater people.)

He trembles when he must descend his ladder and dash through the "menschenleeren Straßen" on the way to the town where the next performance will be held. The Impresario takes special care that all obstacles to the acrobat's hurried return to the heights to which he has become accustomed will be removed – doors opened, aisles emptied. No matter

[32] See Heiri Steiner and Jean Gebser, *Anxiety: A Condition of Modern Man* (New York, 1962).

how fast the train or the "Rennautomobile" flies, however, the manager cannot eliminate "time below" from the acrobat's life. These journeys on the earth excite in the trapeze artist a certain nervousness which deepens until it spreads throughout his being as "existence-threatening" anxiety. Even separated by a tall ladder from the world of daily struggle, a man cannot live *ungestört* in isolation: there will always be unavoidable journeys through the world of men and eventual involvement in the "irdischen Plage" (p. 291) from which Josephine on the last page of this cycle, is finally *erlöst*.

The trapeze artist attempts to solve his problem of isolation and lack of relationship by a half-way measure: perched on the luggage rack, he dreams (*träumte*) of performing on two trapezes. Like taking an aspirin when surgery is required, this pseudo-solution will merely assist the disease by prolonging the cure. It distracts him momentarily from his real problem – his inability to relate, to communicate with normal human beings. On the train he whispers his request to the Impresario. What he is really saying on the metalingual level of gesture, tone, and other observable signals, is "Help me. I am lonely. I am isolated". But the manager takes his request for two trapezes at face value, and grants it immediately.

The trapeze artist realizes that he has not communicated. He tries again in a demanding tone, "so als wolle er es zeigen, daß hier die Zustimmung des Impresario ebenso bedeutungslos sei, wie es etwa sein Widerspruch wäre" (p. 243). Either would be a meaningless response because both miss the real meaning the acrobat wants to convey. Again, the manager consents to the acrobat's urgent demand, and buttresses the acrobat's words with further reasons of his own. This too avoids the real level of the attempted communication.

"Da fing der Trapezkünstler plötzlich zu weinen an" (p. 243). Deeply shocked, the Impresario begins to notice the real distress signal which the acrobat is sending out. Gradually he becomes aware that the subject of conversation has shifted from artistry and acrobatics to life and death. The trapeze artist speaks the language of dreams when he blurts out, "Nur diese ein Stange in den Händen – wie kann ich denn leben!" (p. 244).[33]

Though the Impresario cannot quite conceptualize the acrobat's inner plea, he at least recognizes its seriousness. He showers attention on the creature in the luggage rack to calm him temporarily, realizing all the

33 This could be another appearance of Kafka's *ur*-bachelor, deadly afraid of marriage, yet immensely disturbed by living alone.

while that the acrobat's vague fears of separation and isolation will return with greater force and cause more fundamental alterations in his way of life then a mere doubling of trapeze bars ever could. "Mußten sie [solche Gedanken] sich nicht immerfort steigern? Waren sie nicht existenzbedrohend?" (p. 244). The manager shares the acrobat's anxiety, if not because of his own fatherly feeling for this child who is now experiencing his "first sorrow", then at least because the manager's own economic security is threatened by some future possible radical shift in the *Lebensweise* of his means of support – the trapeze artist.

At key structural junctures in "First Sorrow", Kafka has set up verbal signposts by which we may see the direction of the dialectic of anxiety and inner calm. The first paragraph tells us that *die Umwelt* found the acrobat's unusual way of life no particular inconvenience. Still it was "ein wenig störend" that during other program numbers he drew an occasional glance from the crowd, "trotzdem er sich in solchen Zeiten meist ruhig verhielt" (p. 241). Here, *ruhig* and *störend* do not carry the psychological significance they acquire at the beginning of the second major portion of the story. They simply mean "still", *i.e.*, "not moving" and "distracting" respectively.

The shift from this first peaceful scene to the story's frantic conclusion occurs over two paragraphs (the third and fourth). The first and last sentences of this section use forms of *stören* which penetrate beneath mere external distraction to indicate psychic disturbance. The occasions which bring to a head the acrobat's anxiety are journeys through the streets of man. The third paragraph opens:

> So hätte der Trapezkünstler ungestört leben können, wären nicht die unvermeidlichen Reisen von Ort zu Ort gewesen, die ihm außerst lästig waren. (p. 242)

And the fourth paragraph concludes: "die Reisen waren, von allem anderen abgesehen, für die Nerven des Trapezkünstlers jedenfalls zerstörend" (p. 243). During this section, too, one sees that the Impresario shares in the *Leiden* of the acrobat through his meticulous care to satisfy all the performer's needs: "Zwar sorgte der Impresario dafür, daß der Trapezekünstler von jeder unnötigen Verlängerung seiner Leiden verschont blieb", and "es waren doch immer die schönsten Augenblick im Leben des Impresario, wenn der Trapezkünstler...endlich, wieder oben an seinem Trapez hing" (pp. 242-243).[34]

[34] One should note too that the journeys which are "Leiden" to the acrobat are

In the final scene, the acrobat's vague fears are expressed in lip-biting, whispering, assumed imperiousness, and contracted weeping. The Impresario finally succeeds in comforting him: "So gelang es dem Impresario den Trapezkünstler langsam zu beruhigen.... Er selbst aber war nicht beruhight..." (p. 244).

The innocent uses of *ruhig* and *störend* in the first section of the story give way to an intensification and deepening of their meanings in the second; but nervousness during a journey develops, in this third section, into existential *Angst*. The trapeze artist's dream-experience is not only disturbing, but also *existenzbedrohend*. For the present, however, the Impresario has succeeded in soothing him into a "scheinbar ruhigen Schlaf" – a highly unsatisfactory synthesis to the dialectic of the calm/anxious antinomy. Sleep, like childhood, must wake to new and more frightening anxieties. The trapeze artist's weeping has subsided into sleep, but his sleep (a temporary alleviation from anxiety) must wake again into weeping.

2. "*A Little Woman*"

"A Little Woman" presents existence-threatening anxiety from the limited subjective rather than from the omniscient objective viewpoint. The first-person narrator builds labyrinths of evasive syntax and involved negative passages ostensibly designed to lead the reader away from the central issue – his own deep disturbance. But both structure and texture of the story speak a metalanguage similar to that used by the trapeze artist perched in his luggage rack. The narrator does not address a second person, not even the reader. He speaks to himself, coaxing himself into calm.

The little woman may or may not actually exist. Almost certainly, she does not exist precisely as the narrator describes her. The fact that she always appears in the same dull-colored clothes, that the narrator stringently denies any connection with her except her own vexation, and that the occasions of her vexation repeat themselves almost exactly, indicate a solid possibility that the little woman is either a recurring dream or an hallucination. Even though the narrator underplays the *Sache* when he relates it in a few words to a friend, the friend considers the situation critical, or at least important enough to warrant a relaxing journey. The narrator rejects this advice, refusing to let the affair seep over its present

---

"peinlich" for the Impresario. This verbal distinction between two depths of anguish occurs also in "Eine kleine Frau".

contained boundaries. Apparently, he has been able to function many years as a useful member of society: no one has considered him psychotic, schizophrenic or paranoid. If, however, he should begin publicizing this relationship which is no relationship, he might well rouse the general rancor against himself. He may well be considered a mental case or a freak. And this he must avoid at all costs.

Everything about this story – most especially the web-work of opinions and subjunctive speculations meticulously picked apart and rejected – warns us to sift the narrator's words and intentions carefully. It is not necessary, however, to construe the woman as an hallucination or a recurring dream. She may well be a real woman whom the narrator endows with characteristics which he sees as representing either his own inner anguish or the causes of it. Whether hallucinatory or real, the woman as presented is an objectification of the narrator's anxiety, and embodies in her movements and alleged attitudes everything which disturbs his otherwise peaceful existence. She functions as a diminished negative catalyst in a way somewhat similar to that of Mephistopheles in Goethe's *Faust*. Perhaps we should not say she is real OR imaginary, but real AND imaginary.

The general structure of the story, as outlined above, is: (1) positive description, containing seeds of negation; (2) reflection (*Nachdenken*), in which the implications of the early ambivalent statements are fully explored and the precise force of their ambivalence developed; and (3) a summary of the situation as it appears at present (accompanied by a brief, questioning look to the future), which returns the story to its beginning. The theme of anxiety temporarily controlled works out its dialectic within this framework.

The dreamlike description of the little woman in the first paragraph departs from realistic descriptive practices. "Es ist eine kleine Frau" could indicate that the narrator, before opening his story, had been thinking of something else. When he attempts to give his feeling form, he objectifies "it" as a little woman. The description is placed above time by such phrases as "ich sehe sie immer im gleichen Kleid", where "sehe" could as easily point to dream or hallucination as physical sight; and "immer" indicates typical and/or repeatable experience; "sie ist immer ohne Hut" – again, the time-transcending "immer". The little woman's gestures are unfeminine: hands on her hips like an army sergeant, overdone swiftness of movement, and so forth. Still, she appears as much a real and normal woman ("es ist eine völlig normale Hand") as Gregor Samsa had appeared a real and normal insect in *Die Verwandlung*.

After the introductory description, the narrator immediately highlights the source of his own anxiety, though he tries to direct his remarks away from himself to the woman:

Diese kleine Frau nun ist mit mir sehr unzufrieden, immer hat sie etwas an mir auszusetzen, immer geschieht ihr Unrecht von mir, ich ärgere sie auf Schritt und Tritt; wenn man das Leben in allerkleinste Teile teilen und jedes Teilchen gesondert beurteilen könnte, wäre gewiß jedes Teilchen meines Lebens für sie ein Ärgernis. (p. 245)

The declarative statements – that this woman is dissatisfied with the narrator and that he vexes her "auf Schritt und Tritt" – are taken as fundamental fact from which all further reflections grow: "Ich habe oft darüber nachgedacht warum ich sie so ärgere..." (p. 245). The narrator tries to shift responsibility for everything to the little woman. He denies any relationship at all; and in this he is like the trapeze artist: his "lack of relationship", though, is but one of the causes of his disturbance.

The narrator pretends indifference, but worries about the questions the world may ask; he says she cares nothing for his improvements, but he attempts to improve himself in order to lessen her fury; he admits that her objection to him is "grundsätzlich" but continues to treat the affair, on the surface, as trivial; he argues that the "Sache" has not developed in any way over the years, that situations tend only to repeat themselves; his attitude toward the affair, however, has changed – become more composed and manly, yet at the same time slightly nervous. In short, on the one hand he insists verbally that this is but "eine kleine Sache", while on the other hand, we must conclude from his painstaking examination of all the details and consequences, relationships and lack of relationships, that he considers it much more important than he dares to admit on the surface.

All in all, the story reads as an imaginative exposé of the dynamics of anxiety so engaging to the twentieth-century reader. There is no plot in the traditional sense. The development of the story is not a development of the affair but a revelation of the conscious and unconscious shifts of anxious attitudes on the part of the narrator. The dialectic of anxiety and calm, as it works itself out through the involved webwork of *Nachdenken*, comes to a climax in weak subjunctive hypothesis, built up through a faltering flood of conjunctions, adverbs, and verbs of pretended discretion and determination. The preparation:

Von wo aus also ich es auch ansehe, immer wieder zeigt sich und dabei bleib ich, daß...

The subjunctive hypothesis:

wenn ich mit der Hand auch nur ganz leicht diese kleine Sache verdeckt halte, ich noch sehr lange, ungestört von der Welt, mein bisheriges Leben ruhig werde fortsetzen dürfen, trotz allen Tobens der Frau. (p. 254)

The above quotation forms, as a single unit, the final paragraph of the story. By the end of the story, the narrator has indeed viewed the "kleine Sache" from every possible viewpoint he knows. He is determined to stand by ("dabei bleib ich") what has always ("immer wieder") proved to be the case. Still, his weak resolve does not conquer anxiety. He affirms only an hypothesis which brings him back to his position at the beginning of the story. If he keeps his hand lightly over it – not refusing to think about it, but neither allowing others to know about it – then he can live an untroubled life just as he had before. His victory, in other words, is a compromise. He holds his anxiety under temporary control, but has not overcome it.

The appearance of *ungestört* and *ruhig* in this final paragraph, recalls the gradual deepening, as in "First Sorrow", of the meanings of these words through the course of the story. They are not, of course, the only such terms used. "Eine kleine Frau" is flooded, and especially at key structural junctures, with terminology connected with the anxiety/calm syndrome. Some terms, which appeared sparsely in "Erstes Leid", recur in more generous proportions and in more varied forms here: *gestört, ungestört; ruhig, unruhig, beruhigt, beunruhigen; Qual, quäle, gequält; Leid, leiden, leidende, leidet, Leidenschaft; peinlich, Peinlichkeit; Sorgen, Sorgfalt.* At the same time, a few additions expand the vocabulary of inner turmoil qualitatively as well as quantitatively: *Ärger, privater Ärger, öffentlicher Ärger, Ärgernis, ärgern* (in several forms); *unzufrieden, Unzufriedenheit; Schuld, Unschuld, Urteil, beurteilen; Verzweiflung, Aussichtlosigkeit; beschuldige, entscheiden;* and with growing intensity: *Frage, Antwort, gefragt, verantworten, Verantwortung, Entscheidung.* I shall point out in detail a few of these usages.

In the early parts of the story, especially in the second and third paragraphs, the narrator emphasizes the little woman's vexation. He pretends to have a detached, amused attitude toward her; he pities her unreasonable and totally groundless fury; he mentions that he has managed to hint somehow – without establishing any relationship – that she could best free herself from this disturbance by forgetting the narrator's existence. He contrasts his *Peinlichkeit* with her *Leid*; he makes *her* the object of his pity.

In stressing the inner disturbed state of this woman[35] the narrator seems to be disguising his own inner tensions. As in "First Sorrow", when *stören* is first introduced, it means simply "to hinder", "to interrupt": "was sie an mir aussetzt, nicht von einer derartigen Beschaffenheit ist, daß mein Fortkommen dadurch gestört würde" (p. 246) – he never does make clear what her objection to him is!

Only two forms of *ruhig* occur in these first three paragraphs. The first, connected with nervousness, occurs in the question: "Also könnte ich in dieser Hinsicht völlig beruhigt sein?" (p. 248). The answer: no. The second usage substitutes for a copulative verb in an atmosphere of growing nervous tension: "daraus ruht meine letzte Hoffnung" (p. 249).

The fourth paragraph represents a gradual shift from a pseudo-detached presentation of someone else's inner problems to a more intense examination of all the implications this "little affair" may have on the personal life of the narrator. *Ärger* appears in the first sentence of this paragraph, but then drops out of the story until the penultimate paragraph, during which the narrator again seeks to seize control over his existence-threatening thoughts. Now we learn that the narrator once sought to improve himself "um die Frau zu besänftigen" (p. 249), but failed. "Wie wäre es auch möglich? Ihre Unzufriedenheit mit mir ist ja... eine grundsätzliche" (p. 250). They continue to oppose one another without really confronting one another. Both remain silent, separated except for her *Ärger* and his *Nachdenken*.

In the fifth paragraph, the narrator's friend suggests that he take a journey. The narrator, however, rejects the advice categorically, asserting that he must remain *ruhig* where he is, and allow no change of behavior, as far as possible, to be noticed in him. Here, *ruhig* has a double meaning: "quiet" and "undisturbed". The phrase "ruhig zu bleiben, wo ich bin", also operates on at least two planes – the physical and psychological – through the association with the "großen...auffallenden Veränderungen" which the narrator so deeply fears. In this paragraph, he determines to keep the affair "in ihren bisherigen, engen, die Außenwelt noch nicht einbeziehenden Grenzen", which should recall, on second reading, his wish in the final paragraph to continue his "bisheriges Leben ruhig" as before.

[35] In two paragraphs he speaks of her *Ärger* (12 times in various forms), *Leid* (7 times) and *Qual* (5 times).

The changes he fears never come. After closer inspection, he tells himself in the sixth paragraph that, over the years, there have been "keine Veränderungen der Sache selbst", but only "die Entwicklung meiner Anschauung von ihr". His attitude, he goes on to say, has developed toward both poles of the anxiety/calm antinomy: it has become "teils ruhiger, männlicher", and more to the heart of the matter; but at the same time, under the influence of the continued nervous strain which he cannot overcome, he has contracted "eine gewisse Nervosität" (p. 252).

In the seventh paragraph, the narrator tries to make explicit his reasons for becoming more placid about the matter. The paragraph begins with the word *Ruhiger* and ends with *beunruhigen*. His chief consideration throughout is the repetative nature of the matter: when he was young he expected a crisis; he expected the intrusion of the *Öffentlichkeit*, he expected to be called to account. Since none of these things has ever happened, he concludes that it is likely they never will happen: "gewiß nicht morgen und übermorgen und wahrscheinlich niemals" (p. 253). Since he has, he believes, a fair understanding of the dynamics of his relations with the woman, he naturally concludes that it is hardly likely "mich zu beunruhigen" (p. 254).

In the eighth paragraph, he makes more explicit the connection between his becoming "ein wenig unruhig" and the *Ärger* which he causes the little woman: "Man hält es einfach nicht aus, jemanden immerfort zu ärgern, selbst wenn man die Grundlosigkeit des Ärgers wohl erkennt; man wird unruhig..." (p. 254). As the rest of the paragraph shows, the narrator's uneasiness has passed from mere nervousness to a deep-seated vague fear, ultimately, of death: "Zum Teil aber handelt es sich auch nur um eine Alterserscheinung...".

Despite all these reflections, he remains convinced that he has many years of peaceful existence before him, if he can just manage – and perhaps he can – to hold his hand lightly over his existence-threatening anxiety. The situation has been *im Grunde* always the same (see p. 253). It is not likely to change radically at this late date.

3. "*A Hunger Artist*"

Situations which excite and heighten anxiety abound in "A Hunger Artist": the fasting showman is forcibly isolated (in a cage) from the community of man. He is questing toward a goal which he is not allowed to reach. Each step toward that goal leads him closer and closer to death. The shift of interest in fasting threatens the economic security of the Impresario and the stability of the *Lebensweise* of the showman. His audience does not understand the hunger artist. Many of them suspect him of cheating. They lock him in a cage, exhibit him, and limit his freedom.

Felix Weltsch[36] wrote that "A Hunger Artist" actually includes four stories in one. "Im Grunde", he says,

> besteht diese Geschichte aus vier Geschichten, vier Entwicklungslinien mit verschiedenem Sinn, die ineinander verflochten sind; die äußere Geschehen ist ihnen natürlich gemeinsam, aber der Sinn dieses Geschehens ist vielfaltig. Man braucht nur zu fragen: was ist der Sinn dieses Unternehmens, in Schaustellungen vor dem Publikum zu hungern? (p. 80)

Four simultaneous accurate answers can be given to that question, he says, forming four *Sinnlinien* to the story: (1) *Hungern als Sensation* – public fasting provides an outlet for the curiosity of the people; (2) *Hungern als Geschäft* – it provides security for the hunger artist and his manager; (3) *Hungern als eine Angelegenheit der Ehre* – it provides a challenge which the fasting showman is proud to prove he can meet; and (4) *Hungern aus Ekel vor dem Essen* – it is unavoidable. Each of these *Sinnlinien* supplies a convenient basis for analysis of anxiety-factors in the story.

The first, *Hungern als Sensation*, provokes anxiety superficially for the public, the hunger artist, and the Impresario, but serves at the same time to distract them from more fundamental problems. The Impresario has the constant worry of staging a good show, of keeping the audience interested and the hunger artist alive. The hunger artist's contact with the suspicious and disbelieving public; his awareness that the nature of his performance and abilities is being falsified by the manager; and his constant frustration that he can never exercise his talents fully, since he is forced to come out of his cage and take food on the fortieth day – all these cast him into melancholy. At the same time, concern for his reputation distracts him from the more fundamental issue – that if he were actually allowed to fast on and on, he would die. His discontent with the particulars of the show keep him from a too acute awareness of the freakish nature of his death-bearing life.

In the same way, the public's intense concern over the trappings of the show distract them from the normally terrifying condition of its chief actor. The show on the fortieth day of the fast is structured in such a way as to allow the public to gather in calm community before the show-stall

36 *Religion und Humor im Leben und Werk Franz Kafkas* (Berlin, 1957), pp. 79-83.

of a man whose life is a living reminder of the approach of death. The ritual has been carefully arranged. Everything contributes toward calming the crowds: loud triumphant strains blare from the military band; pronouncements of doctors announce facts not about the health of the hunger artist, but about his physical measurements; two chosen women help the artist from his flower-bedecked cage; attendants stand ready to step in when the women's tears of discomfort cause them to relinquish their burden; the Impresario forces food through the teeth of the starving skeleton while keeping up a cheerful patter to distract the public's attention from his condition; finally, a toast is drunk not to the faster but to the public. All this, as well as the official act of watching, was arranged "zur Beruhigung der Massen" (p. 256).

Hungern als Geschäft evokes anxiety superficially in the public but profoundly in the hunger artist and his manager. The public is aware of the financial dimensions of the fasting showman's act; the fact that what he is doing is his business and his mode of support increases the suspicions of those members of the public who are not *Eingeweihten*. The public appoints official watchers to assure individuals (who cannot watch day and night themselves) that the hunger artist has not, indeed, taken any food for forty days. Even then, only a few ever seem really to believe that his show is real and not just a trick. They crowd around his cage day and night to satisfy themselves that they are not being cheated.

The hungering of the fasting showman provides economic security for the showman's manager, who when the shift of interest is setting in, races frantically over Europe trying to reignite the dying spark – but all in vain. He can, however, turn to another job – perhaps managing another kind of show that is in fashion. But the hunger artist is too old to change his profession. Besides he was "allzu fanatisch ergeben" (p. 263) to hungering to change. He still hopes to astound the world by hitherto unknown exhibitions. Never having done anything in his life, since he was so busy letting other people do things to him – he knows only one course of action: fasting on and on. Since *das Publikum* has lost interest in him, however, he has only his motive of honor to comfort him; only his knowledge that he is striving after an unreachable goal, toward unimaginable achievements in the profession of fasting. That brings us to the third *Sinnlinie*, *Hungern als eine Angelegenheit der Ehre*.

While the public busies itself with torchlights and the appointment of official watchers, the initiates realize that "die Ehre seiner Kunst" forbids the hunger artist from taking any food during his fasting period, and that he could not even be forced to eat during this time. The vast majority of the population, however, could not be expected to understand this. When the hunger artist sits melancholy in his cage during the final stages of the fast, well-meaning people try to comfort him with the animadversion that anyone who had fasted so long must surely be out of spirits. This throws the hunger artist into a rage. For he has constantly boasted that he can fast much longer than forty days – indeed almost indefinitely. But the public and the Impresario would not permit this. The Impresario even tried to disprove his boast by photographs. They had robbed him of honor again and again by cutting short his fast. This, he would always contend, was the root of his melancholy. And after he had become only a "Hindernis auf dem Weg zu den Ställen" he strove, without opposition, to reach those goals he had set himself, to fast to the limits of his abilities, which he felt had "keine Grenzen" (p. 259). Despite the occasional remark by a passing skeptic that he was a swindle and a cheat, the hunger artist "arbeitete ehrlich, aber die Welt betrog ihm um seinen Lohn" (p. 266).

The hunger artist openly told his audience that fasting for him was the easiest thing in the world. Only in the final scene, however, did he dare mention to anyone (hardly even to himself) that he was helpless to do otherwise. Sitting alone in his cage, perhaps the realization of his freakish incapacity joined with his other thoughts to cause his sadness and dissatisfaction with himself – which his public attributed to his fasting too long and which he attributed to his not fasting long enough.

In the last portion of the story, the *Sinnlinie*, *Hungern aus Ekel vor dem Essen*, assumes centrality. The hungerer confesses at the end that he had to fast because he could not find the food he liked. During his period of isolation and silence, he has ceased to be proud of his fundamental human defect – the inability to eat. All his other passivities, arguments, boasts, and concerns had helped him to distract himself sufficiently from the important death-threatening and anxiety-provoking fact that he was unfit to live. Left alone far from the crowds, he could no longer turn his face away from the reality of his approaching death. The general public, on the other hand, could always find something else to fill the void left by the hunger artist's death. Soon enthusiastic onlookers surround his cage in which now a fresh life-loving leopard tears raw meat in his teeth.

The anxiety theme, then, is conveyed in "A Hunger Artist" primarily through the changes of circumstances which the passing of time brings with it. Structurally pivotal terminology of anxiety follows a different pattern than that of the first two stories, because it is more prominently the terminology of the passing of time, of misunderstanding, and of unachieved goals. Some of the terms used earlier, however, recur here, though not necessarily at key positions in the story: *Beruhigung der Massen, das beruhigte Publikum, ruhige, Ruhepausen, quälender, störte, unzufrieden, Unzufriedenheit, befriedigt, Trost, Verdächtigungen, Urteil,* and so forth. The emphasis, however, centers on anxiety caused by being a creature of time, a creature whose life is packaged out in boxes of forty-days each, a creature who dreams of fasting without limitation, but whose physical nature sets a limit on all his activities.

4. "*Josephine*"

In "Josephine" an entire population lives under the constant threat of sudden slaughter. *Das Volk der Mäuse*, through watchfulness and cunning, daily wage their *Existenzkampf*, against all threatening forces – ultimately, against death. The unidentified, but unquestionably powerful enemy lurks somewhere above, shattering by his very presence any security which native cunning might have afforded the mice. The mice, then, for whom the anxiety that a sudden attack may totally destroy them is only the most disturbing of many threatening aspects of their lives, seek to bolster their sense of security by mass meetings in which they might become less identifiable as anxious individuals.[37] They also have a heroine behind whom they hide and whose loss they would sorely regret. Further, they have a propensity for blaming fate for any disasters that may befall – thus relieving themselves of the burden of responsibility. The narrator has found still another way of calming himself: he talks away his anxiety.

Kafka has prepared the perceptive reader for the anxiety dimension of his narrative in the first paragraph. He has his narrator admit that this mouse people is accustomed to comfort itself through cunning (*Schlauheit*):

> eine gewisse praktische Schlauheit, die wir freilich auch äußerst dringend brauchen, halten wir für unsern größten Vorzug, und mit Lächeln dieser Schlauheit pflegen wir uns über alles hinwegzutrösten. (p. 268)

We should not be surprised, then, when we find the facts of Josephine's history encased in a multimirrored, many-halled labyrinth of opinions and counter-opinions.

Josephine's recent disappearance has occasioned these involved speculations of the narrator, but he slyly withholds mention of this important

[37] See Steiner, pp. 76-87.

fact until the thirty-first of thirty-four paragraphs – until, that is, he has had time to undercut the feeling, both in himself and in the people, that Josephine was a gifted – even necessary – member of their race. His reflections center around two main questions, one concerning the nature of her song, the other concerning the nature of the people's devotion to her. His own view, which emerges gradually from the elaborate construction of opinions he builds, is that: (1) her song is not essentially different from the common language of the people – "Natürlich ist es ein Pfeifen. Wie denn nicht? Pfeifen ist die Sprache unseres Volkes..." (p. 282); and (2) the people's devotion to her – hardly to be considered unconditional – is the devotion of a protecting parent toward a weak child, not that of a spineless people for a savior-heroine. Only after he has convinced himself (and any other mice who may be listening to or reading his tract) that Josephine really was not as important to the people as she and her flatterers thought, does he dare to reflect openly on what both he and his mouse-audience already know – that despite the frantic search of the entire population to find her, Josephine has disappeared. As far as anyone can tell, she is gone forever.

It is curious to note that the narrator blames her departure (*Hingang*) either on her own proud miscalculations or on the iron hand of destiny. The possibility that she may have been defeated and eaten by the enemy never, apparently, enters his mind. Despite his sly argumentation, however, the narrator and the populace did actually consider Josephine a kind of savior, a heroine – only immensely diminished from the heroes of the *Sagen* and *Lieder*: she is female, not male; her weapon is a song, not a sword; and, of course (for the human reader) she is diminished by being a mouse, not a man.

Throughout this *Bericht*,[38] the narrator lets his readers know, sometimes directly, most often through indirection, that he is seeking peace, security, calm; further, he speaks frequently in the first-person plural, and so claims peace as the primary wish of all the mouse-folk: "Stiller Frieden ist uns die liebste Musik; unser Leben ist schwer..." (p. 268); Josephine's music possesses a power to induce peace, and "Wer sie nicht gehört hat, kennt nicht die Macht der Gesanges" (p. 268). But since Josephine has vanished, the mouse folk must rely solely on their "praktische Schlauheit" to calm their nerves before and after their terrifying struggles to live.

Before the mention of *Schlauheit* in the text, Kafka kept his syntax

38 See Hillmann, pp. 188ff. He applies this term specifically to "Josephine". The narrator reports on events in an apparently detached way, even though he is part of the story process.

simple: all the verbs are indicative, mostly in the present tense; clauses and sentences are short and uninvolved. Immediately after the appearance of *Schlauheit* in the text, however, there occurs also the first negated conditional construction, the first parenthetical remark, and the first use of *vielleicht* to diminish Josephine's importance among the people:

mit dem Lächeln dieser Schlauheit pflegen wir uns über alles hinwegzutrösten, auch wenn wir einmal – was aber nicht geschieht – das Verlangen nach dem Glück haben sollten, das von der Musik vielleicht ausgeht. (pp. 268-269)

According to the narrator, the mouse folk do not care for music. Josephine's disappearance, then, should not disturb them any more than the disappearance of any other mouse. Nevertheless, "mit ihrem Hingang wird die Musik – wer weiß wie lange – aus unserem Leben verschwinden" (p. 269). The narrator devotes some twenty pages of carefully reasoned text to uncover (or perhaps, to cover over) the nature of that music and the relationship of the mouse people to the sole "music-maker" of their race.

He begins his campaign (against the anxiety of having lost a heroine, a comforter, perhaps a savior) by emphasizing how much like ordinary squeaking Josephine's song is: "Im vertrauten Kreise gestehen wir einander offen, daß Josefinens Gesang als Gesang nicht Außerordentliches darstellt" (p. 269). Her singing does not measure up to any of the standards of song, culled as vague *Gesangsüberlieferungen* from the ancient *Sagen* and *Lieder*,[39] which "freilich niemand mehr singen kann" (p. 269). So the people can console themselves that they have lost nothing essential to their well-being. Josephine was just another member of the race of workers; and her song was nothing more than a squeaking: "Natürlich ist es ein Pfeifen. Wie denn nicht?" (p. 282).

Despite the narrator's explicit denial of anything special in the actual song of Josephine, he does concede that a public presentation spreads an aura of art over an otherwise habitual action – like the staging of a nutcracking show. Naturally the people would feel that "was sie hier pfeift, ist kein Pfeifen" (p. 272). But the people also receive this common action as something immensely *außerordentlich*: "Dieses Pfeifen kommt fast wie eine Botschaft des Volkes zu dem Einzelnen" (p. 278). It seems to embody by its very tenuousness that cowering nation which, according to the narrator, has always saved itself:

[39] By implication, the narrator compares Josephine to the heroes of the mythic age. Like Bucephalus over his law books, Josephine's heroics are greatly reduced.

das dünne Pfeifen Josefinens mitten in den schweren Entscheidungen ist fast wie die armselige Existenz unseres Volkes mitten im Tumult der feindlichen Welt. (p. 278)

Etwas von der armen kurzen Kindheit ist darin, etwas von verlorenem, nie wieder aufzufindendem Glück, aber auch etwas vom tätigen heutigen Leben ist darin.... (p. 282)

The fact that the folk will listen to Josephine during times of great stress argues, the narrator says, to her not being a professional singer, for the people would not put up with the performance of a professional singer at such a time. Josephine's chief claim, however, is not that she is a professional songstress, but that she saves the people, or at least gives them new strength by her presence and her song. The narrator dismisses her claims with *ad hominem* remarks, while at the same time he describes the effect her singing has on the harried multitudes:

Josefine bringt diesem so gestimmten Volke noch mehr.... Hier in den dürftigen Pausen zwischen den Kämpfen träumt das Volk, es ist, als lösten sich dem Einzelnen die Glieder, als dürfte sich der Ruhelose einmal nach seiner Lust im großen warmen Bett des Volkes dehnen und strecken. Und in diese Träume klingt hier und da Josefinens Pfeifen... hier an seinem Platze, wie nirgends sonst, wie Musik kaum jemals den auf sie wartenden Augenblick findet... Gewiß, diese Vorführungen wollten wir nicht missen. (p. 282)

Still, the narrator refuses to admit that these performances were peace-producing. The essential thing, he argues, was and is the silent togetherness of the crowds.

But Josephine has vanished – "sie hat uns diesmal völlig verlassen" (p. 290). In the final paragraphs of the story, Josephine's magnetism and charismatic power again come into the narrative foreground. Josephine, acting on miscalculation, has destroyed the "Macht die sie über die Gemüter erworben hat" (p. 290). She has removed herself and her song from the people; singing has vanished – "wer weiß wie lange" – from the race. Nevertheless, says the narrator, the populace will continue, in perfect equilibrium, on its way.

For the loss of Josephine, the narrator comforts the people with a series of conjectural questions:

War ihr wirkliches Pfeifen nennenswert lauter und lebendiger, als die Erinnerung daran sein wird? War es denn noch bei ihren Lebzeiten mehr als eine bloße Erinnerung? Hat nicht vielmehr das Volk in seiner Weisheit Josefinens Gesang, eben deshalb, weil er in dieser Art unverlierbar war, so hoch gestellt? (p. 290)

Josephine has vanished, but her song, perhaps, has not vanished at all. In fact, perhaps Josephine has not vanished at all! "Josefine aber, erlöst von der irdischen Plage...wird frölich sich verlieren in der zahllosen Menge der Helden unseres Volkes...in gesteigerter Erlösung..." (p. 291).

The final paragraphs contain reaffirmations of the positive elements of the story's first paragraph, and conjectural denials of its negative aspects. They reaffirm Josephine's power of song, her character as an exceptional member of the race; but they conjecturally deny that she or her music will be missed, that they have actually vanished from "unserem Leben" at all, since her music was, perhaps, *unverlierbar*, and she herself "erlöst von der irdischen Plage". Again, the people's anxiety is temporarily under control.

Josephine, according to the narrator, does not feel the full weight of the *Existenzkampf*. She works, indeed, like the rest of the mouse-folk, and rises up to sing when they gather for a "Becher des Friedens vor dem Kampf" (p. 277); but since she normally stands at the front of the assembly, she easily escapes when a sudden attack from the enemy materializes and many mice are left dead in the assembly hall. The root of Josephine's anxiety lies not so much in her relationship to the hostile world above, as in her unsettled position as a music-maker among a people known for their "Unmusikalität". Over the years, Josephine has developed a "nervöse Mißbehagen" (p. 278) because her relation to the community has never been clarified. Her all-consuming desire, according to the narrator, is to wrench from the *Volk*[40] "die öffentliche, eindeutige, die Zeiten überdauernde, über alles bisher Bekannte sich weit erhabende Anerkennung ihrer Kunst" (p. 285). Though everything else seems to be within her reach, this garland constantly evades her grasp.

Josephine also shares, of course, the fundamentally insecure existence of all the mouse-folk. But she is even closer to death than her brothers because of the consuming power of her song.

Schon steht sie da, das zarte Wesen, besonders unterhalf der Brust beängstigend vibrierend, es ist, als hätte sie alle ihre Kraft im Gesang versammelt, als sei allem an ihr, was nicht dem Gesange unmittelbar diene, jede Kraft, fast jede Lebensmöglichkeit entzogen, als sei sie entblößt, preisgegeben, nur dem Schutze guter Geister überantwortet, als könne sie, während sie so, sich völlig entzogen, im Gesange wohnt, ein kalter Hauch im Vorüberwehn töten. (p. 273)

40 One never knows who is in command of the mousefolk. Perhaps no one. Perhaps that is one of the more basic reasons why Josephine's efforts are ignored and why she must always fail in her petition.

She can almost be identified with her song, which in turn is "fast wie die armselige Existenz unseres Volkes mitten im Tumult der feindlichen Welt" (p. 278; see also p. 282). Josephine, her frail song, and the "den Tod wohl kennenden" mouse nation share a single precarious existence.[41] No wonder, then, that the narrator takes great pains to suggest that Josephine and her song have "vielleicht" not totally departed from the nation.

The existence-threatening nature of the life of the mouse-folk is itself anxiety-provoking. Recently, however, one of the props of the people's tenuous security, Josephine's peace-giving song, has slipped out from beneath the already frail mutual-support system of the nation. But the narrator, with that "praktische Schlauheit" for which the race is famed, first argues that the prop was non-essential; then, as if not convinced of his own arguments, he suggests that the prop possibly is not really removed at all – that it has always been essentially *unverlierbar*.

In his attempts to calm himself and the people, he naturally uses a number of terms associated with the anxiety/calm antinomy. As in the other stories, the first usages of these terms are often innocent, connoting no deep anxiety or struggle to achieve inner calm. Such, for instance, are the uses of *Angst*, *Scham*, *die Störerin*, *Beleuchtungsstörung*, and *Störungen* in the sixth and seventh paragraphs. In the eight paragraph, however, the discussion passes from "das Kleine" to "das Große".

> Unser Leben ist sehr unruhig, jeder Tag bringt Überraschungen, Beängstigungen, Hoffnungen und Schrecken, daß der Einzelne unmöglich dies alles ertragen könnte, hätte er nicht jederzeit bei Tag und Nacht den Rückhalt der Genossen. (p. 273)

When the troubles come fast and heavy, Josephine rises to bear the burden of a thousand shoulders – a burden, the narrator hints, which her function in society forces her to carry: "manchmal zittern selbst tausend Schultern under der Last, die eigentlich nur für einen bestimmt war. Dan hält Josefine ihre Zeit für gekommen" (p. 273). While her whole body, entering into her song, vibrates so that it seems the slightest breath of wind would cause her death, the people relax, sink into themselves, and dream.

Angst of paragraph six referred to the feeling of the *Störerin* who piped up in the midst of Josephine's song and was shouted down by the assembly. By paragraph eight, *Beängstigungen* and *beängstigend* describe death-threatening situations. Most of the uses of anxiety/calm terminology

41 This seems to be the rationale behind the "Oder-Titel" Kafka gave the story as he sent it to press.

after the eighth paragraph concern the struggle to attain existential or psychological security in a world full of dangers. The *Tagessorgen*, mentioned lightly in the first paragraph, recur in varying froms – *Sorgen, die Sorge um das tägliche Brot, sorgfältig, sorgen, Sorgt, Sorglosigkeit*, and so forth. *Stören* and *ruhig* also reappear, after their first mention, in several forms; for example, *der Ruhelose* (the harried mouse) may relax and dream at Josephine's concerts. In another context, the *Volk* calmly (*ruhig*, [p. 84]) refuses Josephine's request each time she presents it. In the final summarizing section of the story, the narrator says that Josephine destroyed (*zerstört*, [p. 90]) the power she had held over the people. But the *Volk*, described in the eighth paragraph as *unruhig*, is now depicted as continuing calmly on its way: "ruhig, ohne sichtbare Enttäuschung, herrisch, eine in sich ruhende Masse...dieses Volk zieht weiter seines Weges" (p. 290). Through the narrator's structuring of thought and feeling, the people gain control over any anxiety they may feel about the loss of Josephine, the heroine to whom they were (conditionally) devoted. She was but "eine kleine Episode in der ewigen Geschichte unseres Volkes und das Volk wird den Verlust überwinden" (p. 290).

Though the folk as a whole will, according to the narrator's prognostication, live relatively securely forever, the individual must find some other solace for the painful uneasiness that Josephine's brief history must cause. The very idea that the folk may turn a cold, judicial, impenetrable face toward one of their own – one indeed whom it otherwise treated with fatherly affection and care – enters each mouse's conscience as a seed of deeper anxiety. Any individual may become an outsider. The narrator tries to gloss over this issue of pressing concern by suggesting that Josephine has become part of a special community within the larger body of *das Volk*. She buries her identity "in der zahllosen Menge der Helden unseres Volkes" (p. 291). In such company, she and "alle ihre Brüder" can feel accepted, "inside", and safe.[42]

5. *Conclusion*

Each of the four stories, then, patterns its treatment of the anxiety-theme in a dialectic of (1) apparent calm, (2) deepening disturbance, and (3) return to a temporary, unstable calm. The terms used to convey this

[42] Other terms which enrich the texture of the anxiety/calm theme in "Josephine" are: *Drohungen, Gefahren, Feinde, aufgeregten Zeiten, zerstreut, Hoffnungslosigkeit, Kampf, Existenzkampf, quälenden, Leid, ängstlich, Notlagen, Note, Retter, retten, still, stiller Frieden, die Stille, tröstet, Trost, Erlösung*, and *erlöst*.

dialectic alter from story to story. Some of them, however, recur from story to story, and reappear in previously established patterns based on the similar structures of the works. "Josephine", besides implying in its final scene a universalizing return to its opening situation, also points beyond the cycle to the vague possibility of redemption from *Angst* for "alle ihre Brüder". The characters of the four stories were all either outsiders or in dread of becoming outsiders. "Josephine" proposes a community of outsiders – a *Menge der Helden*, all of whom believe that they have been elected for special achievement in some field, and all of whom have been cut off from ordinary life in the community of their peers.

The other dialectical themes, as I mentioned earlier, are closely interrelated with this theme of anxiety. The precise interworkings of the various levels of thematic development are not, however, always clear. Kafka considered the totality of what he was trying to say fundamentally incommunicable: "ich suche immerfort etwas Nicht-Mitteilbares mitzuteilen", he wrote to Milena, "etwas Unerklärbares zu erklären".[43] Whether the story concerns someone striving after an unreachable goal, or deals with the reflections of an involved mind over "eine kleine Sache" or some life-threatening reality, Kafka is often basically portraying the dynamics of anxiety – that vague, apprehensive uneasiness which reaches beyond itself, which yearns toward unexperienced communication or unimaginable heights of achievement, toward self-appropriation or the feeling of being a part of a community, or of having been released from the harrying limitations of time and space. In the same letter to Milena quoted above, Kafka tries tentatively to characterize the "Nicht-Mitteilbares" and "Unerklärbares" that he embodies often in his experimental myths:

> Es ist ja vielleicht im Grunde nicht anderes als jene Angst, vor der schon so oft die Rede war, aber Angst ausgedehnt auf alles, Angst vor dem Größten wie Kleinsten, Angst, kramphafte Angst vor dem Aussprechen eines Wortes. Allerdings ist diese Angst vielleicht nicht nur Angst, sondern auch Sehnsucht nach etwas, was mehr ist als alles Angsterregende. (p. 249)

E. THEME OF THE EXCEPTIONAL AS ORDINARY

This theme might be expressed in a number of ways: the exceptional as ordinary and the ordinary as exceptional; the extraordinary as habitual

[43] *Briefe an Milena*, p. 249.

and therefore ultimately not extraordinary; compromise in striving; artistic talent as abnormality. The first paragraph of "Erstes Leid" introduces the theme for the entire collection. A man is considered *außerordentlich* if he strives to achieve a goal which ordinary men can hardly reach. If, however, activities connected with this extraordinary striving become his habitual *Lebensweise*, the exceptional man fast becomes the eccentric, and the eccentric soon becomes the freak. Not every person who strives for exceptionally elevated goals ends up a freak, though in this collection they all become "outsiders" – they separate themselves from communication with normal men by means of their one peculiarity. Only in "Josephine" is there some hope that the exceptional man may also be a member of the community.

1. "*First Sorrow*"

In the opening paragraph of "First Sorrow", Kafka paints the disconcerting picture of a trapeze acrobat who has decided to remain always aloft, hanging day and night on his trapeze. At first he does this "nur aus dem Streben nach Vervollkommnung" but later "auch aus tyrannisch gewordener Gewohnheit" (p. 241). The minor inconveniences he causes the theater people are forgiven him "weil er ein außerordentlicher, unersetzlicher Künstler war" – a man earnestly striving to work his art up to the peak of its "Vollkommenheit". His art separates him physically and socially from men. He works out "hoch in den Kuppeln der großen Varietébühnen" where the "menschlichen Verkehr" is "sehr eingeschränkt". His art, indeed, is "eine der schwierigsten unter allen, Menschen erreichbaren", according to the narrator, and is honored as such. But, despite its uniqueness, the acrobat's life in the extraordinary world of tent-tops and theater-domes becomes tyranically habitual; the abnormal conditions of living on a single trapeze bar have become the normal conditions of his life.

Soon he finds himself a stranger in the world below. Each second of the "unvermeidlichen Reisen" he feels is a menace to his way of life. He rushes at breakneck speed through the "menschenleeren Straßen" at odd hours, when he will be least likely to meet other men. To alleviate some of the pain he feels at being down below instead of "oben" on the trapeze, he perches "oben im Gepäktnetz". By the symbolism of place, his abnormality becomes evident. For on the trapeze bar he appears as beautiful and exceptional – like Baudelaire's albatross kinging it in the skies. When he lands on earth, he is both grotesque and pathetic.

To live on a trapeze bar for the sake of one's art might pass as eccentric yet still be consonant with one's extraordinary talents. But to perch in a luggage rack can only be regarded as strange. When a man who is *außerordentlich* lets exceptional behavior become *gewöhnlich*, he separates himself from society, becomes an "outsider", and sometimes a freak. The trapeze artist, realizing that something is wrong but unable to pinpoint the problem, demands a second trapeze. He hopes that that will radically change his life which, until the present, he had lived alone on a single bar. The perceptive reader will see, however, that on this thematic level too, the situation at the end of the story represents no significant advancement over its beginning.

2. "*A Little Woman*"

The little woman of the second story, in being a diminished and modified spirit of negation, not only embodies all those traits of personality which cause the narrator uneasiness, but also, in making him dissatisfied with himself, encourages him to improve his character. The narrator denies that the little woman serves this function, even while he admits that he did improve himself in order to lessen her vexation. Still he stops halfway; he finds it impossible to meet her requirements. In the language of a man satisfied with his present *Lebensweise* – despite its limitations – he argues that he is helpless to improve his character, that what this woman objects to is not of a nature to hinder his development, that there must exist a fundamental incompatibility of natures between him and the woman, and that even the removal of himself would not overcome this fundamental incompatibility.

The woman is often described as feeling vexation because the narrator takes no pains to improve himself. He, however, denies that she is interested in his improvement at all; she merely wants revenge for the suffering he has caused her. Despite the narrator's protests, a good case can be made to show that the woman (real or imaginary) actually is interested in his becoming *außerordentlich*, in his escaping from the narrow limits of his own *Gewohnheit*.

When the narrator begins speculating on the reasons for her discomfort, he suggests that it may be because everything in him contradicts "ihrem Schönheitssinn, ihrem Gerechtigkeitsgefühl, ihren Gewohnheiten, ihren Überlieferungen, ihren Hoffnungen". Her objection to his present state of mind is "eine grundsätzliche". Further, she would be furious if he should commit suicide – "ihre Wutanfälle etwa bei der Nachricht meines

Selbstmordes wären grenzenlos" (p. 250). The very fact that the narrator refuses to rouse himself from his own style of "tyrannisch gewordener Gewohnheit" disturbs and vexes the little woman. Her judgment differs from the judgment of society, which finds him not particularly objectionable: "die Öffentlichkeit wird niemals so unendlich viel an mir auszusetzen haben..." (p. 247). But this very use of the term *Öffentlichkeit* – most often in a context of vague fear or overly protesting assurance – shows that his relationship with society is fundamentally antagonistic. The narrator feels tacitly accepted by society only because he has never allowed himself to be noticed: "wenn ich aber nicht durch besondere Brauchbarkeit ausgezeichnet sein sollte, werde ich doch auch gewiß nicht gegenteilig auffallen" (p. 248).

The woman, he says, is not interested in his improvement. Yet his own uneasy conscience poses in advance several questions which he might expect the world to ask him if this "kleine Sache" ever appeared openly before *die Öffentlichkeit*; and in these questions his own *Unverbesserlichkeit* appears as the source of the woman's torments:

> Es kommt die Welt und wird mir die Frage stellen, warum ich denn die arme kleine Frau durch meine Unverbesserlichkeit quäle... wenn mich die Welt so fragen wird, es wird schwer sein, ihr zu antworten. (p. 248)

Again, when in former times the narrator thought a crisis might be imminent, his conscience disturbs him with several other questions which the world's tribunal might one day summon him to answer:

> ich habe mich tatsächlich öfters gefragt, ob mich denn mein gegenwärtiger Zustand so befriedige, das ich ihn gar nicht ändern wolle, und ob es denn nicht möglich wäre, gewisse Änderungen an mir vorzunehmen.... (p. 249)

He had, in fact, undertaken several reforms but found it impossible to satisfy the little woman. Now, he settles for compromise, for the comforting thought that he had brought about a few changes. Then, with a shrug of the shoulders, he tries to slip back into his comfortable "bisheriges Leben".

Part of the narrator's technique in presenting this "kleine Sache" is verbal diminution. What normally might be considered extraordinary, he underplays, cutting even the ordinary down to less than ordinary. The title itself carries overtones of this mock-epic approach. In his description of the little woman in the first paragraph, he emphasizes her ordinariness: she wears the same dull-colored clothes, her hair is "glatt und nicht unordentlich", and her hand is "ein völlig normale Hand". As the story progresses, however, the hidden references of the woman's peculiarities (in the first paragraph) – her hair "sehr locker gehalten", and the fact that she overdoes her "Beweglichkeit" – grow into the picture of an extraordinary, or at least eccentric, person: a person of great sensitivity, easily disturbed, quickly growing pale and trembling, fainting, rising weak from sleepless nights, and so forth. To her feelings, actions, attitudes, and functions, the narrator assigns elevated vocabulary, selected to differentiate himself from her. He tries to show that she over-reacts – "sie übertreibt freilich diese Beweglichkeit" – and so her reactions can be sifted, diminished, and (by and large) discarded. The narrator imagines his own life as cut into tiny pieces ("in allerkleinste Teilen"); still, "jedes Teilchen meines Lebens", he says, would be for her "ein Ärgernis". He dignifies her inner suffering with the term *Leid*, but applies *Peinlichkeit* to his own: "ich erkenne, daß alle diese Peinlichkeit nichts ist im Vergleich mit ihrem Leid" (p. 246).

This process of verbal diminution continues when the narrator mentions the "Sache" to a good friend:

> nur nebenbei, leicht, mit ein paar Worten, ich drückte die Bedeutung des Ganzen, so klein sie für mich nach außen hin im Grunde ist, noch ein wenig unter die Wahrheit hinab. (p. 251)

He seems shocked when the friend suggests taking a trip (the very thing which in "First Sorrow" had pained the acrobat so). The situation is a minor, personal matter, he decides, and must remain so.

In the early years, the narrator had waited in fear for the *Entscheidung* – "Dachte ich immer, nun sei die Entscheidung" (p. 252). Later he smiles at the word itself: "Und die Entscheidung selbst, warum benenne ich sie mit einem so großen Wort?" (p. 253).

Perhaps he has also dignified his own conscience, his anxiety, or his own negative spirit which goads him toward goals which his present habits make "unerreichbar" for him, by calling it "meine kleine Richterin" (p. 252). At any rate, he decides to keep his hand over this "kleine Sache" so that he can continue to live his "bisheriges Leben" calmly, "trotz allen Tobens der Frau" (p. 254).

3. "*A Hunger Artist*"

The four *Sinnlinien* which Weltsch noted in "A Hunger Artist" (and which we used above as hinges for our discussion of the anxiety-theme in that story), also form a convenient basis for an analysis of the exceptional-as-ordinary theme. Here, too, all four levels of meaning interpenetrate one another.

The man we know only as a *Hungerkünstler* could never find the food he liked (fourth level); the Impresario capitalized on this (second level) by putting this otherwise ordinary sick man on display; the crowds found fasting shows exotic and fascinating; they came in droves to see the shows (first level); the fame which his *Lebensweise* brought him encouraged him to try even more amazing feats of endurance, and so to become the greatest faster of all time (third level).

But his manager and the public limit him each time to forty days. Eventually, interest in his malady's display wanes (first level) and business dies almost over night (second level). With two external motivations removed from him, he has only his interior drives (third and fourth levels) to support his determination to climb to the heights of fasting. Outside the circus tent, he continues to fast, intent on breaking all records. But no one changes the placards telling how many *Hungertage* have elapsed (first level), and no barker attracts crowds to his cage (second level). Eventually, even he loses track of his achievement. He no longer considers it a glory to have fasted longer than any living man (third level). As he dies, he knows that he still fasts, but he is no longer proud of the fact. He admits that the only real inducement he ever had for fasting was his distaste for all food, his illness – *der Ekel vor dem Essen.* The final scene with the leopard in the hunger artist's cage suggests the beginning of a new story which we might call "The Eating Artist", and which would have at least three *Sinnlinien: Essen als Sensation, Essen als Geschäft,* and *Essen aus Liebe vor dem Essen.*

The people's praise convinces the hunger artist that he is an exceptional fellow, that he stands out from the crowd by dint of his extraordinary abilities. The truth is that he is a man with a malady who, by "Erhöhung der Wirkung" (p. 255), is made to seem *außerordentlich.* But overfamiliarity removes the uniqueness from his performances. Times change. Soon the exceptional becomes not only ordinary but uninteresting.

> Man gewöhnte sich an die Sonderbarkeit, in den heutigen Zeiten Aufmerksamkeit für einen Hungerkünstler beanspruchen zu wollen, und mit dieser Gewöhnung war das Urteil über ihn gesprochen. (pp. 265-266)

Even among his recently acquired peers in the cage-world of the menagerie, the hunger artist has nothing to recommend him to the attention of the visitors. Voracious eating is much more exciting than fasting; robust good health more astounding than prolonged illness; restless pacing ("die Unruhe der Tiere") more engaging than quiet listlessness.

In the early phases of the fasting showman's history, he loved to display the effects of his "extraordinary ability" to fast (which was really an extraordinary inability to eat) by thrusting his arms through the bars "um seine Magerkeit befühlen zu lassen" (p. 255). Sometimes he would sit up all night telling stories, just to show people that he was fasting "wie keiner von ihnen es könnte" (p. 257). He would never touch food during his fasting period – "die Ehre seiner Kunst verbot dies" (p. 256). He needed to prove beyond all suspicion that he too, like the trapeze artist of the first story, was an "außerordentlicher, unersetzlicher Künstler" (p. 241).

Nevertheless, he was never satisfied with himself, since "für seine Fähigkeit zu hungern fühlte er keine Grenzen" (p. 259). Since he considered himself to be "der größte Hungerkünstler aller Zeiten" (p. 259), he longed for freedom to fast to the limit of his limitless abilities. But on the fortieth day, despite his initial stubborn resistance, he was always removed from his cage and forced to eat the "Krankenmahlzeit" (p. 259) the people had prepared for him.

Before the change of interest had driven the populace to the stalls of wild beasts at the circus, the hunger artist's famed name drew thousands to his cage. Afterwards, he was just one of the numberless throng of "Menschen und Tieren und Apparaten" (p. 263) for which the big circus somewhere, somehow, finds a place. The shift of interest had nothing to do with the hunger artist's ability – he felt he was still "auf der Höhe seines Könnens" (p. 263) and would soon astound the world by terrific new feats, would even surpass himself "bis ins Unbegreifliche" (p. 259). The *Fachleute* smiled. "Man gewöhnte sich an die Sonderbarkeit..." (p. 265). The people were too familiar with such boasts to be interested. Even the accusations of cheating, which an occasional passerby let slip, lacked their original verve. Only the children who had never heard of fasting shows could gaze amazedly at him.

In the early times, people thought him exceptional, *außerordentlich*; now, he seems less than common, *gewöhnlich*. Before, he was in the center of a large hall or out in the open surrounded by eager crowds; now, he is "draußen" in a narrow lane leading to the animal cages. He has become an "outsider", "ein Hindernis auf dem Weg" (p. 265), a misfit in society – too old to change, and "vor allem dem Hungern allzu fanatisch ergeben" (p. 263) to want to.

In the final scene, the hunger artist himself draws the distinction between a man who is extraordinary because he is positively talented and one who is extraordinary because he is exceptionally sick. He had posed as the former, and he begs forgiveness now for his hypocrisy. The people should not have admired a sick man, who fasted because food nauseated him. Dying, he continues to abstain from food, but knows that this is no claim to fame. Crowds press round the leopard that moves into the hunger artist's deserted cage. Ovbiously, they marvel at his normal *joie de vivre*, but again are guilty of elevating the common to the level of the extraordinary. Furthermore, since they have cruelly removed this beast from his natural habitat, they console themselves with the thought that he carries his freedom around with him. And so the cycle begins again.

4. "*Josephine*"

In tracing the anxiety theme in "Josephine", I have already noted the narrator's attempt to ease his own and his people's anxiety at the loss of their sole *Sängerin*. To this end, he frequently employed (like the narrator of "A Little Woman") the technique of diminution. In the first paragraph, Josephine is placed on a pedestal. Her power of song is almost indescribable: "Wer sie nicht gehört hat, kennt nicht die Macht des Gesanges" (p. 268). In all the race of cunning unmusical mice, "nur Josefine macht eine Ausnahme" (p. 269). Here we have a marvel indeed – a singing mouse!

But, surprisingly, the narrator immediately asserts that "Josefinens Gesang als Gesang nichts Außerordentliches darstellt" (p. 269). She squeaks like any other mouse. Squeaking "ist die eigentliche Kunstfertigkeit unseres Volkes" or rather "eine charakterische Lebensäußerung" (p. 270). Everybody squeaks. If Josephine's squeaking distinguishes itself in any way from the everyday speech of the people, it does so by being weaker than theirs. Hers is "ein gewöhnliches, höchtens durch Zartheit oder Schwäche ein wenig auffallendes Pfeifen" (p. 270).

Yet Josephine, according to the narrator, wants to be admired for her squeaking. So she stages performances – like putting on nut-cracking shows. The people admire her singing, set loose as it is from normal speech situations: "Wir bewundern an ihr das, was wir an uns gar nicht bewundern". Even the opposition, when they sit before her, must admit: "was sie hier pfeift, ist kein Pfeifen" (p. 272).

What is ordinary and what extraordinary can never be determined. Throughout the story, the nature of Josephine's singing and its precise effect on the people remains doubtful. The two main opinions – (1) Josephine's and her flatterers', that her gift is both exceptional and valuable to the community; and (2) her opponents', that her "Gesang als Gesang nicht Außerordentliches darstellt" – maintain themselves in ambivalent tension.

Conflicting opinions gravitate toward one or the other pole of the extraordinary/ordinary antinomy. The two poles show up verbally as pairs of value-words which stress the dynamics of the antinomy. Such, for instance, are the pairs: *außerordentlich/gewöhnlich; Gesang/Pfeifen; die Sonderbarkeit/das Übliche; Höhe/Gemein; perlend/stoßend; Kunstfertigkeit/Lebensäußerung; Musik/unmusikalisch; Kunst/Gewohnheit; Gesangsvorführung/Volksversammlung; Kräfte/Schwäche; Kunst/Arbeit; Künstlerlaufbahn/Existenzkampf; Schmeichler/Gegner; Einzelner/Volksgenossen; Josefine/das Volk der Mäuse.*

The poles of each of these sets of antinomies entail value judgments concerning the two central questions around which the narrator's *Nachdenken* revolve: what is the nature of Josephine's song? And what is the relation between Josephine and the people? Even though the narrator's opinion – which he poses also as the people's opinion – leans heavily toward the right-hand members of each set of antinomies, the true nature of Josephine's song and of her relation to the community remain questionable. In earlier parts of the story, the narrator occasionally draws careful distinctions between *Gesang* and *Pfeifen* – for instance, "nicht Gesang – reden wir nicht von Gesang – aber...das landesübliche Pfeifen..." (p. 273). But in the penultimate paragraph, the narrator uses both *Pfeifen* and *Gesang* to describe Josephine's song. Both occur in interrogative constructions:

> War ihr wirkliches Pfeifen nennenswert lauter und lebendiger, als die Erinnerung daran sein wird?... Hat nicht vielmehr das Volk in seiner Weisheit Josefinens Gesang, eben deshalb, weil er in dieser Art unverlierbar war, so hoch gestellt? (p. 290)

His only answer to his final series of questions is a conjectural paragraph – all of its statements governed by the initial "Vielleicht" (p. 290). The dialectical antinomies maintain their strained balance even in this final paragraph.

5. *Conclusion*

"Josephine" brings to a climax the extraordinary-ordinary theme of the collection. In "First Sorrow" striving to excel in the most difficult art attainable by man separated the trapeze artist from men. In "A Little Woman" the refusal to answer one's inner call gives the narrator an unsteady security in a world of diminished events. The hunger artist in the third story excelled only in being exceptionally ill, yet achieved fame –

"an unparallelled career" – by displaying his malady before the wondering and admiring eyes of the crowds. Josephine's talent for song both separates her from the community and sends her into its very heart. She is no mere showcase object like the trapeze acrobat and the hungering expert. But at the same time she does not shrink from public display of her abilities, as the narrator of "A Little Woman" may be doing. She claims to save her people with her singing – or at least to give them new strength to survive the vagaries of the *Existenzkampf.* As "unsere Sängerin", she is both insider and outsider: insider as a working member of the community, outsider by reason of her gift for music among a people who are totally unmusical, and cannot, therefore, be expected to understand her.

Of the four central characters in the stories, Josephine alone achieves partial success at bridging the gap between the ordinary and the extraordinary. She is an important figure in the community as well as an unusual creature who demands that her uniqueness receive public and unambiguous recognition. She alone has gained a power over the community which she herself decides to break – according to the narrator – by refusing to sing. She boasts, too, that she can make her song a real delight to the people, not by the standards merely of her unmusical audience, but by her own standards – and that without falsifying "das Höhe" nor pandering to "dem Gemeinen" (p. 287).

Her role in the community and the community's reactions of respect, dedication, and silent attention, spread an aura of the heroic over the figure of Josephine – a dimension altogether absent from the first three stories. As a female mouse singer instead of a male human warrior, her mythic proportions must be somewhat diminished. Though her song does not fully match, according to the narrator, the *Gesangsüberlieferungen* which can be culled from the *Sagen* and *Lieder* of earlier times, still, the whole people gather around her when she rises to sing in times of greatest peril. Her voice (like the battle-cries of heroes of the epics?) probably attracts the enemy. But the people forgive her the deaths she may cause. They rush to assemble any time and any place she decides to sing. Their devotion to her is firm; the fact that it is not also unconditional is not a reflection on Josephine's prominence but on the pusillanimity of the people:

> bedingungslose Ergebenheit kennt unser Volk kaum; dieses Volk, das über alles die freilich harmlose Schlauheit liebt, das kindliche Wispern, den freilich unschuldigen, bloß die Lippen bewegenden Tratsch, ein solches Volk kann immerhin nicht bedingungslos sich hingeben.... (p. 275)

Unconditional devotion would be too open, too straightforward, too bold an action for these childish, innocent, cunning creatures. From one point of view, they are incapable of heroism: "das fühlt wohl auch Josefine, das ist es, was sie bekämpft mit aller Anstrengung ihrer schwachen Kehle" (p. 275).

Josephine claims she saves these people and gives them new strength. When danger lurks, the people do rally around Josephine. But save them? This the narrator would never agree to: "sie retten uns nicht und gibt uns keine Kräfte, es ist leicht, sich als Retter dieses Volkes aufzuspelen...das sich noch immer irgendwie selbst gerettet hat" (p. 277). In the last paragraph, however, he places her among the "Menge der Helden unseres Volkes".

When Josephine's war to attain recognition from the people makes no progress against their stony, impenetrable front, she cannot retreat from her position (possibly as Achilles could not retreat from his demands). Perhaps she has always known she was reaching for the unreachable:

> Sie greift nach dem höchsten Kranz, nicht weil er im Augenblick gerade ein wenig tiefer hängt, sonder weil es der höchste ist; wäre es in ihrer Macht, sie würde ihn noch höher hängen. (p. 287)

Josephine never grasps her garland. Though for her "gibt es kein Altern und keine Schwächen ihrer Stimme", she disappears after a final furious campaign to win recognition from her own people. Her disappearance is described as a "Hingang" (possibly toward the Western Isles?). She disappears. She has not been defeated by the enemy. She follows either her own miscalculated judgment or the directives of destiny. She passes, music passes, and perhaps the final tiny traces of heroism pass forever from the mouse nation – and possibly, from the nation of modern man. An extraordinary figure among her contemporaries, she was nevertheless "ein kleine Episode in der ewigen Geschichte unseres Volkes". She joins the throng of heroes of the race in the leveling land of forgotten deeds.

F. THEME OF FAILURE TO COMMUNICATE

The theme of failure to communicate emerges from the basic *Erzählsituation* of each story. Those who interpret this cycle as a study of the plight of the artist, misunderstood and outcast by society, have perceived only a small part of the truth of Kafka's experimental myths. The central "artist" figures of the story share responsibility with society for the division between themselves and their contemporaries. They have contributed generously to their own exile, to the misunderstanding that stands like an impenetrable shield between themselves and their fellow man.

1. "*First Sorrow*"

The trapeze artist decides to remain "Tag und Nacht auf dem Trapeze". Naturally, then, his social life develops within the very narrow limits which he himself has imposed. He relaxes only with a rare *Turnerkollege* who takes the trouble to climb the high ladder and sit chatting on the narrow bar – both formidable obstacles to communication with the *Umwelt* below. People must climb to the acrobat's kingdom; he will not descend to theirs.

Living *oben* becomes such a habit that the trapeze artist performs very clumsily when he is forced to remain *unten* very long. The final scene in the train shows him interiorly flailing about, trying to communicate across the few feet that separate him from his manager. He whispers, biting his lips, softly demanding two trapeze bars. The manager responds immediately to his words ("sofort einverstanden") and even feels that another level of meaning might lie behind the whispered sounds. The artist reiterates his demand; but even then, the manager's consent ("nochmals sein volles Einverständnis"), like the mousefolk's refusal of Josephine's petition, counts for nothing – indeed, misses the real point of the attempted communication. The acrobat is trying to break out of himself, to free himself from that "narrow bar" on which he lives. When words fail, violent emotion pours out in the artist's tears. Again the manager must climb up to the acrobat's perch, press his face against the tear-stained cheeks, and praise and caress the acrobat to calm him.

No understanding is reached. The men inhabit two worlds which are far apart. Only a sympathetic vibration passes from the trapeze artist to the Impresario. When the acrobat sleeps, the manager watches; having succeeded in calming his charge, the manager finds that he himself is "nicht beruhigt". Anxiety alone has been communicated. It has spread, more like a disease than like a message, from the man on high to the man below.

2. "*A Little Woman*"

The narrator of "A Little Woman" insists on nothing so strongly as the lack of any real relationship between himself and the subject of his thoughts. He and she live in separate worlds (though, as I suggested before, her world may be the world of his dreams). At first, he categorically denies all connections: "Es besteht ja gar keine Beziehung zwischen uns..." (p. 245). Later, he qualifies this statement by his comment that "die einzige Beziehung, die zwischen uns besteht, der Ärger ist, den ich ihr bereite", which he diminishes ever further by adding, "oder vielmehr der Ärger, den sie sich von mir bereiten läßt..." (p. 246). Since this *Ärger* of hers causes her *Kopfschmerzen*, the narrator feels "eine gewisse Verantwortung" for the stranger.

If his part in her illness should ever attract the attention of the public, the world would come and ask: why do you torment this woman? do you want to drive her to her death? when will you show common ordinary human decency ("das einfache menschliche Mitgefühl") and stop torturing so weak a creature?

If he were to answer those questions truthfully (he implies), he would say: I don't believe in her sickness; even if I did, I would have "nicht das geringste Mitgefühl" for her, since she is a total stranger "und die Beziehung, die zwischen uns besteht, nur von ihr hergestellt ist und nur von ihrer Seite aus besteht" (p. 248). But the world would suspect a *Liebesbeziehung*, and would cling to its prejudice, "trotzdem es bis zur äußersten Deutlichkeit zutage liegt, daß eine solche Beziehung nicht besteht" (p. 249).

So not only is there a failure of communication between the narrator and the woman, but also between the narrator and the world. The circle of broken circuits is made complete by the little woman's inability to communicate her *privaten Ärger* to the *Öffentlichkeit*. She would be ashamed openly to publicize "diese unreine Sache" (p. 247); so, in *ihrer Frauenschlauheit* she strikes upon a compromise: she attempts to communicate through *äußern Zeichen* – by turning pale, shuddering, and fainting. But over the years, she fails. No *Entscheidung* disturbs the narrator's relatively calm existence. He is never forced to establish communications either with the little woman or with the world. He may continue to live his life, like the trapeze artist, keeping it within its "bisherigen, engen, die Außenwelt noch nicht einbeziehenden Grenzen" (p. 251).

The vocabulary of communication and non-communication in this story reveals a dialectic which moves toward a substitute compromise. The antinomial thesis/antithesis and the compromising synthesis of the failure-at-communication theme in "A Little Woman" reveals itself in such word-patterns as: (1) *Beziehung/keine Beziehung/einzige Beziehung: Ärger;* (2) *besprechen/schweigen/Mittelweg: äußern Zeichen;* (3) *glauben/nichts glauben/verdächtigen*; (4) *verstanden/nie verständigen/ärgern und Nervosität.*

The unsatisfactory *Mittelweg* yields no better results than direct attempts at establishing or breaking communications. Only the woman's *Ärger* succeeds in setting up in the narrator similar (though hardly sympathetic) vibrations of psyche – "eine gewisse Nervosität". Again, as in "First Sorrow", only anxiety – vague, formless fear; unreasonable uneasiness – has been communicated.

3. "*A Hunger Artist*"

Expressions and situations which convey the failure-to-communicate theme flood the pages of "A Hunger Artist". The initiates know that the hunger artist will take no food during his fast, but "nicht jeder Wächter konnte das begreifen" (p. 256). So professional watchers are created to assure the masses that there is nothing edible in the cage. With watching come suspicions which the hunger artist must learn to accept as part of his profession. The series of questions which he broods over while stubbornly refusing to exit from his cage indicate not only a fundamental misunderstanding between the hunger artist and his public, but also a fundamental misconception of the hunger artist about his "art":

> ...warum gerade jetzt aufhören?... Warum wollte man ihn das Ruhmes berauben?... Warum hatte diese Menge...so wenig Geduld mit ihm; ...warum wollte sie es [his continued fast] nicht aushalten? (p. 259)

Later, in the final scene, the *Aufseher* asks: "Du hungerst noch immer? Wann wirst du denn endlich aufhören?" Ironically, only the *Aufseher* "understood" – in the sense of registering interiorly – the words the hunger artist whispers; at the same time, he signals to the bystanders that the man in the cage is insane, thus cutting off any possibility of further communication.

The most disturbing thing the hunger artist must endure – even while living "in scheinbarem Glanz, von der Welt geehrt" (p. 261) – is "daß niemand sie [his moods] ernst zu nehmen verstand" (p. 261). Everyone thinks him sad because he has fasted too long; he feels sad because he is not allowed to fast to the limits of his abilities. (Both reactions overlook the fact that his "abilities" are an illness, not a talent.) The Impresario's "Verdrehung der Wahrheit" serves only to increase the hunger artist's conviction that communication is impossible: "Gegen diesen Unverstand, gegen diese Welt des Unverstandes zu kämpfen, war unmöglich" (p. 262).

Neither the hunger artist nor the Impresario had been aware of the "geheimen Einverständnis" against fasting shows. But soon the crippling decrease of attendance at performances forced the performer himself to sign up – without reading the contract – with a circus. He considered it *selbstverständlich* that his cage would be outside and to the side of the main events, but did not expect the total lack of interest and appreciation in those who pushed and shoved their way past him to get to the animals. The ones in back did not understand (*nicht verstanden*) why they were being held up; while the ones in front paused, "nicht etwa aus Verständnis", but rather to assert themselves against the charging mob. The occasional child who stopped to stare at him looked on "*verständnislos*" (p. 265).

The dialectic of unachieved communication between starvation artist and people moves from renewed attempts to be understood to new occasions of frustration. Each attempt must continue to be frustrated as long as the one communicating does not really understand what it is that he wishes to communicate. The vocabulary of "A Hunger Artist" shows the public searching for other kinds of responses to the fasting performances which might serve as compromise substitutes for true understanding. As we saw in the first three paragraphs of this section, all words connoting achieved communication appear in negative contexts (*e.g.*, *nicht verstanden, nicht glauben, nicht begreifen*).

The words connoting a compromise substitute for understanding occur with increasing frequency; for instance: (1) neutral words: *Interesse, Teilnahme, teilnahmen, Besichtigungen, Fragen, Bewachung, wachten, seinen Willen, lassen*; (2) positive words: *stauen, bewundern, ehren, loben, sorgen, trösten, verziehen*; and (3) negative words: *verdächtigen, Verdächtigungen, Verdrehung der Wahrheit, Abneigung gegen das Schauhungern, Gleichgultigkeit, Bosartigkeit, Lächeln, Lüge, Urteil.* The most serious of all the negative responses, however, is overfamiliarity (*Gewohnung*) which leads to forgetfulness and neglect. Even suspicion had been better than this. Paradoxically, however, only when *Interesse* passed into *Gewohnung* and forgetfulness, could the hunger artist see his own life clearly enough to base his world on something more substantial than public concern; only then could he penetrate to the core of his confused life; only then could he see that his strivings and his sorrows had been constructed on a maze of misunderstanding.

For the hunger artist's entire career is founded on a complexus of confusions. He cannot find the food he likes, so he abstains (fourth level – *Weltsch*). When the Impresario discovers that people are willing to pay to witness this starving man's progress toward death – provided it be halted after forty days – he makes a business of staging performances (second level). People come in droves to watch with increasing interest (first level), which in turn half-convinces the starving man that he is a "hunger artist" and so must perfect his art by pursuing his talents to their utmost limits, by reaching beyond himself "bis ins Unbegreifliche" (third level).

Several times this misdirected "artist" tries to clarify the basic confusion by hinting that he finds fasting easy. But even the *Eingeweihter* cannot understand. Some watchers praise his modesty in making such a statement; others call him a swindler or a publicity seeker. Try as he may, he can convince no one that at the root of his sensational career lay a misunderstood malady. Dying, he whispers the shocking secret to the *Aufseher*, but the *Aufseher* merely listens with casual attention, making no attempt to understand the meaningless words of a lunatic.

Because the public so enthusiastically misinterprets the hunger artist's condition, he begins to regard himself as an expert. His confusion about his own abilities and inabilities receives no ultimate clarification until the final scene. "Immerfort wollte ich, daß ihr mein Hungern bewundert", he tells the polite but non-interested *Aufseher*. "Ihr solltet es aber nicht bewundern...weil ich hungern muß" (p. 267). He admits that both his own view that he was worthy of praise for his talents, and the public's encouragement of such a view were false. He expresses what has to be expressed: that he is a sick man. But the *Aufscher* interprets his sickness as lunacy, and so pays no attention to the actual meaning conveyed.

The public, having learned nothing about themselves from their extended experience with the hunger artist, press around the cage of the leopard. The final paragraph focuses on the public's initial misinterpretation of this new object of interest. Kafka carefully repeats the word to indicate how the public has accustomed itself to be satisfied with appearances: *schien*: "nicht einmal die Freiheit schien er zu vermissen; dieser edle... Körper schien auch die Freiheit mit sich herumzutragen: irgendwo im Gebiß schien sie zu stecken" (p. 268). A new maze of misunderstanding is in the making. The public will treat the leopard with the same insensitivity as it treated the hunger artist.

4. "*Josephine*"

The failure-to-communicate theme in "Josephine" brings to its peak the problem of communicating the irrational, the ambivalent, the fundamentally incommunicable. In "First Sorrow" the emotional outburst which accompanied the acrobat's words demanding two trapeze bars sufficed to transfer his anxiety to the Impresario. In the second story of the cycle, groundless *Ärger* becomes the means by which the little woman impresses her existence on the withdrawn narrator, whose meager response manifests itself as "eine gewisse Nervosität". The hunger artist finds frustrating his attempts to explain his experience of hungering to a healthy, peripherally concerned crowd: "Versuche, jemandem die Hungerkunst zu erklären! Wer es nicht fühlt, dem kann man es nicht begreiflich machen" (p. 266).

In "Josephine", two chief problems of communication confront the reader: the singer's difficulty in conveying what she wishes to convey through her singing; and Kafka's problem in conveying the ambivalent relationship of singer and people through the syntax and choice of words of his first-person narrator.

Josephine tries to communicate the incommunicable through music. She does not impart anxiety and uneasiness to her audience, as had the central figures of the first three stories of the cycle. Rather, she communicates peace, inner calm – which the narrator admits is the kind of music mice like best: "Stiller Frieden ist uns die liebste Musik" (p. 268).

Her music, however, is also mystery. People feel its effects, but (*ihrer Meinung nach*) no one really understands it. Perhaps she herself, like the hunger artist, does not really understand her own art. At any rate, she has given up all hope of any real communication with her unmusical race: "auf wirkliches Verständnis...hat sie längst verzichten gelernt" (p. 273). She easily accepts the disturbances of her performance which cause her to heighten the effects of her "Triumphpfeifen" (p. 272), because these disturbances serve "die Menge zu erwecken, sie zwar nicht Verständnis, aber ahnungswollen Respekt zu lehren" (p. 273). Like *Interesse* in "A Hunger Artist", *Respekt* substitutes for real understanding as a bond between the people and the singer.

To understand Josephine's song, says the narrator, one must sit before her: "es ist zu Verständnis ihrer Kunst notwendig, sie nicht nur zu hören, sondern auch zu sehn" (p. 270). In fact, being present before her automatically insures one of understanding her: "und wenn man vor ihr sitzt, versteht man sie" (p. 273); but by that he obviously means one feels that Josephine is doing something at least slightly different from ordinary squeaking: "wenn man vor ihr sitzt, weiß man: was sie hier pfeift, ist kein Pfeifen" (p. 272).

Whether or not the people understand Josephine's song is the central question during the first nine paragraphs of the monologue. The answer will determine the solution to be offered the second central question about the relation of Josephine and the people. For if her song is "außerhalb seines Fassungsvermögens" (p. 283), then she herself must stand "außerhalb seiner Befehlsgewalt" and "außerhalb des Gesetzes" (p. 283). As a representative of the people and a member of Josephine's opposition, the narrator must argue that Josephine's song is "natürlich...ein Pfeifen. Wie denn nicht?" (p. 282).

But Kafka's narrator never succeeds in conceptualizing either Josephine's song or his own "understanding" of it. His reflections take shape in involved sentences which allow full play to the irrational forces that control the ambivalent relationship of songstress and people. His approach, while couched in carefully reasoned phrases, hinges on feeling. Her song, he says, represents "nichts Außerordentliches" because that "Gefühl des Außerordentliches" which one would need to have, is lacking: "ich fühle es nicht und habe auch bei andern nichts dergleichen bemerkt" (p. 269). Vaguely, he compares Josephine's song to a "notion" of singing of which past legends and ballads might inform him, if someone could only sing them; but no one can. Still, he concludes: "Eine Ahnung dessen, was Gesang ist, haben wir also, und dieser Ahnung nun entspricht Josefinens Kunst eigentlich nicht" (p. 269).

Immediately following his introductory "Ich habe oft darüber nachgedacht", the narrator capsulizes in a sentence that central mystery, never solved, from which the entire story on this level, ultimately unfolds:

> Wir sind doch ganz unmusikalisch; wie kommt es, daß wir Josefinens Gesang verstehn oder, da Josefine unser Verständnis leugnet, wenigstens zu verstehen glauben. (p. 269).

Though the two opinions – Josephine's and the people's – oppose one another in drawn battle, no one ever really clarifies what the war is about. The folk, though unmusical, claims to understand Josephine's music. Josephine claims it does not. But what is it to understand? Is not the entire problem predicated on a false premise – that music can be "understood"? What can it possibly mean for the mouse folk to "understand" Josephine's music?

Because of the limited suspicious point of view which controls all information that the reader receives, one can never be sure if Josephine is a real artist or not. If she really is an artist, then the narrator's final judgment that her song is merely "ein Pfeifen...Pfeifen ist die Sprache unseres Volkes" (p. 282) – proves the narrator's complete misunderstanding of Josephine's song. Though he may experience its effects, he does not know how to begin to evaluate it. If Josephine ever spoke, she might repeat, almost verbatim, a line from "A Hunger Artist": "Versuche, jemandem den Gesang zu erklären! Wer es nicht fühlt, dem kann es nicht begreiflich machen" (*cf.* p. 266).

Through his first-person suspicious narrator, Kafka does not try to communicate any single idea or theme, but rather a complexus of balanced meanings which in themselves argue to the impossibility of arriving at any apodictic statement of truth. Complexities, obscurities, tensions of opposities constantly warn the reader to re-evaluate. The fact that the narrator concludes his *Bericht* with a series of unanswerable questions and a conjectural paragraph argues strongly that no single interpretation can be superimposed on this story or on the cycle. Ultimately, he leaves ambiguous the relationship of Josephine and her people, as well as the true nature of her song.

A further indication of this appears in the choice of connecting and adverbally modifying words by which the narrator makes transitions from one thought to another.[44] The most common of these are: *aber*, *meine Meinung nach*, *vielleicht*, *vielmehr*, *doch*, *oder*, *sondern*, *nur*, *wie es mir scheint*, *wenigstens*, *kaum*, *selbst*, *sogar*, *trotz*, and *freilich*. These words operate in the text in such a way that, even though one should feel he has a full understanding and a solidly formed opinion about any matter, yet the other side may be presented with an equal persuasiveness so that one is forced to alter his previously formed opinion.

Kafka's narrator also employs conditional clauses to help capture the ambiguities and ambivalences of living. Hillmann has outlined three clearly observable uses of this construction in "Josephine": (1) an if-then construction in which the then-clause becomes pure illusion because the if-clause must be categorically negated; (2) conditional phraseology which, in the negative answer of a question suggests that the answer could as well be "yes" as "no"; and (3) the situation: "if, then; but no", often followed up by "and even if, then still no".[45]

All these devices are part of the story's design. In themselves, they argue both to the narrator's craftiness (*Schlauheit*) as a member of Josephine's opposition, and to Kafka's care to present, with as full a force as his choice of narrator will allow, both sides of Josephine's struggle for understanding and recognition.

[44] See Hillmann, pp. 118-120; also Martin Walser, *Beschreibung einer Form* (München, 1961), p. 94.

[45] See Hillmann, especially pp. 269, 270, 283, and 286.

G. SUMMARY AND CONCLUSION

The questions raised at the beginning of this chapter concerned the aesthetic patterning of the collection *Ein Hungerkünstler*. During the major portion of my analysis, I have tried to point out in detail the similarities of structure of the stories in the cycle and the dynamic development of the cycle as a whole. But I have limited myself to only three of the themes or meaning-sets in the collection: the theme of anxiety temporarily controlled but always ready to break out again; the theme of the exceptional as ordinary, or of the ordinary as exceptional, in which the points of view of the alleged exceptional characters are contrasted with those of the apparently ordinary individuals; and the theme of failure to communicate, in which the tension between the lack of matter and the lack of manner confuse the basic reason behind the lack of communication.

I have treated only three of the structurally relevant themes. Other themes expressive of the ambiguities and ambivalences of life which Kafka has structured dialectically as a struggle between two goods, are: the theme of man in society (*Einzelner/Publikum – Volksgenossen*); the theme of freedom within the law (*Freiheit/Gesetz – Erlösung*); the theme of the childish grown-up (*Kind/Erwachsener – das Volk*); and the theme of time-passing (*Jugend/Alter – ewige Geschichte*).

Kafka's narratives are "experimental myths" which embody the opposition and dialectic of these and other attitudes, values, and judgments of the human situation. He presents each side of opposing points of view with a cogency which draws the reader first toward one pole and then toward the other. But Kafka himself does not throw the weight of his rhetoric unambiguously toward either side of the balance. The tension between the individual and society is not solved, for instance, by a vindication of the individual nor by a eulogy of society. The antinomy resolves itself into a partial synthesis, a precarious balance between the two: a *Menge der Helden*, a society of individuals.

Kafka sides neither with the separated individual nor with the faceless throng; he exalts neither total freedom from law nor total submission to the law; he does not sentimentalize the careless joys of childhood nor paint a rosy picture of an idyllic old age; he refuses to praise previous ages to the neglect of the present or to laud the present to the disservice of the past – and he speculates about the future with caution.

Kafka's experimental myths, at bottom, embody the fundamental ambiguities and ambivalences of human existence. Kafka himself cannot be said to make any "statement" about life in this collection. About the "poetic meaning" of his book one can only say with assurance that it shows, through situation and counter-situation, evaluation and counter-evaluation, that human experience is ambiguous and that human values evoke ambivalent attitudes.

This "poetic meaning" emerges through Kafka's structure and rhetorical technique. Opaque depth, expressive of man's confusion in the face of an uncertain life-situation, is achieved through the multileveled movement of theme. Each theme, as I have shown in detail, represents both an oscillation between two poles of a truth or value-antinomy, and a dialectic which progresses toward an unsteady synthesis, which again is but a renewed thesis. But the complexities of Kafka's narrative do not stop there. For each of the three themes I have examined, as well as the other themes I have discussed briefly, interweave with one another, so that the truth or value-pole of one antinomy is supported or negated by that of another.

Abstractly stated – a dangerous enterprise, I admit – the "poetic meaning" of Kafka's collection would consist in mere generalizations of the shifts of opinion and value judgments that the various narrators engaged in during the span of their stories. The generalizations would turn on such phrases as "and yet", "still", "nevertheless", "but", and so on. A pattern such as the following might be detected: to strive to achieve a goal above the common reach of man is admirable; but one must beware lest in becoming extraordinary, he also become a freak, unable to communicate with other men; still, other men are not really interested in what the exceptional person wants to communicate – they are incapable of understanding; but if they do not understand, then they should not have any power over the exceptional individual; the individual, however, is not above the general law – the law of the *Existenzkampf* which governs all living beings; and yet, perhaps the exceptional person actually is a hero in that battle, and so saves his race from the enemy; but what is one man to an entire race? Surely, the *Volk* is a fatherly protector to the childish individual; but it is also a judge; yet it does not, ultimately decide the fate of the exceptional individual; time passes and the individual passes; youth was a time of gaity, the early times were ages of peace, calm, heroism; but youth is overeager, looking all the time for crises or astonishing phenomena; but as time passes, one becomes used to the astonishing; the extraordinary becomes the ordinary; as the child becomes the adult, he loses his love for music, his ability to be astonished by such feats as hungering, his readiness to consider every change a crisis; as time goes on, such alterations in the lives of individuals will continue to occur – some caused by a shift of interest, some by a necessary shift of location – but history rolls on, even though "people learn little from others' experiences"[46] so that history will continue to repeat itself without any solid hope of significant progress.

Obviously, I have not summarized all the truth and value judgments of the narrators of the four stories; I have merely attempted to indicate in what way the various thematic levels of the collection interact.

Earlier critical works on Kafka have often attempted to apply biographical facts or allegorical meanings to the myths he has created. My study has not yielded any new biographical insights or discovered any new allegorical referents. As I stated at the beginning of this chapter, my purpose has been to seek an understanding of the dynamic patterns of the collection – to trace the design in the weave, not to unwind the fabric. The "poetic meaning" of the collection IS the collection itself – with all its complex interconnections of theme, situation, and structure.

Finally, I have proposed this collection as representative of one kind of short story cycle. I have shown that the reader's experience of each of the stories is significantly modified by his experience of the other stories in the cycle, since their patterning reveals the simultaneous development of several interconnected themes. But why choose *Ein Hungerkünstler* for this illustrative purpose? The two chief reasons which dictated the choice were: (1) that Kafka is perhaps one of the most significant of all twentieth-century writers; and (2) that the patterning of several interconnected themes assumes priority as a unifying principle in these stories of Kafka, but is sometimes merely secondary in other collections. Kafka's cycle does not have a unifying central character, such as one finds in *My Name Is Aram* or *The Unvanquished.* Nor can its unity be said to hinge upon a single realistically detailed locale or the presentation of an emerging community, both of which operate strongly in *Winesburg, Ohio.* Only one unifying principle predominates in *Ein Hungerkünstler*: the structurally similar recurrent development of several interconnected themes.

46 From T. S. Eliot, *Murder in the Cathedral.*

IV

WILLIAM FAULKNER: *THE UNVANQUISHED*

The Unvanquished (1938)[1] consists of seven short stories, the shortest being about 6,000 and the longest 12,000 words. Five of them (the first five of the collection) made their debut in *Saturday Evening Post* in groups two years apart in their publication date: the first group in 1934 (three stories: "Ambuscade", "Retreat", and "Raid"; September 29, October 13, and November 3, 1934); the second in 1936 (two stories: "The Unvanquished" [later changed to "Riposte in Tertio"] and "Vendée", November 14 and December 5, 1936). "Skirmish at Sartoris", the sixth story in the book version, appeared first in *Scribner's Magazine*, April 1935. The final story of the collection, "An Odor of Verbena", was published first in *The Unvanquished.*

In the change of address from magazine to book, three of the stories (4, 5, and 6) changed little other than their address – two gained 500-1000 words, and "Skirmish at Sartoris" lost about 500. But the three 1934 stories (1, 2, and 3) underwent major revisions: in the Random House edition, "Ambuscade" occupies 39 pages, 12 of which are completely new to the book version. Of the 45 and 47 pages in "Retreat" and "Raid", 9 pages in each story have no counterpart in the magazine versions.

The purpose of these revisions[2] seems to be to bring the thematic content of the earlier stories more closely in line with the serious direction of the later stories from "Riposte in Tertio" through "An Odor of Verbena". The revisions bring out the serious impact of the war on the game-world of Bayard and Ringo and on the polite world of Rosa Millard. They prepare with more precision the march to freedom of the Negroes, and bring out the relation of the Negroes to the Whites, both southern and northern. They show too how large, how grand, how mythically immense the figure of John Sartoris appeared to Bayard at the age of twelve,

[1] (New York: Random House, 1938). All page references in the text which refer to *The Unvanquished* correspond to the pagination of this edition.

[2] Most critics overlook the extent and importance of these revisions. A notable exception is James B. Meriwether in his unpublished docotral dissertation, "The Place of *The Unvanquished* in William Faulkner's Yoknapatawpha Series", (Princeton University, 1958).

and how the stature of that man shrank as Bayard himself reached upward toward physical and spititual maturity. They develop the intimate ties that join Bayard to Ringo and stress each one's determination to experience more than the other – a competition which Bayard finally settles by his action as The Sartoris in "An Odor of Verbena". Finally, the revisions serve to enrich the background of characters (such as Buck McCaslin) that are to take an important role in some later story, and to connect *The Unvanquished* with other Yoknapatawpha sagas.

A. STRUCTURAL LINKS

The direction of the revisions, then, leans toward a tightening of substance and symbol. But the unrevised stories already possessed several important structural and thematic links. First, there is the recurrence of characters. Most important structurally is the character Bayard Sartoris, the narrator-participator. From the distance of achieved maturity, he narrates all the events in which he, as a boy of twelve, thirteen, fourteen, fifteen, and as a young man of twenty and twenty-four, took part. Though the events are presented as perceived by a maturing adolescent and young man, Bayard's distanced objectivity casts a uniform and reflective hue over them all.

Even in the first three revised accounts, Bayard the narrator modifies, from an ironic perspective, the romanticized view of war and heroics which inundates the child view of Bayard the participator. In the last story, he maintains and deepens his distance so that it seems as if the narrator is not Bayard at twenty-four, but almost a different person who has reflectively assimilated this experience into his outlook.

The narrator is not the only character who appears in all the stories. Miss Rosa Millard (Granny) and Colonel John Sartoris, either as active living beings or as active spirits, recur in every story. Granny dominates the scene in most of the early stories, until her death in "Riposte in Tertio". Bayard is still an adolescent, almost still a child, until the moment of her murder. In "Vendée" he tracks and kills Granny's murderer, Grumby, and in so doing tastes blood for the first time in his life. An inverse pattern orders stories 6 and 7: Colonel John Sartoris, who occupied a portion of the center stage in the first two stories, returns home at the end of "Vendée" to find that his son has just killed Grumby – an act Bayard at fifteen felt obliged to perform both because at that time he was the only male Sartoris at hand and because he felt at least partially responsible for allowing Granny to go senselessly to her death at the hand of a coward. "I could have held her", he says near the end of "Riposte in Tertio". "[But]...I sat there in the wagon in the cold rain and let her walk on into the wet twilight and never come out of it again" (p. 174).

In the last two stories, John Sartoris, though he protests that he wants to establish peace, law, and order, continues to perpetuate the habits of war. He is not punished for killing the carpetbaggers because he had forced them to shoot first. Caught by his war habits, he lacerates even a brave man's peacetime reputation until that man feels obliged to shoot him. Here again, Bayard is faced with the killer of a relative – his father this time. As Granny's spirit was crying for vengeance, John Sartoris' spirit cries for "moral housecleaning" – "I'm tired of killing men no matter what the necessity nor the end" (p. 266), he had told Bayard shortly before he was shot. Bayard's calm courage in "An Odor of Verbena" executed in deed what John Sartoris only wished he could do. John had killed too many men. Bayard had killed only one, and would never forget it.

Besides Granny and Father, Bayard's constant companion, Ringo, grows and matures with Bayard throughout the seven stories. In one of the additions to the book version of "Ambuscade" Bayard says:

> Ringo and I had been born in the same month and had both fed at the same breast and had slept together and eaten together for so long that Ringo called Granny "Granny" just like I did, until maybe he wasn't a nigger anymore or maybe I wasn't a white boy anymore, the two of us neither, not even people any longer: the two supreme undefeated like two moths, two feathers riding above a hurricane.... (pp. 7-8)

The contest between Ringo and Bayard is almost a race toward maturity. Born on the same day, they burst from the starting stalls with an open track before them. Throughout the cycle, they (first Ringo, then Bayard) nose ahead of one another by experiencing what the other has not. In the first story, they run neck and neck: whatever one does, the other does too. Syntactically, the subject of an action done is either "we" or "Ringo and I" or both: "We – Ringo and I – ran as one, in midstride out of frozen mobility..." (p. 8).

In the first three stories, the narrative "we" (meaning primarily "Ringo and I") occurs more often than the narrative "I". In "Raid", Bayard, the distant narrator, elaborates on the kind of competition that existed between the two boys (this section is new to the book version):

> That's how Ringo and I were. We were almost the same age, and Father always said that Ringo was a little smarter than I was, but that didn't count with us,

> anymore than the difference in color of our skins counted. What counted was, what one of us had done or seen that the other had not, and ever since that Christmas I had been ahead of Ringo because I had seen a railroad, a locomotive. (p. 91)

But in the following story, "Riposte in Tertio" Ringo speeds ahead of Bayard so far that Bayard feels he may not be able to catch up with him. Bayard is not intimately involved in the "business" Granny had arranged with Ab Snopes. But Ringo is: he shows up with the letterheads of the Union Army; he scouts the Yankee troops in the area and brings back information about their mules and officers; he shows himself competent to handle stress situations; he learns to draw, forges the signatures of various Yankee officers, and keeps, with Granny, accurate accounts of their transactions. Ringo had seen many more Yankee officers by this time than Bayard had; and Ringo was first to realize that Ab Snopes had tricked them all in pursuit of his own interests.

As Knoll pointed out,[3] the separation of the "I" from the "we – Ringo and I" first occurs significantly in the passage where Bayard begins to take upon himself the responsibility for Granny's death:

> We tried. I keep on saying that because I know now that I didn't. I could have held her, turned the wagon, driven away, holding her in it. I was just fifteen, and for most of my life her face had been the first thing I saw in the morning and the last thing I saw at night, but I could have stopped her, and I didn't. (p. 174)

Still, when Bayard undertakes to track and kill Grumby, Ringo, without hesitation, includes himself in the venture. Uncle Buck goes too since he is a man, a relative, and has a pistol. "Vendée" shares several similarities with "Ambuscade", but with important differences: the atmosphere of "game" in the earlier story yields here to foreboding. Rain falls from burgeoning and brooding skies with a determination not unlike the will to vengeance. While in the first story, Ringo's back had supported the barrel of the musket and Bayard had fired, here Bayard fires the pistol without assistance. Still, without Ringo's help, Bayard may never have had the opportunity to shoot, since Grumby had pinned him to the ground. Further, Ringo participated in the ritual retributive act of vengeance – the severing of Grumby's hand, the nailing of his body to the compress where he had murdered Granny, and the impaling of his hand on Granny's headstone.

So, in the last analysis, Ringo and Bayard still acted as one. The use of

3 Robert E. Knoll, "'The Unvanquished' for a Start", *College English*, XIX (May, 1958), 338.

"we" in the concluding pages of the story emphasizes their togetherness, their evenness in the race toward experiential maturity: "what we had to carry", "we rode through Jefferson", "we unwrapped it... and fastened it to the board", "we both began to cry", "we came to the cabin", "we could see the big fire...", "we went to bed", "Ringo and I went to bed in our clothes on the pallet, and went to sleep all in one motion", "Father holding me, and Ringo and I held to him", "Drusilla kneeling and holding me and Ringo, and we could smell the rain on her hair..." (pp. 210-212). At the story's close, however, Uncle Buck praises Bayard's action without mentioning Ringo: "Ain't I told you he is John Sartoris' boy? Hey? Ain't I told you?" From that time on, Bayard begins to think and act independently.

Bayard IS John Sartoris' boy, but not in the sense Uncle Buck McCaslin meant. In "An Odor of Verbena" Bayard shows that he has a mind of his own and a courage to carry out his convictions. In the second section of that story, Drusilla evokes for him her version of John Sartoris' dream. "He is thinking of this whole country which he is trying to raise by its bootstraps", she tells him,

> so that all the people in it, not just his kind nor his old regiment, but all the people, black and white, the women and children back in the hills who don't even own shoes – Don't you see? (p. 256)

But Bayard does not see. Father had just shot a man, a neighboring hill man who had been in the first infantry regiment when it voted him out of command. Father said the man looked like he was going to rob him, but no one could tell since Father had shot too quick. All anyone knew was that the man

> had a wife and several children in a dirt-floored cabin in the hills, to whom Father the next day sent some money and she (the wife) walked into the house two days later while we were sitting at the dinner table and flung the money at Father's face. (p. 255)

Bayard has developed, out of disgust for his own killing of Grumby, a greater respect for human life than his father or Ringo had.

In "An Odor of Verbena", Ringo seems to feel that he leads Bayard in the race, that he is more mature, more "experienced". Bayard notices it with chagrin:

> Ringo was waiting; I remember how I thought then that no matter what might happen to either of us, I would never be The Sartoris to him. He was twenty-four too, but in a way he had changed even less than I had since that day when

we had nailed Grumby's body to the door of the old compress. Maybe it was because he had outgrown me, had changed so much that summer while he and Granny traded mules with the Yankees that since then I had had to do most of the changing just to catch up with him. (p. 248)

During the forty-mile ride home, Ringo and Bayard exchange words only once. Ringo suggests: "We could bushwack him,...like we done Grumby that day." "No" says Bayard, and they ride on. Later, Bayard rejects Ringo's help as well as his attitude toward handling Redmond. This final burst of self-directed experience decides the race. Ringo had mounted and, unasked, had followed Bayard into Jefferson, carrying in his shirt the gun that he and Bayard had wrenched from Grumby's hands. As they dismount in town, Bayard says, "Wait for me here", but Ringo answers defiantly, "I'm going with you." The dialogue is brief and decisive:

"No you ain't", I said.
"Yes I am".
"No you ain't". So I walked on, along the street in the hot sun. (p. 283)

From that moment, Ringo disappears rapidly into the background. The last we see of him, he is performing menial tasks – unlocking the pasture gate for Bayard and bringing water to him in his hat. Bayard refuses the water and goes to the stream himself. He has extricated himself from his childhood; he has surpassed his adolescent competitor; he has asserted himself as The Sartoris of the future.

Loosh and other Negroes also occur in several of the stories. In the early tales, Faulkner made Loosh into a type of Southern Negro who believed that the Yankee troops offered immediate liberation from the conditions slaves faced in the Civil War South. In "Ambuscade" Loosh knows before any one else that Vicksburg has fallen and that the Yankees are already in Corinth. In "Retreat", Loosh shows the incendiary Yankee troops where the Sartoris' silver is buried – just as Granny dreamed he would. When he packs his bundle, and is about to leave, Granny accosts him:

"Loosh", Granny said, "are you going too?"

"Yes", Loosh said, "I going. I done been freed; God's own angel proclamated me free and gonter general me to Jordan. I don't belong to John Sartoris now; I belongs to me and God". (p. 85)

In "Raid" the identity of Loosh is swallowed up in the numberless throngs of Negroes who are singing "Glory! Glory! Hallelujah!" (p. 119) as they march out on the bridge the Yankee soldiers will momentarily blow up.

When the Union troops find they have hoards of "freed" Negroes on their hands, they frantically search for ways of disencumbering themselves. Granny asks them for Loosh and Philadelphy, so they foist off on her a hundred and ten Negroes.[4] After that, Loosh drops out of the book for over a hundred pages. In "An Odor of Verbena", however, we find him again established as caretaker of the livery stable at the Sartoris place (p. 279), while the South struggles to reconstruct not necessarily the old order, but a livable one.

Other characters who serve to connect the stories are Drusilla Hawk, Ab Snopes, and Uncle Buck McCaslin. Drusilla figures prominently in three stories: "Raid", "Skirmish at Sartoris", and "An Odor of Verbena". Each time she appears, she fills a different role, while maintaining her unique character as the woman of active and violent courage, rather than of passive resistance. In "Raid" she functions as a man, because her "man" – her fiance – has been killed in the war. The war has taught her endurance – an endurance which seems to abrogate sleep. She wants to join John Sartoris, to live on the battlefield and fight with other soldiers. In "Skirmish at Sartoris", however, now that the war is done, Drusilla must succumb to the pressures of her mother and of other Southern ladies. She is forced to wear a dress. But the spirit of war and adventure has not left her. Election day and wedding day fuse into a galloping, shouting confusion so that when she returns triumphant but unmarried to Sartoris' place, brandishing her election box, the only excuse she can offer to her astonished mother is "I forgot" – and the story confirms this excuse as the actual fact!

Her two roles – violent warrior and valiant bride – merge with and are overshadowed by her role in "An Odor of Verbena" as "the Greek amphora priestess of a succinct and formal violence" (p. 252). In a scene that consciously mimics ritual, she offers the dueling pistols to Bayard, exulting in the fact that she has been privileged to perform the task of the gods. "Do you feel them? the long true barrels, true as justice, the triggers...quick as retribution, the two of them slender and invincible and fatal..." (p. 273). When Bayard's act of courage surpasses anything which her limited view of heroism could encompass, she leaves him the laurel – the sprig of verbena which alone can be smelled above the smell of horses

4 Whether wittingly or unwittingly is never clarified. The botched order of the commanding general transliterates Old Hundred and Tinney – the two mules – into "one hundred and ten mules"; the Negroes Loosh and Philadelphy become twisted into the phrase "captured loose near Philadelphia in Mississippi", so that Negroes, too, are requisitioned to the number of one hundred and ten.

and courage – and retires to Hawkhurst, realizing that new – yes, and better – gods have taken over the temple at Sartoris.[5]

Ab Snopes enters the collection in the story in which Granny is killed – the story which was originally entitled "The Unvanquished" and which, except for its title, changed little other than its external relationships as it became part of the collection which stole its name. As a title within the collection, "Riposte in Tertio" carries much more meaning than "The Unvanquished" would have. *Riposte* is a fencing term (basically deriving from the Latin *respondere*, "to respond"). It means a fencer's return thrust after a parry, or a warding off of a blow.[6] A *riposte* is a new attack made in the same sweep and motion of warding off the other's blow.

The "riposte in tertio" of the title seems to refer to the third-party parry-thrust of Ab Snopes and his associates, Grumby and Grumby's men. Granny has been trying to defend herself and the entire Southern community against the invasion of the Union forces. A large portion of this story concerns Granny's distribution of the mules and money which she manages to requisition from Yankee troops on Union Army stationary that Ringo got from God knows where. The Union invasion is the first thrust, the primary attack. Granny parries the attack adding a *riposte* – she requisitions from the Yankees and then sells back to them 246 mules. Ab Snopes, unable to sell the last batch of mules at full price to the evacuating armies, makes a deal with a Yankee lieutenant and shows him the pen where the mules are hidden. The opportunity Granny had had, to give John Sartoris (on his return) some money to start again, vanishes.

5 Critics who have compared the character of John Sartoris to that of Agamemnon, and the rhythms of *The Unvanquished* to that of the Oresteia trilogy have done so not from mere whim, but on the basis of an entire field of associations. See especially John Lewis Longley, Jr. *The Tragic Mask: A Study of Faulkner's Heroes* (Chapel Hill, 1963).

6 Faulkner seemed romantically attracted to the manly art of dueling. Fencing terminology often insinuates itself into his writings. In an earlier section of *The Unvanquished* (in a passage added after the publication of the magazine version), he describes the battle of the two trains and comments: "this [was] no poste and riposte of sweat-reeking cavalry which all war-telling is full of..." (p. 108). One finds the expression also in the early pages of *The Hamlet*: "All poste and riposte of humor's light whimsy", and again in *Knight's Gambit* in a passage actually describing a fencing situation, though not with two rapiers: "One day Sebastian took a hearth-broom and parried through two ripostes until Max jerked the button off and went at him with the bare point..." (p. 123, Signet edition). Despite his apparent fascination with the art, Faulkner's terminology is not always accurate. There is no such fencing motion as the "poste", but only the "riposte". Faulkner seems to have formed "poste" on some kind of analogy: act-react: poste-riposte. But *riposte* derives from *respondēre*. If Faulkner had posed the false analogy: ponse-response: poste-riposte, he may have questioned his melodic phrase "poste and riposte of sweat-reeking cavalry".

On Ab Snopes' advice, she tries to parry the blow. She has Ringo forge a requisition for four horses – which Ab Snopes says Grumby has stolen from stables in the South. But her last desperate thrust does not work. Grumby murders her: the *riposte in tertio* – a death blow from an adversary she expected to fall under her own attack.

Uncle Buck has to disillusion Bayard from his false notion that Ab Snopes killed Granny. Uncle Buck is a traditionalist, an upholder of Southern gentility, as well as a man with advanced ideas for freeing the slaves and for collective farming.[7] His angry praise and respectful cursing of John Sartoris in the second story come to the fore again in the fourth and fifth as ties to action and theme.

Other characters, too, weave in and out of the action of the various stories: Louvinia and Joby, the two faithful Negroes of the Sartoris spread, are contrasted with Loosh and Philadelphy. Colonel Dick, himself the father of three boys, serves almost as a stereotype of the Union officer disillusioned with the war. His parting comment in "Ambuscade" strikes an ominous note in an otherwise humorous episode: "I won't apologize; fools cry out at wind or fire. But permit me to say and hope that you will never have anything worse than this to remember us by" (p. 38). In the next story, the Yankees burn the Sartoris house, steal their mules and chest of silver, and put an outlaw's price on Colonel John Sartoris' head. Again, in "Raid", Colonel Dick expresses his horror at the frustration of his earlier hopes by the simple phrase, heard after every battle and after every new account of martial destruction: "Damn this war. Damn it. Damn it" (p. 124).

Besides sharing point of view and the rhythm of repeated characters, the stories develop against the backdrop of a broader action – the action of the Civil War (which we will discuss later); and of a definite general locale: Yoknapatawpha County in Mississippi. The Sartoris residence radiates prominence as the center of action. It is the place from which all journeying proceeds and to which all journeying ultimately returns. In every story, the Sartoris house stands starkly in the foreground, prominently, whether as a stronghold against the enemy (as in "Ambuscade", "Riposte in Tertio" and, in another sense, "Skirmish at Sartoris"); or as the scene of destruction or sorrow (as in "Retreat" and "An Odor of Verbena"). It is a house that must be rebuilt by the fortitude and planning of

[7] See the account of him Faulkner gives in the first story of *Go Down, Moses*. That story ("Was") had originally been narrated by Bayard Sartoris, as Roth Russell has shown in "The Brennan Papers: Faulkner in Manuscript", *Perspective*, II (Summer 1949), 219-224.

the living Sartorises, a house whose fortunes emblemize the fortunes of the Sartorises themselves.

Another important element of the book's unity lies in the mere chronology of central actions. Faulkner carefully recalls the action of the previous stories in each succeeding one. This chronology, however, does not run smoothly or continuously, like a river, but progresses in discrete packages, in time-units. The main events of later stories follow those of earlier ones, but not immediately. And, within a single story, the narrator may jump from the central action to an associated action of four or eight years before (as in "An Odor of Verbena"); or from the present summer to the preceding spring (as in "Ambuscade"); or from this Christmas to a Christmas before the war (as in "Raid"). Faulkner's discrete chronological sequence does not prevent such use of flashbacks.

B. BAYARD SARTORIS

The primary unifying force in the work, however, is the emergence of a theme-embodying character through discrete thematically oriented actions. Bayard is that character who, in the mature actions which he undertakes in opposition to family and Southern friends, embodies a redirectioning of Southern mores. In those actions too, he emerges as an independent, morally responsible Southern leader. His decision shapes the future Sartoris tradition and ritually frees the community of its habits and traditions of violence. The necessity of courageous action remains, but courage must now be based on personal convictions suited to a postwar world. As its temporary representative, Bayard releases his community from the necessity of vengeance-killing without weakening the traditional foundations of courage, honor, and human dignity. Further, he repersonalizes the (wartime) depersonalized view of man, but does not yield to sentimentality. He exemplifies in his decision to face Redmond unarmed, the possibility of building a new order without rejecting what was valuable in the old order. And he tries to redirect men's minds from the continuing of an old war to the building of a new peace.

Bayard represents his community not by consistently occupying the center of the stage, nor merely by inheriting the glamorous past of an almost legendary father. Rather, he allows himself to be affected by the lives of all those about him – and then transcends them. Bayard takes their attitudes and traditional responses upon his shoulders. He experiences, in part at least, the same struggles and suffering and hardships they experienced. He breathes air filled with the smoke of discharged muskets and burned houses and with the smell of freed Negroes marching to their Jordan. Much like George Willard of *Winesburg, Ohio* and Aram of *My Name Is Aram*, Bayard assimilates fictionally something of the lives of all those with whom he lives, plays, suffers, works, struggles – even kills. Only from the vantage point of his reflective assimilation – of his rejection and acceptance respectively of bad and good – can he assume the role of The Sartoris: the role of a shaper of the South.

Bayard does not, indeed, occupy a central position in all of the stories. In fact, he can be said to be a true protagonist in only three stories ("Ambuscade", "Vendée", and "An Odor of Verbena"), and the sole protagonist only in the last, "An Odor of Verbena". The dynamic structure of "An Odor of Verbena" shows Bayard picking and choosing the extent to which he will allow his own previous responses, and the attitudes and insights of his family, relatives, and associates – to influence the action which will either establish him as The Sartoris or delay, perhaps stunt forever, the process of his becoming a man.

"An Odor of Verbena" is built in four large sections. The first lays the foundation for the "present" action of the story: Ringo brings the announcement of John Sartoris' death to Bayard at Professor Wilkins' house in Oxford, Mississippi, where Bayard is finishing his third year of law school. Bayard mulls over the decision he must make and the principles according to which he must choose to act; his reflections hint at the enormity of the obstacles he will have to cast aside if he is to act as he sees fit.

At least this will be my chance to find out if I am what I think I am or if I just hope; if I am going to do what I have taught myself is right or if I am just going to wish I were. (p. 248)

When Mrs. Wilkins' figure recalls Granny to him, his reflections show that he basically accepts Granny's prewar moral stance. He rejects the proffer of Professor Wilkins' gun – a civilized educated man condoning violence. He rejects, with a simple "no", Ringo's suggestion that they bushwack Redmond "like we done Grumby". The first section also recalls the six previous stories and places the action of each in the context of a more mature, more educated, more reflective Bayard. Bayard's princicples, which he found enunciated in the Bible, urge him to peace, based on God's fifth commandment:

If there was anything at all in the Book, anything of hope and peace for His

> blind and bewildered spawn which He had chosen above all others to offer immortality, *Thou shalt not kill* must be it, since maybe even he believed that he [Professor Wilkins] had taught it to me except that he had not, nobody had, not even myself since it went further than just having been learned. (p. 249)

Bayard's innate moral center contrasts significantly with the violent ardor with which Drusilla will attempt to inspire him. She will try to initiate him into a rite of "succinct and formal violence" (p. 252), by presenting the dueling pistols through which justice, retribution, and vengenace will be achieved.

The second section of the story comprises several flashbacks to times other than "time present". At the end of section 1, Bayard and Ringo are riding toward the house and at the beginning of section 3, they arrive. The second section counters present with past. Here, Faulkner enriches the context of Bayard's motivation by showing past incidents, connected most often with Drusilla, in which Bayard comes gradually to the convictions which ride with him as he jogs on toward the house.

In the first flashback, Bayard at age twenty strolls with his stepmother, Drusilla, in the garden. Drusilla conjures up for him John Sartoris' dream for Yoknapatawpha County. As counterpoint to this rhythm, Bayard the narrator fills in details of Drusilla's character, of verbena symbolism, of the relationship of Father to Ben Redmond, of the personal meaning of the Grumby episode to him, of the story behind Colonel Sutpen's dream of the violence (condoned by Drusilla but condemned by Bayard) which goes with the Sartoris dream ("A dream" she says, "is not a very safe thing to be near..." [p. 257]); and of Bayard's concern for human lives as opposed to Drusilla's absorption in a vague vision of the future ("There are not many dreams in the world, but there are a lot of human lives" [p. 257]).

During this first flashback complexus, Bayard remarks that he has grown taller than Drusilla and that he remembers being taller than she even when she was riding Bobolink in the midst of the panicked Negroes in "Raid". Throughout the book, Faulkner uses physical height as an indication of the possibility of moral superiority or at least of moral independence. Bayard, as he goes through the process of maturing, begins to notice that he towers above Granny, then outgrows his own Father; Ringo is at one point taller than Bayard. Here, Bayard remarks how much taller he is than Drusilla – he is more mature, more independent morally of the Southern mores and of Drusilla's brand of pseudo-religious indoctrination.

A second flashback unit recounts the events of "last summer, last

August" (p. 258).[8] Bayard is twenty-four. His father has just won a landslide victory over Redmond in a race for the State legislature. To Bayard, John Sartoris looms as a tragic, ruthless figure caught in the postures of life which had frozen around him during times of war, unable to extricate himself from them in times of peace. Everyone knew Redmond to be a man of courage who would have fought in the war had he not been serving the Confederacy in an equally important capacity. But

> Father would taunt him with not having smelled powder. He was wrong; he knew he was when it was too late for him to stop just as a drunkard reaches a point where it is too late for him to stop.... (pp. 258-259)

George Wyatt had told Bayard how John had completed the railroad after buying Redmond's partnership, and how he continued senselessly to badger a brave man. "I know what's wrong", George Wyatt told Bayard. "He's had to kill too many folks, and that's bad for a man" (p. 260).

Redmond contrasts starkly with Grumby. He is no coward as Grumby was. By the time he was fifteen, Bayard had known that "you might frighten a brave man, but...nobody dared frighten a coward..." (pp. 172-173). Granny had walked unarmed into the den of a coward and was killed. Bayard would walk unarmed into the office of a brave man, and he knew he would not die.[9]

That afternoon the scene returns to the Sartoris garden. Bayard is twenty-four. He talks about George Wyatt's notions concerning his

[8] The chronology here, as in other parts of *The Unvanquished*, is confusing. Faulkner has often repeated that the artist should have complete control over time. If, in retelling a story, he decides to shift the relations of time which had operated in the first telling, he is perfectly free to do so. Few critics have remarked the apparent and real contradictions in the time structure of *The Unvanquished.* James Meriwether in "Appendix C" of his dissertation separates all those time relations in the cycle which must be reconciled. His summary of the chronology of the stories agrees, in the main, with my own. Dorothy Tuck's chronology, in *A Handbook of Faulkner* (London, 1965), would place the first story in 1862 – a date I cannot accept because of the fall of Vicksburg. Below I list Tuck's chronology briefly and compare it with Meriwether's dating. I have used numbers for the titles of the stories:

Tuck	*Meriwether*	Bayard's age:
1. Summer 1862	1. July 1863	12
2. 1863	2. Summer 1864	13
3. Summer 1863	3 August 1864	14
4. 1864	4. October-December 1864	15
5. 1864-1865	5. December 1864-February 1865	15
6. 1865	6. Spring 1865	15
7. 1874	7. October 1873	24

[9] See p. 250: "who would not die (I knew that) but who maybe forever after could never again hold up his head".

father. Drusilla tries to tilt the planes of his moral consciousness: "There are worse things than killing men, Bayard". But Bayard's moral imperative, "Thou shalt not kill", drowns her out. Drusilla counters: "Have you forgotten Grumby?" "No", Bayard says, "I never will". But the Grumby adventure had led him to conclusions altogether different than those of Drusilla. Suddenly, Drusilla presses Bayard to kiss her. Bayard refuses twice. Then when she tries to resist, he folds her in against his body, feeling her stiffness yield. Afterwards, Drusilla removes a verbena sprig from her ear and gives it for a first time to Bayard.

Bayard determines to tell his father, but John Sartoris shows no interest in Bayard's love-making with Drusilla. John changes the subject to speak of his dream and of Bayard's role in it: "you, trained in the law, can hold your own – our own". He defends as necessary his actions during the terrible and confused days of the war and its immediate aftermath. "I acted as the land and the time demanded", he said.

> But now the land and the time too are changing;...Yes. I have accomplished my aim, and now I shall do a little moral housecleaning. I am tired of killing men, no matter what the necessity nor the end. Tomorrow, when I go to town and meet Ben Redmond, I shall be unarmed. (p. 266)

Section 3, returning to time present, opens with Bayard's and Ringo's midnight arrival at Sartoris. Bayard, realizing that he "*won't even have until tomorrow in which to begin to resist*" (p. 267), continues to reject offers of advice, assistance, protection. One after another, those he has known proffer arms; each time he refuses. George Wyatt offers to take the whole matter into his hands. Bayard rejects his offer. Drusilla presents the dueling pistols in the same tone as she had said "Kiss me" the summer before. Again she presents him with a sprig of verbena and kisses his right hand but then recoils in horror as she realizes he has no intention of killing Redmond. Bayard pauses to glance at his father's coffined body. Perhaps his father, like the dead Agamemnon in Aeschylus' *Libation Bearers*, struggles to influence him from beyond the grave. Bayard rejects his father's spirit of violence and intolerance while at the same time preserving his honor. Aunt Jenny alone seems to accept Bayard's maturity of judgment. She encourages him to stand firm in the decision he has made, allowing consideration of no one else to uproot his own firmly planted will.

> Don't let it be Drusilla, a poor hysterical young woman. And don't let it be him [Father], Bayard, because he's dead now. And don't let it be George Wyatt and those others who will be waiting for you tomorrow morning. (p. 276)

The fourth section of the story recapitulates Bayard's rejection of all violent influences while carrying the action forward through brief encounters with each of the major proponents of killing. All the while, Bayard respects the attitude of Aunt Jenny, thankful that she does not pity him, nor treat him as a child. Drusilla laughs at him, but he turns and walks away, giving no explanation or apology. Carrying Grumby's gun, Ringo tries to intrude himself into the scene, but Bayard steadily and decisively stymies him. George Wyatt offers his gun and when he (like Drusilla) realizes Bayard does not intend to shoot Redmond he blurts out, "By God, if you don't kill him, I'm going to." Bayard answers calmly, "I'm tending to this. You stay out of it. I don't need any help." (p. 284). So George Wyatt and his men drop into the background.

Bayard's encounter with Redmond wins George Wyatt's approval: "You ain't done anything to be ashamed of.... Maybe you're right, maybe there has been enough killing in your family" (p. 289); and that of Ringo, who brings him a hatful of water; and of Aunt Jenny, who cries with tears of joy and pride and pained involvement: "Oh, damn you Sartorises! ... Damn you! Damn you!" (p. 292). He even wins approval of Drusilla – the war hawk – who has left him a final sprig of verbena "which she said you could smell alone above the smell of horses and courage".

Bayard, then, emerges through seven stories – in only one of which he is the sole protagonist – as a theme-embodying character. The significance of "An Odor of Verbena" is not that it introduces a new theme into the work – as some critics[10] have remarked – but that in it the themes of the collection come to maturity in the coming to maturity of Bayard Sartoris. Some critics, too, have thought that the book is "trivial", "Grade A magazine fiction, but nothing more",[11] humorous but not significant. A single reading of the book might conceivably lead one to this conclusion,

[10] Critics, however, who have treated the book as a novel, emphasize that "An Odor of Verbena" draws together the themes of earlier sections of the book. Waggoner, for instance, remarks: "'Ambuscade' introduces all the themes that are to be developed and even the criticism of the code that is the subject of 'An Odor of Verbena.'" (*William Faulkner* [Lexington, 1959], p. 175). And Cleanth Brooks: "'An Odor of Verbena' completes the novel by drawing together the themes of the preceding sections and by marking the culmination of Bayard's development in one significant dramatic action. It is the concluding act in his long initiation in the moral responsibility that goes with manhood." (*William Faulkner* [New Haven, 1963], p. 92). Peter Swiggart, on the other hand, sees "little thematic unity" in the stories (*The Art of Faulkner's Novels* [Austin, 1962], p. 36).

[11] Bernard De Voto, "Faulkner's South", *Saturday Review of Literature*, XVII (February 19, 1938), 5. See also: Louis Kronenberger, "Faulkner's Dismal Swamp", *The Nation*, CXLVI (February 19, 1938), 212, 214; and William Van O'Connor, *The Tangled Fire of William Faulkner* (Minneapolis, 1954), pp. 101ff.

since in the first three and a half stories and in the sixth story, humorous events and reactions are described in Faulkner's usual emotion-savoring style. But a second reading should certainly make one aware of the serious intent of the book and of the way Faulkner typically used humor as a means of conveying his complex view.

C. THEME COMPLEX

The central theme of the book is an involved one. The exigencies of war introduce serious disorder into human living on several levels: on the physical level – the ravaging of land and property; on the moral level – habits of lying, stealing, cheating, killing; on the psychological level – depersonalization, limiting the variety of human responses to a single kind of response, distortion of character; on the political level – gun rule, justice through vengeance, disregard for law; on the sociological level – the breakdown of family life, and the disruption of Negro-White relations. As the war continues, the unnatural conditions under which its participants must live become the custom, the rule rather than the exception. The deeds of disorder which war encourages in men become habits which, even after the last cannon stands silent and the last Yankee soldier has departed, remain imbedded in the Southerner's soul, ready to rise to the surface at the drop of a challenger's threat. In such men as Colonel John Sartoris, the habits of war become so deeply ingrained that, despite his determined effort, he is unable to break them – just as the drunkard cannot turn from his drink. Nevertheless, the conditions of war can be alleviated, the habits of war can be replaced by habits of peace; an order can be established which is neither the pre-war order come back to life, nor the war order itself continuing unabated. In the person and committed action of Bayard Sartoris – The Sartoris – the South (and "man" – who will prevail) succeeds in reestablishing order – a new order solidly based in responsible moral choice and buttressed by an understanding of civil law, of the dignity of the human being, of the worth of the land, of the character of Southern Negroes, and of the nature of courage.

The book leads us through the most brutal years of the Civil War – the only one of Faulkner's works to do so. In "Ambuscade", war begins as a game Ringo and Bayard play behind the smokehouse. They feel it as little more than a game when they lift down the long musket and fire on the Yankee soldiers who have come onto the Sartoris homestead. In this story, only a horse dies and a mere pile of wood chips behind the smokehouse lies in ruin, demolished by the sweep of Loosh's arm. In "Retreat", however, the meaning of war begins to intrude more and more on the consciousness of Granny and the two boys. A chest of silver and a team of mules are stolen; two Negro slaves pack a bundle and march toward freedom; the little white lies Granny was forced to tell in "Ambuscade" have ceased to shock her. War theft acquires the polite name "borrowing". John Sartoris wears a price on his head like an outlaw. And when the Yankees burn the Sartoris house, Granny joins Ringo and Bayard in their rhythmic cursing: "The bastuds! The bastuds!"

As Granny and the two boys ride toward Hawkhurst in "Raid", they see more burned houses, families uprooted, Whites crouched now in Negro cabins. The house of Granny's sister is in ashes. The railroad that used to run through Hawkhurst lies in ruin. On the road, displaced Negroes tramp in stunned groups toward "Jordan" and freedom. They rush the bridge over which the Yankees have just marched, only to have it blown up. Negroes, mules, and captured supplies flood the Yankee camp. "Damn this war!" Colonel Dick mutters when he sees Granny, who has just been rescued from the river. "Damn it. Damn it."

Colonel Dick tries to repair some of the damage the Union troops have wreaked on the Southern people. He requisitions a hundred and ten mules and Negroes to Granny, along with ten chests of silver.[12] But Granny makes use of his generosity and of the wartime situation to establish a business. Forgery replaces the lying, borrowing, and cursing of the early stories. Granny makes a virtue of necessity – her business actually is stealing on a broad basis, but is justified (she believes) by wartime conditions. Nevertheless, those who live by trickery may die by it. Granny conquers the Yankees, but is vanquished by "southern gentlemen" – "because she still believed that what side of a war a man fought on made him what he is" (p. 170).[13]

[12] This is one of the incidents in the book that stretches credulity.

[13] As a title for this story, "The Unvanquished" would seem to indicate through irony that Rosa Millard, though triumphant in her war against the Yankees, could be vanquished only by the underhanded deeds of her alleged compatriots. When Faulkner gave the title *The Unvanquished* to his cycle about the Sartoris family and the Sartoris spirit, he necessarily broadened its significance. He also baffled French translators of the book, who were forced to choose one of four possible translations of the title: *L'Invaincu*, *L'Invaincus*, *L'Invaincue*, and *L'Invaincues*. The first would point to Bayard as "the unvanquished one" of the cycle. The second would indicate that the Southern people as a whole, or the Southern Army, even though it had lost the war, yet remained "unvanquished". The third French title would place Granny's exploits and Granny's person at the center of the book's action. The last title (preferred by some French translators) would give the laurel of endurance to the Southern women. My own opinion

As the war ends, the breakdown of all order affects Bayard profoundly. No legal system, no civil court of justice, no representative of law and order can be found to retaliate against the crime of Grumby and his band of thieves and murderers. With some help, Bayard tracks down his man, scares his companions out of Mississippi into Texas, and kills his grandmother's murderer. Then he and Ringo nail Grumby's body to the compress door and his hand to Granny's grave marker. Later, Bayard remarks that in being forced by circumstances to have to kill Grumby he had had to perform "more than should be required of children because there should be some limit to the age, the youth at least below which one should not have to kill" (p. 254).

In "Skirmish at Sartoris", – an important linking story, and not merely an appendage, as some commentators have thought [14] – Faulkner clearly shows that the ruthless habits of war have not been rooted out of a people pursuing peace. Bloodshed and lawlessness hover like hawks above the new young life which peacetime should bring. Neither the North nor the South had found a successful means of making the transition from war to peace. The election – in which a Negro is apparently the sole candidate for marshall – merely provides another kind of battlefield. Still, the opponents fight with guns, not ballots. Ironically, after John Sartoris has shot the two carpetbaggers, he makes bond to the sheriff while overriding George Wyatt's objections with the query, "Don't you see we are working for peace through law and order?" (p. 239).

Each time John Sartoris surmounts peace-time problems by wartime tactics, the narrator Bayard notes that the cheers which follow his success resemble the cheers that followed his heroic escapades during the war. It was "like the Yankees used to hear it" (pp. 238 and 242). Further, John does not wait upon the formalities and legalities of that "law and order" through which he is striving to obtain peace. He forces the carpetbaggers to fire first so that his case will stand as self-defense. He appoints Drusilla (by what authority Faulkner does not say) to be the "voting commissioner until the votes are cast and counted" (p. 238), and proclaims that the

---

is that Faulkner's title refers to the Sartoris spirit, the spirit of the Sartoris family, and ultimately to the heroic-constructive spirit of man, who "will prevail". I shall leave it to the French, however, to decide whether this spirit can best be described as masculine or feminine, as singular or plural.

14 This story, as we have already remarked, had been published in *Scribner's*, while the others appeared in *Saturday Evening Post*. It is set in the period of the Reconstruction, not in that of the Civil War itself, as are the first five stories in the collection. John Sartoris and Drusilla are the central figures, not Bayard or Ringo or Granny.

election will be held at his home. There, he stands brazenly over the ballot box and then proclaims the outcome of the election without counting the votes. Father's troops express their approval of his actions in war-whoops: "It came back high and thin and ragged and fierce, like when the Yankees used to hear it out of the smoke and the galloping: 'Yaaaaay, Drusilla!... Yaaaaaay, John Sartoris! Yaaaaaaay!'" (pp. 241-242).

The events of "An Odor of Verbena" transpire nine years after those of "Skirmish at Sartoris". Flashbacks fill in motivational gaps by relating incidents which shaped Bayard's character during that interval. The distance and increased knowledge of Bayard's character help make believable Bayard's dissociation of himself from the community's atmosphere of gallant unconcern for true peace and from his father's attitude of dictatorial supremacy. Bayard, the law student of the University of Mississippi, enters the scene from a background of education and cultivated sensibility. From that vantage point, he can initiate the real reconstruction of a war-torn South.

By the time Bayard reaches manhood, the recultivation of the soil has already begun. Verbena grows in the garden, the pastures are covered with grass, flowers bloom in the yard. Then, too, John Sartoris has built a railroad to replace the one the Yankees destroyed, and the Sartoris house, burned to the ground in "Retreat", stands once again on its old landsite.

Disorders on many other levels, however, still run rampant. Shortly before the story opens, John Sartoris has killed two carpetbaggers and a neighboring hill man. Bayard clearly rejects his father's ruthlessness and disregard for human life. In Bayard's dream for the South, concern for human dignity would surely be the cornerstone.

Many Southerners regretted John Sartoris' treatment of Redmond. His constant taunting of a man with a clear record, the backbiting and slandering he employed not even as an election tool, but merely because it had become a habit with him, all this repelled Bayard. John had acquired Redmond's share of the railroad, too, by means which were more suited to a Snopes than to a Sartoris. This, too, Bayard rejected.[15] Colonel John Sartoris talked a good game of "moral house-cleaning". He said that he would not be armed when he went to meet Redmond, yet he wore his derringer under the coat-sleeve of his right arm, even if, as George Wyatt testifies, he made no move to fire it. Bayard wore no weapon when he confronted Redmond.

[15] Recall too that Bayard had not been actively involved in the mule-business with Granny and Ringo. He constantly refers to the mules as "Granny and Ringo's Yankee mules".

Colonel John Sartoris has come to regard law as an intellectual battlefield. He prepares himself to give up killing only because he feels that with Bayard's prowess at law, he will be able to obtain what he wants THROUGH legal means rather than OVER them. "I have not needed you in my affairs so far", he tells Bayard,

> but from now on I shall.... What will follow will be a matter of consolidation,of pettifogging and doubtless chicanery in which I would be a babe in arms but in which you, trained in the law, can hold your own – our own. (p. 266)

Bayard rejects this notion of law too. The first law is the law of personal responsibility and of respect for others. "Thou shalt not kill", he feels is solidly based in man's nature. He would probably feel the same about lying, stealing, and cheating as he does about killing.

Throughout the early phases of the war, a tendency to regard other human beings not as persons but as forces or things begins to twist the Southern personality. Bayard and Ringo consider the Yankees merely as "the bastuds", for which expression they are made to wash out their mouths with soap. Granny sees a difference between officers and the regular soldiers until, at the command of one officer, her house is burned. Then she joins the two boys in her depersonalized judgment of all Northern forces as "the bastuds".

The Negroes go through a similar depersonalization: from "Loosh and Philadelphy" they become the singing, trudging mass, void of all personality, of all individuality. They are herded together with mules, requisitioned along with the mules and trunks of silver. In "Skirmish at Sartoris", Ringo says "They ain't no more niggers, in Jefferson nor nowhere else", because "niggers" have been abolished. Still the South treated Cassius Q. Benbow not as an individual, but as a "nigger". And so Ringo remarks, "This war ain't over. Hit just started good" (p. 229). In all these instances of depersonalization, only Bayard's relation with Ringo stresses individuality above racial qualities: "What counted was, what one of us had done or seen that the other had not..." (p. 91).

Bayard's emphasis on the dignity of the human being, his stress of individual worth, becomes most obvious in the flashback conversations with Drusilla recorded in "An Odor of Verbena". Drusilla says Father's dream is to benefit all the people of the South. Bayard replies, "But how can they get any good from what he wants to do for them if they are – after he had –". "Killed some of them?" Drusilla asks; "I suppose you include those two carpetbaggers he had to kill to hold that first election, don't you?" Bayard answers: "They were men. Human beings." Drusilla will not grant the point. "They were northerners, foreigners.... They were pirates" (pp. 256-257).

Bayard's method of handling his father's murderer again shows a tremendous respect for the individual. Though he could not have walked unarmed into Grumby's den, he feels he can enter Redmond's office carrying no weapon. Redmond shot his father in front, not in the back. His father was armed and expected trouble. Redmond was courageous; he had almost been forced, because of John's brutal taunting, to take the course he did in order to salvage his reputation. Redmond was one of those few men Bayard could face unarmed and escape unscathed.

If Bayard concretizes the new South's respect for the individual, so also does he direct the South toward a new respect for law. In "Skirmish at Sartoris", we see mock elections, stolen ballot boxes, infiltration of carpetbaggers, and the countermeasures of violence agreed on by the Southern Whites. Bayard himself, in "Vendée", had considered himself a minister of justice. Now, in the time of the new peace, law and order need to be reestablished. Gun rule must be relegated to the crises of war; vengeance must yield to due process of law; even the prewar custom of death-dueling must fall into the dead past. Redmond, ironically, is an attorney-at-law; Bayard, a law student. Yet no trial is held; no arrest is made. They merely confront one another – without bloodshed. The code-law of "a life for a life" crumbles and on its ruins can emerge a new South, respecting law and order rather than trying to control the processes of law.

Bayard, indeed, solves few problems in the course of the stories. But his process of maturation embodies the kind of maturation necessary to the South, if it is ever to create a new order on those several levels of human living treated above, where disorder had raged.

D. *THE UNVANQUISHED* IS NOT A NOVEL

In the first part of this chapter, I have shown that the stories in *The Unvanquished* are connected through chronology, locale, and theme; that they show a consistency in point of view and in the repetitive appearance of a central group of characters; and that throughout the stories, Bayard Sartoris, a theme-embodying character emerges into mature leadership for the new order. However, despite the comprehensive interconnectedness of these stories, the book is not a novel "in the traditional sense" but a composed, mythically oriented short story cycle.

Criticism of this book (and of other twentieth-century short story cycles) has been plagued by an either/or mentality which makes a sensible approach to its nature and structure almost impossible. Either the book is a "mere collection of short stories" or it is a "novel". Some critics seem to decide by flipping a coin. If they call it a "mere collection" of stories, most of which were written for "slick" magazines,[16] they find little good to say about it. Still, no one, to my knowledge, has bothered to criticize any of these stories as an independent unit; at least no analytical journal articles have appeared on any one of them.

The other side of the critical coin bears a different stamp. Most of those who say the work is a novel are forced to the conclusion that it is a "loosely jointed" novel,[17] not a novel in the ordinary sense. Even Waggoner,[18] who has offered the best published study to date of the unity of the book, seems falsely to equate "unified work of fiction" with "novel". Only a few critics – none of whom treat *The Unvanquished* at length – have managed to escape the mire of muddy terminology. Olga Vickery[19] proposed the term "story-novel" for *The Unvanquished, Go Down, Moses, Knight's Gambit*, and *The Hamlet*. Stanley Tick[20] used the more inclusive term "blend" for those same works, as well as for *Absalom, Absalom!* and *The Wild Palms*. In his article on the unity of *Go Down, Moses*, Tick writes:

If *The Unvanquished* (or *Go Down, Moses*, or any other work) is considered to be a collection of short stories – random or associated, but essentially independent – then critical judgment will receive and assess the volume on these terms.... And if *The Unvanquished* (or the others) is considered to be a novel, or a blend – composed of units not essentially independent – then critical judgment can avail itself of other, more useful terms to evaluate the volume. (pp. 68-69)

[16] See footnote 11 above. See also Michael Millgate, *William Faulkner* (New York, 1961) who calls the book "essentially a sequence of stories...reprinted here with, for the most part, only minor revisions" (p. 67).

[17] Exceptions to this general rule are H. H. Waggoner; Cleanth Brooks (both mentioned earlier); Stanley Tick in "The Unity of *Go Down, Moses*", *Twentieth Century Literature* VIII (Juli 1962), 67-73; and Edmond L. Volpe, *A Reader's Guide to William Faulkner* (New York, 1964).

[18] See Waggoner, pp. 170ff.

[19] Olga W. Vickery, *The Novels of William Faulkner: A Critical Interpretation* (Baton Rouge, 1959, 1964). Professor Vickery does not devote a major section of her book to *The Unvanquished*. But in the summation of her critical approach she divides Faulkner's novels into "story-novels" (*The Unvanquished, Knight's Gambit, Go Down, Moses*, and *The Hamlet*); "novels of juxtaposition" (*The Sound and the Fury, As I Lay Dying*); "counterpoint novels" (*Wild Palms, Light in August, Requiem for a Nun*); and "fused novels" (*Absalom, Absalom!*)

[20] "The Unity of *Go Down, Moses*", 1962, pp. 68-69.

Critical evaluation of a work often depends heavily upon one's basic understanding of the structure of that work. Commentators from the time of the first review in 1938[21] to the most recent evaluations of the work have misjudged the nature of *The Unvanquished* – having no *tertium* term to interpose between "mere collection" and "novel in the traditional sense". I propose that the most operative critical term, the term most descriptive of the structure and dynamism of the work, is the term "short story cycle".

In her deeply perceptive study of Faulkner's novels – in which, however, she gives no thorough analysis of *The Unvanquished* – Olga Vickery presents many valuable insights into the nature of Faulkner's fiction. She realizes, for instance, that "the short story for Faulkner is not only a genre but an element of structure" (p. 305). In her discussion of what she calls "story-novels",[22] she remarks further that previous criticism of these books has often been irrelevant, since critics use "the criteria of the well-made novel in discussing a form which deliberately rejects that particular tradition" (p. 306). Faulkner, she says, was "creating a new form" – just as Anderson was.

But is there any evidence that Faulkner realized he was putting together a book that was more than a mere collection of short stories and yet not a novel? William Van O'Conner[23] had wondered if Faulkner knew what the last story would be before starting the first one. The answer obviously is no.

At the end of the magazine edition of "Ambuscade" an editor's note informs the reading public: "This is the first of a series of stories by Mr. Faulkner in which these same two boys will appear." As we noted above, the first three stories of the collection appeared in *Saturday Evening Post* that year, but the fourth story of the book was not due to hit the presses

21 See bibliography for a list of reviews of *The Unvanquished.*

22 While Vickery's term "story-novel" (I have also seen the term *Kurzgeschichtenroman* in German critical works) approximates the form of *The Unvanquished, The Story of Gösta Berling, Tortilla Flat,* and other works which crowd near the novel-extreme of the short story cycle spectrum, it seems less adequate than my own term for expressing the kind of unity one finds in *Knight's Gambit, The Pastures of Heaven* (closer to the center of the cycle spectrum) and completely inadequate for coming to grips with the kind of unity one finds in *Ein Hungerkünstler* and other works at the opposite extreme of the spectrum. My term, then, draws within one critical perspective, on the basis of shared characteristics, a larger number of problematical twentieth-century works.

23 William Van O'Connor's *William Faulkner* in the UMPAW series (Minneapolis, 1965) is one of the least perceptive discussions of *The Unvanquished* to date. O'Connor makes such obvious mistakes as that of saying *The Unvanquished* "is composed of five [sic!] fairly long stories, each involving Bayard Sartoris' experiences in the Civil War [sic!]" (p. 30).

until November 14, 1936. It seems likely, then, that the "series of stories" announced by the editor of *Saturday Evening Post* was a series of three, and not until after the publication of "Skirmish at Sartoris" in *Scribner's* (April, 1935) did the notion come to Faulkner of showing the cumulative effect of the war years on Bayard and his father, as well as Bayard's decision firmly to face up to the war tradition, continuing in peacetime through his father's ruthlessness.

The nature and extent of the Faulkner revisions of the magazine versions confirm this supposition. "Skirmish at Sartoris" met minor revisions only – revisions which were primarily removals from the story of data which had already been provided in earlier stories. Furthermore, "Riposte in Tertio" and "Vendée" already show a rich interweaving of serious thematic material with less serious – even before revision. The first three stories, however, as mentioned earlier, acquired in the transition from magazine to book large quantities of richly thematic material, of character enroundment, and of personality contrasts.

That the idea of the book grew from a small series of short stories to which others were gradually added, Faulkner confirmed in a conference he held with the freshman class of the University of Virginia on April 28, 1958. A student asked him:

> When you were writing those short stories did you have the idea in mind that these would make a novel eventually, or did they just appear after they appeared in short story form to fit together so naturally it was necessary to make a novel out of them?

To which question, Faulkner replied:

> I saw them as a long series. I had never thought of it in terms of a novel, exactly. I realized that they would be too episodic to be what I considered a novel, so I thought of them as a series of stories, that when I got into the first one I could see two more, but by the time I'd finished the first one I saw that it was going further than that, and then when I'd finished the fourth one, I had postulated too many questions that I had to answer for my own satisfaction. So the others had to be... written then.[24]

Faulkner did realize, then, that what he was writing was not a novel – not even what HE considered a novel.[25]

[24] Frederick L. Gwynn and Joseph L. Blotner, eds. *Faulkner in the University* (New York, 1965), p. 252.

[25] And Faulkner had even considered his revised *Go Down, Moses* a novel. In response to questions put to him at the University of Virginia, Faulkner said: "'The Bear' was a

The structural difference between a short story cycle and a novel may be more clearly seen if we compare the movement of Faulkner's novel *Sartoris* with that of his short story cycle *The Unvanquished*, both of which deal with the Sartoris family though at different periods of their development.

Sartoris (1929) was the first of Faulkner's books to deal with the Yoknapatawpha County and its people. In it Bayard Sartoris, the boy of *The Unvanquished*, appears as a grandfather of sixty years – the only male Sartoris ever to have achieved that age. The main action – none of it too violent or bizarre – takes place immediately after World War I. Another Bayard, the old Bayard's grandson, comes home from the war in which he and his twin brother, John, had flown fighter planes against the Germans. In one of the last engagements of the war, John's bravado had brought his plane crashing to the ground under enemy fire. John himself was killed.

The "present" events of the book center around Bayard's return home, his deeply disturbed broodings about his responsibility for his brother's death, his recuperation from various senseless stunts (such as his automobile wreck), and his marriage to Narcissa Benbow. There follows another wild automobile ride in which Old Bayard dies of heart failure, and after which young Bayard departs. He wanders listlessly, recklessly, and finally kills himself test-piloting a plane that his pilot friends all knew was unsafe.

The book begins with an evocation of Colonel John Sartoris – the spirit and mythical hero of the Sartoris clan. It ends with Aunt Jenny's trip to the cemetery where the Colonel's straight-backed statue watches over the graves of all the dead Sartorises: three Bayards and three Johns and some of their wives and birth-dead children. The survivors are Aunt Jenny, Narcissa Benbow Sartoris, and Narcissa's child (whom she named Benbow over Aunt Jenny's decision to call him John). The real action of the book, then, is not merely the action of a central character, but of a family, of a tradition.

---

part of a novel. The novel was – happened to be composed of more or less complete stories, but it was held together by one family, the Negro and the white phase of the same family, same people. *The Bear* was just a part of that – of a novel." (Frederick L. Gwynn and Joseph L. Blotner, eds. *Faulkner in the University* [New York, 1965], p. 5). One would think that the description "a novel that happened to be composed of more or less complete stories" would apply to *The Unvanquished.* But for that volume Faulkner uses the term "series of stories". Faulkner's remarks are not, however, the first instance of a writer's inconsistencies in explaining his own craft.

Besides those events in which young Bayard figures most prominently, several "sub-plots" move forward steadily, paralleling or counterpointing the actions of the reckless twin. Cutting across young Bayard's story comes the occasional mention of Old Bayard's weak heart, of Narcissa Benbow's anonymous love letters from Byron Snopes, and stories, related by Miss Jenny and others, of the wild exploits of past Sartorises whose spirit seems still to influence the actions and attitudes of the present generation. Less immediately connected with Bayard's struggle toward self-destruction are: the relationship of Horace Benbow and Belle Mitchell, the financial troubles of Simon and the members of the First Baptist Church, and the frustrated attempts of the Negro Caspey to assert his individuality and freedom.

The book is built in five parts (I-V) each of which has several numbered sections (I has 2 sections; II, 6; III, 9; IV, 5; V, 3). The book's 380 pages are apportioned: I, 50; II, 111; III, 109; IV, 81; V, 29. None of the five major parts contains a "complete action". Each merely introduces or adds to or concludes a number of strands of action. The same is true of each of the numbered sections within the larger parts, and of other unnumbered sub-sections (indicated by breaks in the text). They all present fragments of the continuous, multiple "action" which is the novel.

Lengthy and leisurely descriptive passages which would overload a short story sprout up everywhere in the novel. Descriptions of the Sartoris house, reminiscent of the "house of Atreus", enrich the symbolic dimensions of the work: "the house John Sartoris had built", with its "iron gates" and curving drive, its "white simplicity" standing out "unbroken among ancient sunshot trees". As Old Bayard enters, the Negro maid Elnora moans like a Greek chorus or a captive Cassandra. Individual rooms, settings expressive of character, also receive full treatment.

Faulkner occasionally hands his narrative over to Miss Jenny, who tells stories about the Sartoris past. Her reminiscences and those of Bayard make the past live in the present. Old Bayard muses over his father's life in that dark room which John Sartoris had used for entertaining but which now has fallen into disuse. Many events central to *The Unvanquished* appear as the musings of an old man in *Sartoris*.[26]

The first section of Part I concerns itself, by and large, with Old Bayard, his present and his past. Beginning with Section 2, Faulkner introduces

[26] The names and dates are not always perfectly consistent in Faulkner's two accounts of the Sartoris tradition. Faulkner felt he had, as sole proprietor of Yoknapatawpha County, complete liberty to manipulate names, dates, and events as the needs of each fictional account required. See Gwynn, p. 29.

Simon in the buckboard, Miss Jenny Du Pre at her club meeting (held at the symbolically described Mitchell house), and Narcissa Benbow in her relationship with Miss Jenny. He touches upon the tottering union of Harry and Belle Mitchell, and also the insecure relationship of Narcissa and her brother Horace. A sub-section brings together Old Bayard, Aunt Jenny, and Simon, three strongly independent representatives of three stratas of the old South. Under the cloak of darkness, Young Bayard appears on the scene, passes a few words with Old Bayard and Aunt Jenny, then goes to his room which is described as "treacherously illumined by the moon" (p. 47).[27]

In this entire first part, the characters are presented gradually, not at peak moments but in their ordinary tasks, their daily occupations – except for Young Bayard, whose arrival home from the war is but little more than ordinary. No complete "action" runs its course, no thorough insight into character emerges.

The first section of the second part is equally diverse in its subject and treatment. Aunt Jenny argues with and cajoles her Negro workers; Narcissa receives several anonymous love letters and takes them to Aunt Jenny for advice; and Bayard makes acquaintance with Narcissa. The second section juxtaposes Old Bayard's heart and wart condition with Young Bayard's buying and trying out his new car. The third section is full of reminiscences which burst like clouds of dust from the old chest which "had not been opened since 1901, when his [Old Bayard's] son John had succumbed to yellow fever and an old Spanish bullet-wound" (p. 90). The chest is full of Civil War articles, of John Sartoris' trophies of glory – the derringer, the rosewood case with dueling pistols, the Confederate coat, and the silver oil-can which commemorated the completion of the railroad. Bayard recalls his father saying: "the man who professes to care nothing about his forbears is only a little less vain then the man who bases all his actions on blood precedent" (p. 92) – a theme Bayard in *The Unvanquished* had himself embodied. Before this third section concludes, Old Bayard's health again comes up for discussion by Dr. Alford and Dr. Peabody.

The fourth brief section catches Narcissa and Miss Jenny at the bank, where the teller, Byron Snopes, perspires as he notices his secret letter in

[27] This was the room Bayard's twin brother had shared with him, the room which he and his wife Caroline had occupied during their brief marriage before her death in childbirth: "the walls held, like a withered flower in a casket, something of that magical chaos in which they had lived for two months, tragic and transient as a blooming of honeysuckle and sharp as the odor of mint" (p. 48).

Narcissa's purse. Snopes pays a boy, Virgil Beard, to write another letter for him.

In the fifth section, young Bayard seems death-bent. He drives his car recklessly over bad roads and then, having escaped unscathed, mounts an unbroken horse for a head-splitting ride.

In Section 6, Dr. Peabody bandages Bayard's head, but Bayard removes the bandage, and before long rides out with a Negro band to serenade all the single girls in town. When he arrives at Narcissa's, the scene shifts to treat Narcissa's three visitors: formal – Dr. Alford; informal – Bayard; and anonymous – Byron Snopes. As Part II ends, Bayard expresses his disgust that life lasts so long.

Part III introduces Horace Benbow's nascent affair with Belle Mitchell – a new plot line. The first three sections insinuate him gradually into the action; his arrival is followed by his conversations with Narcissa, his visits to Belle, and his (symbolic) interest in glassware. Section 4 shifts suddenly to young Bayard, pinned under his car in a stream and rescued by two Negroes. Narcissa comes out to sit with him every few days while he is recuperating.

Section 5 records a conversation between old man Falls and Old Bayard. Will Falls recounts John Sartoris' exploits in the war,[28] and Bayard asks him "Will, what the devil were you folks fighting about, anyhow?" to which Falls answers: "Bayard, be damned if I ever did know" (p. 227). Two subsections of Section 5 show Byron Snopes in his clandestine dealings with Virgil Beard. Section 6 draws together Simon, old man Falls, and Dr. Alford. Section 7 explores the deepening relationship between Narcissa and young Bayard. Section 8 draws tighter various threads of the action – those of Narcissa with her anonymous letter writer, of Horace and Belle Mitchell, of Narcissa and Bayard. Bayard and Narcissa's subsection ends with their embrace. In Section 9, then, Snopes beats Virgil Beard, breaks into the Benbow house, and steals back his letters to Narcissa.

Enough has been said now to have shown in detail that *Sartoris* moves in one continuous *multiple* action, its several subplots being carried along strand for strand, as the main action develops. Part IV continues the same process, and Part V concludes it, tying all the plots and subplots, the actions and reactions, together, or at least, bringing them definitely to a close: Horace marries Belle Mitchell and leaves town, Old Bayard dies of heart failure on a wild ride with his grandson, Bayard kills himself in a

28 These are retold with different details in *The Unvanquished.*

test-pilot run of an unsafe aircraft, and Simon is found dead in the house of a disreputable mulatto woman. Miss Jenny, then, collects all the dead together in her memory when she visits the Sartoris plot in the graveyard, and Narcissa through the birth and personage of her little son, Benbow, offers some hope for the future of the Sartoris clan.

In *The Unvanquished*, each "chapter" is a complete, discrete unit, circumscribing a single "action". The structure of each of the seven sections follows the structure of a Faulknerian short story, not of a chapter of a novel. The action of each story connects with the action of each of the other stories to the extent which I have outlined in the first part of this chapter. But the connection is not one of strands of action, but of strands of significance, of myth, overlaying the discrete actions. Each story develops its own central action, but the significance of *The Unvanquished* accumulates from story to story through the achievement of successively higher viewpoints embodied in the gradually maturing reflections and actions of Bayard Sartoris.

As present action passes from inception to completion in each short story, the significance of past action may be marshalled toward the understanding of the present. In the novel, we noted, the flashbacks or reminiscences range over multiple time-ranges of the past. This is not generally the case in the short stories;[29] the flashbacks or reminiscences of the seven short stories of *The Unvanquished* usually contrast one or two significant past scenes with the single action of the present.

In "Ambuscade", for instance, two discrete times are juxtaposed: the present (summer, 1863), and the not too distant past (the preceding spring). In the interval between "last spring" and "this summer", Vicksburg has fallen; and so the entire spirit of the war has shifted radically. The feel of triumph, "the smell of powder and glory" (p. 11) in Father's clothes, the glamorous stories of the battles, full of "the cannon and the flags and the anonymous yelling" (p. 17) – all contrast with Father's return "this summer": his slow jog up the drive on Jupiter, the tensely calm greeting from Granny, the silent awed reception from the boys, Father's termination before inception of storytelling time, his anxiousness, his haste in building a new stock pen and in burying the old silver. All of this enriches the basic thematic action of the story: the intrusion of the actual war on the war of Bayard's and Ringo's game world. Now, they confront the real war and the world of defeat, destruction, and doom.

[29] An exception must be made for the mythic character sketches, most of which were added to the short stories when they were to be bound together into the cycle form.

Still another time level, however, operates in "Ambuscade" – dream-time. The boy Bayard had fallen asleep listening from a distance to Father's account of the fall of Vicksburg. Bayard the narrator remarks: "somewhere between waking and sleeping I believed I saw or I dreamed that I did see the lantern in the orchard" (p. 21). In "Retreat" Granny says she dreamed she saw a Negro man going to the place where they had buried the trunk. The Negroes, Loosh and Ringo, do not need to dream in order to "know"; Loosh knows about Vicksburg before Father gets home to tell the story; and Ringo ceases his play, even though Bayard, as General Pemberton, throws dust at him. "Because it was that urgent, since Negroes knew" (p. 7).

Dream-time refers to day-dreaming as well as night-dreaming. An important incident of its occurrence in "Ambuscade" expresses Bayard's juvenile admiration for his father's gallantry and indominable energy. At supper, Father announces "Now we're going to build a new pen." The narrator remarks "when he said that, Ringo and I probably had exactly the same vision" (p. 13) in which Father appears as a mighty general commanding the household troops from atop his charger. The narrator tells his vision in the imperfect tense, as if it were actually happening in the present-past immediacy of dream-vision.

> He was on Jupiter now; he wore the frogged grey fieldofficer's tunic; and while we watched he drew the sabre. Giving us a last embracing and comprehensive glance he drew it, already pivoting Jupiter on the tight snaffle; his hair tossed beneath the cocked hat, the sabre flashed and glinted; he cried, not loud yet stentorian: "Trot! Canter! *Charge*!" (p. 13)

And with that, he attacks the saplings and mows them down; shears, trims, and lops them; lays them in neat windrows, so that they need "only the carrying and placing to become a fence" (p. 14).

In this instance, dream-time fuses time present and time past – mixes in the mind of a boy the simple daily task that must be performed and the magic of the glorious old days when the South was winning the war. Other dreamlike scenes (*e.g.*, the boys racing in what seems to them slow motion toward the house) are mere psychological distortions of present time. So that, primarily, two times – time before the fall of Vicksburg (*i.e.*, last spring) and time after the defeat (*i.e.*, this summer) play off against one another and fuse in dream-time to show the sudden intrusion of the reality of war on the dream-play existence of the Sartorises at home.

The movement of stories 2, 4, and 5 ("Retreat", "Riposte", and "Vendée") is, by and large, discretely chronological. "Raid" intermingles the events of time present with two other events of the past: that Christmas before the war when Bayard visited Hawkhurst and the railroad was still operative (1860), and that date in the recent past when the Yankees burned the house and destroyed the railroad, after the Confederates' locomotive had outrun them in one of the most intriguing encounters of the war.

The growing destruction and desolation of wartime living contrasts with the peace and beauty of life at Hawkhurst before the war: houses now are nothing but charred chimneys; livery stables are gutted; that once beautiful railroad "with those two little threads that didn't look strong enough for anything to run on running straight and fast like they were getting up speed to jump clean off the world" (p. 99), lies now mangled and twisted around the trunks of pine trees.

Faulkner selects carefully those few events of the past which, in a short story, he can effectively juxtapose with the action of the present. He does not generally range freely over a character's entire past or over the past of a family; he does not generally allow for relating of lengthy sub-stories in the midst of these short story units – and when he does (as when he allows the retelling of the great locomotive chase in the revised version of "Raid") the passage sometimes sticks out like a bruise.

The form of the short story, which Faulkner himself admits is the most difficult form for a fiction writer to master, will not allow leisurely development of character, lengthy spinning of yarns, or inclusion of even slightly extraneous material. The exceptions he makes – and this is immensely significant – concern the mythic background or total significence of the cycle. As long as the matter added for the benefit of the entire cycle does not destroy the fundamental singleness and economy of the short story form, Faulkner will insert passages which solidify the totality of the myth and place the present action within its context. An example of such revision occurs in the first paragraph of "Ambuscade" which in the magazine version merely gives a quick start to a single story. But the first paragraph of the cycle *The Unvanquished* introduces an entire book.

MAGAZINE VERSION:	BOOK VERSION:
Behind the smokehouse we had a kind of map. Vicksburg was a handful of chips from the woodpile and the river was a trench we had scraped in the	Behind the smokehouse that summer, Ringo and I had a living map. Although Vicksburg was just a handful of chips from the woodpile and the River a trench scraped into the packed earth with the point of a hoe, it (river, city, and terrain) lived, possessing even in miniature that ponderable though passive recalcitrance of topography which outweighs artillery,

packed ground with a hoe, that drank water almost faster than we could fetch it from the well. This afternoon it looked like we would never get it filled, because it hadn't rained in three weeks. But at last it was damp-colored enough at least, and we were just about to begin, when all of a sudden Loosh was standing there watching us. And then I saw Philadelphy over at the woodpile, watching Loosh.

against which the most brilliant of victories and the most tragic of defeats are but the loud noises of a moment. To Ringo and me it lived, if only because of the fact that the sunimpacted ground drank water faster than we could fetch it from the well, the very setting of the stage for conflict a prolonged and wellnigh hopeless ordeal in which we ran, panting and interminable, with the leaking bucket between wellhouse and battlefield, the two of us needing first to join forces and spend ourselves against a common enemy, time, before we could engender between us and hold intact the pattern of recapitulant mimic furious victory like a cloth, a shield between ourselves and reality, between us and fact and doom. This afternoon it seemed as if we would never get it filled, wet enough, since there had not even been dew in three weeks. But at last it was damp enough, damp-colored enough at least, and we could begin. We were just about to begin. Then suddenly Loosh was standing there, watchings us. He was Joby's son and Ringo's uncle; he stood there (we did not know where he had come from; we had not seen him appear, emerge) in the fierce dull early afternoon sunlight, bareheaded, his head slanted a little, tilted a little, yet firm and not askew, like a cannonball (which it resembled) bedded hurriedly and carelessly in concrete, his eyes a little red at the inner corners as Negroes' eyes get when they have been drinking, looking down at what Ringo and I called Vicksburg. Then I saw Philadelphy, his wife, over at the woodpile, stooped, with an armful of wood already gathered into the crook of her elbow, watching Loosh's back.

One can argue with the quality of the revision, but its direction is unmistakable. No longer are we dealing with a mere childish incident – two boys shooting at a Yankee and killing his horse. Rather we have moved onto the fields of "ponderable though passive recalcitrance of topography which outweighs artillery, against which the most tragic of defeats are but the loud noises of a moment". Faulkner has marshaled on this first page of his cycle perhaps heavier cannon than the terrain can bear, but his purpose has been to set "the stage for a conflict – a prolonged and wellnigh hopeless ordeal". Like John Sartoris in the real war, Bayard is here trying to ward off defeat by holding "intact the pattern of...furious victory like...a shield between ourselves and reality, between us and fact and doom". In this paragraph, Faulkner does not refer primarily to the action of two boys escaping the hands of the Yankee troops on which they fire, but instead, to the full mythic action of *The Unvanquished* – of Bayard, of the South, and of man, who will prevail against "fact and doom".

Nevertheless the action of each of the stories in *The Unvanquished* is self-contained, complete, and for the most part simple. Bayard does not occupy center stage in each of the stories. Granny upstages him even in "Ambuscade"; the figure of John Sartoris predominates in "Retreat"; Granny, Drusilla, and Ringo are all more prominent in "Raid" than is Bayard; Ringo steps into the limelight with Granny in the early portions of "Riposte in Tertio", while Ab Snopes lurks to left stage center; Bayard must even share with Uncle Buck and Ringo, and even with Ab Snopes and Grumby, the action of hunting and killing Grumby in "Vendée". "Skirmish at Sartoris" focuses on Drusilla and John Sartoris, while Bayard looks on. Only in "An Odor of Verbena" does Bayard emerge as the theme-embodying character of the collection; only then does he act as The Sartoris, upholding what is good in the South. Still, his action in "An Odor of Verbena" would lack depth without the earlier stories of the cycle, without the awareness of those concrete situations and peopled environments through which and because of which he has at last emerged.

In *Sartoris*, on the other hand, Faulkner takes an altogether different tack. *Sartoris* does not progress through separate, discrete, complete actions. It evolves in one continuous, multiple-stranded movement which involves many people. None of the five parts can be said to hold up any one character of the novel as central, for there is no single action to which he would be central. In a few lines of the section of some part, a partial history of one character may be spotlighted, but that serves only to bring forward the entire multiple action of the novel. Since the action of each major part of the book is multiple and diffuse, so too is the treatment of the individual characters.

The unity of a short story cycle, then, is the unity of discrete pieces juxtaposed in such an order that the significances of each story deepen and expand as the reader moves from story to story, in a particular order. The full significance of the cycle is realized only after the final story has been read. In *Sartoris*, on the other hand, multiple actions intertwine to form a multiweave continuity, exhibiting the development of a number of concomitant "actions" in the course of the book, each of which actions moves forward piecemeal. Each story of a cycle is, to some degree, self-sufficient, self-contained, because its action is a complete unity. No part of the traditional novel, however, is a truly discrete, self-contained unit, but an integral part of some larger action.

The two dangers, therefore, which must be avoided when criticizing a short story cycle are (1) that of requiring of them more unity than they profess by their very nature to possess; and (2) overlooking the real and substantial unifying factors which they do by their very nature possess.

E. EVALUATION

From the vantage point of an understanding of the form with which we are dealing, we should be able to make a critical evaluation of this work. Some critics have rejected it, as disjointed and trivial[30] but others have exalted it as more unified than *The Hamlet* or *Go Down, Moses*.[31] Our analysis has shown that *The Unvanquished* succeeds admirably in being what it intends to be: a short story cycle.

Faulkner has tied his stories together with more precision than Anderson's pieces in *Winesburg, Ohio*, or Hemingway's in *In Our Time*. He does not rely merely on similarly treated themes or motifs to give his stories unity, as Kafka, Joyce, and Flannery O'Connor do. Faulkner centers his attention on emergence of character against a mythically significant background. But the experiences that shape the character are not as loosely related as are the experiences of Aram in Saroyan's book, or of George Willard in *Winesburg*. The impact of each of Bayard's earlier experiences operates strongly in his considered decision in "An Odor of Verbena". Neither George Willard nor Aram can really be said to embody the emerging themes of their respective books. Bayard can and does.

An increasing number of critics are beginning to recognize in *The Unvanquished* a serious work of fiction and not merely a collection of stories fit for slick magazines. In my treatment of the central themes of the work, I have given support to that view. Even in the early stories, Bayard the narrator provides sufficient distance from the game-war world of the two boys, sufficient distance from the glorification of Colonel John Sartoris (to whom Bayard the participator, at twelve years old, adds

30 See Kronenberger, De Voto, O'Connor, Longley ("the epithet 'trivial' was in some respects quite fair" [p. 176]), and Tuck ("the episodes tend to be anecdotal, and nowhere is there more than a suggestion of the grimness of war or of despair over a cause obviously lost" [p. 70]).

31 *Cf.* especially Waggoner, pp. 170ff; and Volpe, p. 76: "Most critics have dismissed it as a collection of short stories, though its seven stories have far more structural unity than the stories in *The Hamlet* or *Go Down, Moses*, which are generally accorded the status of novels."

the dimensions of a mythic hero), sufficient criticism both of the "old order" and of the exigencies of war to counteract any feeling of over-romanticized sentimentalism to which those three factors might have given rise in a lesser work of art. From the beginning, Bayard the narrator holds his ironic, objective, reflective distance.

Nevertheless, or perhaps in spite of this objectivity, Faulkner has managed to flood his pages – especially in the early stories and in "Skirmish at Sartoris" – with a genuine humor, a humor which survives and even participates in the most dangerous of situations. The nervousness and fear one feels in positions of danger almost contains the seeds of that kind of tension one feels just before laughing. What would have happened to Bayard and Ringo if the sergeant (not Colonel Dick) had discovered they were hiding beneath Granny's skirts? Perhaps nothing. Perhaps too they might have been taken as captives or hostages, to bring pressure to bear against John Sartoris. Soldiers are not known for gentleness. This tense scene, however, becomes a setting for humor.

Faulkner's quality of humor undergoes a change as the general destruction deepens. The fact that Bayard and Ringo have to wash their mouths out for saying "the bastuds!" though they receive no punishment for shooting a horse, at first merely adds a humorous slant on Granny's morals. But Faulkner's humor evokes "thoughtful laughter" when, at the end of "Retreat" Granny feels justified – because her house is burned, her silver stolen, her slaves deserted, and her son outlawed – to join the boys in their deepening hatred of war, which they express in their phrase: "the bastuds! the bastuds!". The humor of the stories does not approximate that of farce or slapstick. It is part of the experience of the South, part of the treasure which Granny and the boys try to preserve from destruction. But with Granny's death, all humor dies until the murderer is brought to the only kind of justice available at the time: blood-justice.

The Unvanquished, then, is a serious work of fiction. Its language is not as rich nor its design as complicated as that of *The Sound and the Fury* or *As I Lay Dying*. Not all of the stories in the cycle are equally engaging – certainly the most full-bodied is "An Odor of Verbena". But in many ways, *The Unvanquished* stands as an unique achievement among the works of Faulkner. It remains his only book to deal primarily with the Civil War and its aftermath. Despite its tragic subject, no other work of Faulkner ends on such a positive note. Here too, Faulkner has created a positive hero who tells his own story – a young man who relates with detachment and critical distance his own courageous encounter, unarmed, with his father's killer. Since Dostoevsky's *Notes from Underground* (and before), writers have found it much easier to write in the first person (principal participant) only if their central character is an anti-hero or a misfit or is somehow psychologically disturbed. Few authors of past or present have been able to create a believable "good and noble" first-person narrator who tells about his own bravery.

For this purpose, a short story cycle gave Faulkner his best chance of success. In a cycle, he could allow other characters to occupy the center of action throughout most of the book. His first-person narrator's normal function would be to relate and comment upon the actions of others. He would not constantly be talking about himself but about Granny and Father and Drusilla and Loosh. As we pointed out earlier, Bayard in the early stories most often refers to himself as somehow congealed with his close companion Ringo. So he is able to relieve a certain amount of narrative pressure from his own person by speaking of "we" and "Ringo and I" as a plural unit.

These narrative devices, as I have shown, are functional. As Bayard begins to break away from composite action, as he separates his personal approach to life from that of his friends, ancestors, and neighbors, the narrative "we – Ringo and I" breaks down until finally the "I" stands alone, prepared for the brief span of the final story to draw toward itself the primary interest of the narration.

I agree, then, with Lytle, Knoll, Waggoner, Brooks, and Volpe,[32] that *The Unvanquished* deserves to be read and evaluated as a serious work of fiction by the most important fiction writer America's first half century has produced. Knoll places the book "just behind the very best of Faulkner" (p. 339), a judgment which I find sound. The "romantic atmosphere" which some critics have deplored in the early stories, is, as Waggoner suggests, "clearly functional" (p. 175).

Finally, *The Unvanquished*, perhaps better than any other book by Faulkner, embodies in its portrayal of character and its optimistic,

[32] Andrew Lytle, "The Son of Man: He Will Prevail", *Sewanee Review*, LXII (Winter 1955), 114-137. Volpe is correct in saying that "*The Unvanquished* is a serious assessment of the Southern legend" but goes too far when he suggests that it is also "a declaration of a moral – if not social and emotional – independence from the past". (p. 86). John Sartoris' spirit in *Sartoris* seemed to express (to Bayard sitting by the chest of Civil War articles) Faulkner's real attitude: "the man who professes to care nothing about his forbears is only a little less vain than the man who bases all his actions on blood precedent" (p. 92). Bayard in his facing Redmond both upheld and transcended the Southern legend which he had seriously assessed.

positive direction, the notions of man which Faulkner expressed to all the world in his speech of acceptance of the Nobel Prize:

I decline to accept the end of man.... I believe that man will not merely endure: he will prevail. He is immortal, not because he alone among creatures has an inexhaustible voice, but because he has a soul, a spirit capable of compassion and sacrifice and endurance. The poet's, the writer's, duty is to write about these things. It is his privilege to help man endure by lifting his heart, by reminding him of the courage and honor and hope and pride and compassion and pity and sacrifice which have been the glory of his past.[33]

[33] James Meriwether, ed. *Speeches and Public Letters by William Faulkner* (New York, 1965), p. 120.

V

SHERWOOD ANDERSON: *WINESBURG, OHIO*

Winesburg, Ohio is Sherwood Anderson's only universally admired book.[1] It comprises twenty-five semi-impressionistic short stories which concentrate on significant "moments" in the lives of characters whose histories are intimately bound up with the fictive town of Winesburg in Ohio. William Phillips has shown, from his examination of the manuscripts in the Newberry Library in Chicago, that "the Winesburg stories were written during a relatively short period of time, one leading to another, and

[1] (New York, 1919). The Chicago papers (*Tribune*, *Daily News*, *Evening Post*, and *Chicago American*) reviewed the volume favorably in June, 1919. Approving reviews also appeared in *New Republic*, *Pagan*, *Liberator*, *Bookman*, *New York Call*, *San Francisco Chronicle*, *Boston Evening Transcript* – all in 1919. Only the *New York Sun* and the *Post* panned the book; the *Sun's* anonymous reviewer called it "A Gutter Would Be Spoon River". When the book appeared from London's Jonathan Cape publishing house in 1922, favorable criticism of it spotted the pages of the *Times Literary Supplement*, *London Evening Standard*, *London Observer*, and *Glasgow Herald*. The book was soon translated into other languages, the earliest being two from Russia (*Uinsberg Okhaio*, tr. S. D. Matveyev, Moscow, 1924; and *Uainsberg*, *Oghaio*, tr. P. Okhrimenko, Moscow/Leningrad, 1924). In France, reviews were enthusiastic. The critics of the early twenties in America (Crawford, Boyd, Crane, Lovett, Manly) continued to regard Anderson's work as a "searching study of American life" (John M. Manly and Edith Rickert, *Contemporary American Literature* [New York, 1929], p. 40). Many American critics reacted against Anderson in the mid-late twenties and thirties. See, for instance, A. H. Quinn, *American Fiction* (New York, 1936), pp. 656-660; and Camille McCole, "Sherwood Anderson – Congenital Freudian", *Catholic World*, CXXX (November, 1929), 129-133. (Later, this article was expanded into a chapter of McCole's *Lucifer at Large* [London, 1937], pp. 125-152.). Yet, although many critics opposed Anderson's writings in general, many were careful to exclude *Winesburg* from their strictures. See, for instance, Alyse Gregory, "Sherwood Anderson", *Dial*, LXXV (September, 1923), 243-246; Lawrence S. Morris, "Sherwood Anderson: Sick of Words", *New Republic*, LI (August 3, 1927), 277-279; Paul Elmer Moore, "The Modern Current in American Literature", *Forum*, LXXIX (January, 1928), 127-136; Rachel Smith, "Sherwood Anderson: Some Entirely Arbitrary Reactions", *Sewanee Riview*, XXXVII (April, 1929), 159-163; Clifton Fadiman, "Sherwood Anderson: the Search for Salvation", *Nation*, CXXXV (November 9, 1932), 454-456. These reactions carried over into the forties, as is evidenced in Michael Gold, *The Hollow Men* (New York, 1941), p. 69; and Lionel Trilling, "The World of Sherwood Anderson", *New York Times Book Review*, (November 9, 1947), p 1.

The 1922 reprint of *Winesburg, Ohio*, put out by The Modern Library, made greater sales than the 1919 edition had. Anderson, in his *Memoirs* and *Letters*, indicates that he continued to be surprised by the great sale of his book and by the praise it had received even from those who discredited his earlier work. A Penguin Books reprint also appeared in 1946. In 1960, Malcolm Cowley edited the first new edition of *Winesburg* to appear since Huebsch's original one.

that this period of time was late 1915 and early 1916".[2] Between February 1916, and December 1918, ten of the stories[3] appeared, sometimes in a modified form[4] in the journals *Masses*, *The Little Review*, and *Seven Arts*. After the collected volume of stories had been rejected as "too gloomy" by John Lane (the publisher of Anderson's previous books),[5] B. W. Huebsch took it under his wing and, in 1919, issued it with a title he himself had proposed to Anderson: *Winesburg, Ohio: A Group of Tales of Ohio Small Town Life.*[6]

The first three stories written were first to be published in the magazines and stand first in the collected volume. Anderson apparently wrote the final three stories of the *Winesburg* volume for the precise purpose of rounding off the book's diverse actions, themes, motifs, and structures.

A tabulation (my own) of the comparative orders of writing and of final arrangement of the stories in the *Winesburg* volume will help to illustrate the nature of certain regroupings of the stories and, at the same time, will serve as a convenient table of contents for our discussion of the book's structure.

The page references to *Winesburg* in my chapter refer to the Cowley edition (New York: Viking Press, 1960). Cowley has altered some things in the text, and I have in my possession a detailed list of those alterations. Cowley does not mention, however, that he has dropped the book's subtitle. It was Cowley's hope that the Viking edition would become the standard text of Anderson's stories.

[2] William Louis Phillips, "How Sherwood Anderson Wrote *Winesburg, Ohio*", *American Literature*, XXIII (March, 1951), 13. Phillips shows that the first eighteen stories were written in three discernible groups, which I have indicated below.

[3] "The Book of the Grotesque", *Masses*, VIII (February, 1916), 17; "Hands", *Masses*, VIII (March, 1916), 5, 7; "The Philosopher", *Little Review*, III (June-July, 1916), 7-9 (this story appears as "Paper Pills" in *Winesburg*); "The Strength of God", *Masses*, VIII (August, 1916), 12-13; "'Queer'", *Seven Arts*, I (December, 1916), 97-108; "The Untold Lie", *Seven Arts*, I (January, 1917), 215-221; "Mother", *Seven Arts*, I (March, 1917), 452-461; "The Thinker", *Seven Arts*, II (September, 1917), 584-597; "The [sic] Man of Ideas", *Little Review*, V (June, 1918), 22-28; "An Awakening", *Little Review*, V (December, 1918), 13-21.

[4] In the magazine version of "Hands", the first two paragraphs of the book version are redistributed in five paragraphs of a different order than the sequence given in the book. Also, "The Untold Lie" acquired a first person narrator for the version that appeared in *Seven Arts*, but lost him when it was subsumed once more into the more congenial environment of the cycle.

[5] *Windy McPherson's Son* (1916), *Marching Men* (1917), and *Mid-American Chants* (1918).

[6] Anderson consented to the new title, though he had planned to call the book, after its first story, *The Book of the Grotesque*. Huebsch, by the way, had a few years earlier issued Joyce's *Dubliners* from his press. He was to publish four other Anderson books: *Poor White* (1920), *The Triumph of the Egg* (1921), *Horses and Men* (1923), and *Many Marriages* (1923).

WINESBURG MANUSCRIPT (1915-1916)[7]	WINESBURG, OHIO (1919)
I. *First Group:*	
1. The Book of the Grotesque	The Book of the Grotesque
2. Hands	Hands
3. Paper Pills [The Philosopher][8]	Paper Pills
4. Tandy	Mother
5. Drink	The Philosopher
6. Mother	Nobody Knows
7. Surrender (Part III)	Godliness, Part I
8. Nobody Knows	Godliness, Part II
9. Respectability	Surrender, Part III
10. The Thinker	Terror, Part IV
11. Terror (Part IV)	A Man of Ideas
II. *Second Group:*	
1. Godliness (Part I)	Adventure
2. Godliness (Part II)	Respectability
III. *Third Group:*	
1. Adventure	The Thinker
2. The Strength of God	Tandy
3. The Teacher	The Strength of God
4. Loneliness	The Teacher
5. An Awakening	Loneliness
IV. *On Yellow Advertising Paper:*	
1. "Queer"	An Awakening
2. The Untold Lie	"Queer"

[7] The *Winesburg* manuscript, now deposited in the Newberry Library, consists of drafts of all twenty-five tales. The manuscripts of the last seven tales listed here were written on advertising paper. No writing appears on the back, and so the order of these tales is somewhat open to question. The other stories, however, were written on the backs of twenty previously rejected sketches of Anderson, varying in length from two to thirty-three pages. For a detailed account showing the correspondence of the *Winesburg* writing and the discarded manuscript, see William Louis Phillips, "Sherwood Anderson's *Winesburg, Ohio*" (unpublished dissertation, University of Chicago, 1950), pp. 203-206. (This work is available in microfilm only through the University of Chicago Library.)

[8] In the *Little Review*, this story was entitled "The Philosopher", but yielded that title to the story about Dr. Parcival when it was decided that both stories – one written early and the other late – were to be included in the same collection.

3. A Man of Ideas	The Untold Lie
4. The Philosopher	Drink
5. Death	Death
6. Sophistication	Sophistication
7. Departure	Departure

"Surrender" and "Terror" apparently came to Anderson as integral parts of the story cycle. It would seem likely that the events of "Terror" inspired him then to write "Godliness", Parts I and II, to which he later joined "Surrender" and "Terror" as Parts III and IV, respectively.[9]

The stories from "The Strength of God" through "An Awakening" were written as a unit and retained their solidarity in the published volume. "Adventure", which shares with "The Strength of God" a sympathetic presentation of a naked woman's frustrated desire to get out of herself, was separated from Group III to serve a new function both in relation to Wash Williams' story in "Respectability" and to Tandy Hard's desires in "Tandy". If "Respectability" is taken as the mathematical center of the volume, one can begin to see some justice in Anderson's grouping the four "Godliness" stories in the first half and the four stories in the "Strength-of-God" unit in the second half. As the action of "Godliness, Part I" completes its ironic course in "Godliness, Part II", so does the action of "The Strength of God" find its ironic fulfillment in "The Teacher". And, as we shall see later, the relationship of "Surrender" to "Terror" is similar to the relationship of "Loneliness" to "An Awakening". The same can be said of the two-story units "A Man of Ideas"/"Adventure" and "The Thinker"/"Tandy". More significantly, the juxtaposition in the published volume of "Paper Pills" and "Mother" in the early pages of the cycle[10] prepares for the brief but passionate communion of Dr. Reefy and Elizabeth Willard in "Death" near the end of the cycle. Finally, as many commentators have noted, just as "The Book of the Grotesque" introduces the volume as its prologue, so does "Departure" serve it as epilogue and conclusion.

9 Jarvis A. Thurston in "Anderson and 'Winesburg': Mysticism and Craft", *Accent*,, XVI (Spring, 1956), 107-128, thinks that the four "Godliness" stories were to form the basis of a novel that Anderson discarded. It is clear, however, that – whatever Anderson's intention may have been after the first and second part of "Godliness" had been written – the third and fourth parts at least were composed as an integral part of the first eleven stories. Perhaps, too, Anderson saw that his "novel's" story was over after the action of "Terror". At any rate, "Godliness I and II" were included to provide an historical perspective to the cycle and background material for "Surrender" and "Terror".

10 This was done by relocating "Tandy" and "Drink" to positions later in the volume.

Phillips has already given convincing proof that, in its manuscript form, *Winesburg*

> was conceived as a unit, knit together, however loosely, by the idea of the first tale, "The Book of the Grotesque", and consisting of individual sketches which derived additional power from each other, not, as anthologists repeatedly suggest, a collection of short stories which can be separated from each other without loss of effect.[11]

What I intend to show in this chapter is that the form of the published *Winesburg* volume demands that it be approached from the vantage point of an accurate awareness not only of the fact that the stories have some kind of loose unity, but of the precise nature of that unity. Here is no mere bundle of disparate stories; neither do we have here a tightly structured novel about George Willard. The unity of *Winesburg, Ohio* is the unity of a short story cycle, both in the sense of a connected series and in the sense of a recurring development in a set of narratives. The action of the book consists in the gradual emergence, from conception in "The Book of the Grotesque", to maturity in "Departure", of a fictive community in the distortive memory of the book's single narrator; and of a return, in "Departure" to the initial (now modified) situation – which had been presented in "The Book of the Grotesque".

Underlying all the stories and forming part of the weave, like threads in a carpet, run various connective devices. One of the most important is the consistent narrative voice which controls the tone and angle of vision in every story. Another is the repetition of words, phrases, situations, and thematic patterns. The pseudo-realistic locale, which really exists only in the mind of the narrator, serves as a framework against which the distorted figures of the narrator's fancy think, speak, and gesture. Finally, throughout the book, George Willard prepares for his mythic journey out of the land of fragmented personalities and ruined dreams into manhood and maturity.

It should be clear, then, that even though Anderson's book has been shaped and molded with the aid of such outside influences as Turgenev's *A Sportsman's Sketches*, Masters' *The Spoon River Anthology*, the post-impressionist painters (Cezanne, Van Gogh, Gauguin), Gertrude Stein's broken textures of language, Mark Twain's American colloquial conventions, the archaic speech patterns of the King James Version of the Bible, and the men and women whom Anderson knew both in Clyde, Ohio, and in his rooming house, 735 Cass Street in Chicago – nevertheless,

11 Phillips, in *American Literature* (March, 1951), p. 7.

there is an important sense in which *Winesburg* is one hundred percent Anderson.[12] He has not copied any previous form, nor merely photographed the people he knew. Like every other significant artist, he has assimilated his heritage, his environment, and his own intense psychic life; and from the chaos of his multiple experiences, he has created a unique and permanent artwork.

From his rostrum of literary prestige, Anderson encouraged younger writers to consider the advantages of the "new looseness" of his *Winesburg* form, which he described as "lives flowing past each other, the whole however, to leave a definite impression".[13] "What is wanted", he told the upcoming generation of writers,

> is a new looseness, and in *Winesburg* I had made my own form. There were individual tales but all about lives in some way connected. By this method I did succeed, I think, in giving the feeling of the life of a boy growing to manhood in a town.[14]

Perhaps the younger writers listened to him and adapted to their own artistic needs Anderson's "new looseness" of form. One thinks immediately of Hemingway's *In Our Time* (1925), Steinbeck's *The Red Pony* (1937), Saroyan's *My Name Is Aram* (1940), and Faulkner's *Go Down, Moses* (1942) – all of which unite the ebb and flow of loosely connected lives with the education of a young boy into life.

A. PREVIOUS CRITICISM

From the beginning, possibly prompted by Anderson's numerous remarks about his "*Winesburg* form",[15] critics have been aware that some unifying

12 Phillips also mentions, in his dissertation, the possible example of the *Decameron* and *The Canterbury Tales* as an influence on the structure of *Winesburg, Ohio*. In England, one finds also Dickens stories of Pickwick and Burrow's collections of gypsy episodes. In America during the nineteenth century, Seba Smith, Benjamin Schillaber, Augustus Baldwin Longstreet, Johnson J. Hooper, George W. Harris, Harriet Beecher Stowe, and Joel Chandler Harris all wrote collections of tales in a humorous vein about related characters. Anderson himself makes special mention in his *Memoirs* (p. 286) of George Burrows, Balzac, Flaubert, Turgenev, and George Moore, all of whom he had been "reading assiduously" during the period before the publication of *Winesburg*. Anderson spoke especially of Turgenev's *A Sportsman's Sketches* as "one of the great books of the world" and as "the sweetest thing in literature".

13 Quoted in James Schevill, *Sherwood Anderson* (Denver, 1951), p. 97.

14 *Sherwood Anderson's Memoirs* (New York, 1942), p. 289.

15 Anderson has described the "*Winesburg* form" on a number of occasions. His

principle draws the stories of *Winesburg, Ohio* together. Cleveland Chase, author of the first full-length study of Anderson (1927), saw the stories as a whole expressing

the intricacy and subtlety that exists in the relationship of an individual to his physical environment and to other people.... In exploring this field Anderson incidentally shows the loneliness, the essential isolation of all people, however far they may or may not have gone toward orienting themselves in life.[16]

Waldo Frank's reappraisal of *Winesburg* in 1941 comments that the most striking impression his re-reading made on him was that the "book as a whole has form; ...the work is an integral whole".[17] A few years later, Pearson added the insight that in *Winesburg* Anderson was seeking "an organic form which might arise out of a parade of minor characters", and would show them "in their struggles, in their gropings, and in their inevitable conflicts with the society against which they stood in tension".[18]

No close analysis of the work had been done, however, until Jarvis Thurston's dissertation (unpublished) in 1946 and William Phillips'

---

descriptions are not always consistent. To Waldo Frank in a letter of December 1919, he wrote that *Winesburg* was "half individual tales, half long novel form" (quoted in Thurston, *Accent*, 1956, p. 125). In an earlier letter to Frank, after he had finished writing the stories, he wrote that he had "a series of intensive studies of people of my home town, Clyde, Ohio", and that there would be "seventeen of these studies". "It is my own idea", he continues, "that when these studies are published in book form, they will suggest the real environment out of which present-day American youth is coming" (letter to Frank, November 14, 1916, quoted in Thurston, p. 125). In his *Memoirs*, he says that, together, the stories make "something like a novel, a complete story" (p. 289). On the same page, however, he says that "the novel form does not fit an American writer...in *Winesburg* I had made my own form". In 1938 (letter to Maxwell Perkins), he describes the form as "a related group of people, their lives touching, never quite touching", and in 1941 (letter to Sergel) goes back to calling it a novel, though he adds: "I invented it. It was mine" (quoted in Schevill, p. 96). In his *Memoirs* he offers, as a model for the form, America itself: "Do we not live in a great, loose land of many states", he writes, "and yet all of these states together do make something, a land, a country. I submit that the form of my *Winesburg* tales...may offer a suggestion to other writers" (quoted in Schevill, pp. 96-97). Even though Anderson sometimes called his work a novel, it is quite evident that he was aware of creating something new, something of his own, a form that could be imitated by other writers, and a form for which he, in the final analysis, found no better term than "my *Winesburg* form".

16 Cleveland B. Chase, *Sherwood Anderson* (New York, 1927), p. 34.

17 Waldo Frank, "*Winesburg, Ohio* After Twenty Years", *Story*, XIX (September-October, 1941), p. 29.

18 Norman H. Pearson, "Anderson and the New Puritanism", *Newberry Library Bulletin*, Second Series, No. 2 (December, 1948), p. 54. He goes on to remark that he thinks George Willard is the central figure in what little story there is.

dissertation (unpublished) in 1950.[19] Phillips had at his disposal the Anderson manuscripts, recently depositied in Chicago's Newberry Library. Taking his cue from Anderson's remark in an unpublished letter to Waldo Frank (December, 1919), Phillips probes in what senses *Winesburg* may be said to be "half long novel form" and in what senses it is "half individual tales". The old writer's theory of "truths" in "The Book of the Grotesque", Phillips argues, unites the tales. This "idea of some seriousness" is embodied in the activities of the group of characters who clamor for the reader's attention, while in the background, against the increasingly detailed locale of Winesburg,[20] George Willard grows toward

[19] Jarvis Thurston, "Sherwood Anderson: A Critical Study" (unpublished dissertation, State University of Iowa, 1946). And William L. Phillips, "Sherwood Anderson's *Winesburg, Ohio*: Its Origins, Composition, Technique, and Reception" (unpublished dissertation, University of Chicago, 1950).

[20] Despite efforts of Harold Toksvig (endpaper of the first edition, 1919) and Evelyn Kintner (in "Sherwood Anderson: Small Town Man" (unpublished M. A. dissertation, Bowling Green State University, 1942), to map out the town of Winesburg, the evidence given by Anderson in the pages of *Winesburg* is insufficient data on which to reconstruct his fictive town. Throughout the cycle, Anderson adds detail to detail, fact to fact; he repeats names of people and places, but these are not meant to cohere into a precise realistic locale. Of Winesburg's 1800 inhabitants, the reader learns the names (and for the most part, the occupations) of over one hundred. Winesburgers who play no important role in any of the pieces are sometimes afforded the luxury of more than a paragraph's character sketch (*e.g.*, John Spaniard, Abner Groff, Will Henderson, Wesley Moyer, Tom Little, Turk Smollet, Hop Higgins, Mook the half-wit, Windpeter Winters, and the old carpenter in "The Book of the Grotesque"). Though we do not know the relationships of building to building, Winesburg's business district is known to possess three banks (Winesburg National, First National, and Winesburg Savings), two dry goods stores (Winney's and the Paris Dry Goods), two saloons (Tom Willy's and Ed Griffith's), three doctors' offices (of Doctors Reefy, Welling, and Parcival), as well as a bookstore, bakery, drugstore, hardware store, shoe repair shop, grocery store, feed shop, shoe store, two harness repair shops, a millinery shop, cigar store, poolroom, two butcher shops, barber shop with two barbers, clothing store, opera house, post office, railroad station, hotel, a notion store (Myerbaum's), a newspaper office, a lunch counter (Biff Carter's), telegraph office, several churches (Presbyterian, Methodist, and "other churches"), and a school. In the surrounding area we see Spaniard's nursery, Comstock's flour mill, King's cider mill, Wesley Moyer's livery barn, the Fair Grounds, Gospel Hill, a number of farms, berry fields, and dining places. In addition to clerks and proprietors of the stores of Winesburg, many of whom are explicitly named, Winesburg also has a jeweler, an express agent, a real estate agent. a baggage man, a Standard Oil agent, a carriage painter, a carpet weaver, a telegraph operator, a quarryman, a court stenographer, a town marshal, a wood chopper, a lamplighter, two ministers (Presbyterian and Methodist), a schoolteacher, a nightwatchman, stable boys, cooks, a lawyer, a railroad conductor, and many farmhands and farmers. Winesburg also is known to have some organizations such as the Epworth League and the baseball team. Nevertheless, the Winesburg community is a community not primarily because it inhabits the environs of Winesburg, Ohio, but because it shares a common origin and destiny in the mind of the narrator and in the context of its mythic relations with George Willard. The Winesburg community is a community of dreamers, of adven-

maturity. Phillips' publication in 1951 of a revised portion of one chapter of his dissertation gave a significant boost to Anderson scholarship.[21]

Two full-length studies of Anderson in 1951 initiated a flood of *Winesburg* articles in the following decade and a half. Irving Howe asserts that Anderson "intended each of [the stories] to be a self-contained unit, as in fact they may still be regarded".[22] The book's "central strand of action, discernible in about half the stories, is the effort of the grotesques to establish intimate relations with George Willard...".[23] He calls the book an "episodic novel" like Turgenev's *A Sportsman's Sketches*, and cites as unifying principles the consistency of setting, mood, and feeling, and the reappearance of some of the characters in several stories. "The ultimate unity of the book", he says,

> is a unity of feeling, a sureness of warmth, and a readiness to accept Winesburg's lost grotesques with the embrace of humility. Many American writers have taken as their theme the loss of love in the modern world, but few, if any at all, have so thoroughly realized it in the accents of love. (p. 164)

James Schevill's book centers more on Anderson's technique than on the themes and symbolic gestures one finds in *Winesburg*. Schevill laments

---

turers, of gesturing figures, of fragmented people, of "unused lives". Throughout the cycle, characters and places recur: George Willard in all but six stories; 33 characters each appear in more than one story (some of them five and six times). Ninety-one characters appear only once in the cycle (ten of these are central protagonists in their stories). Despite all this emphasis on similarity of background, the people of Winesburg live horribly separated lives.

21 "How Sherwood Anderson Wrote *Winesburg, Ohio*", *American Literature*, XXIII (March, 1951), 7-30.

22 Irving Howe's study of Anderson appeared in three places and under different titles: "The Book of the Grotesque", *Partisan Review*, XVIII (January-February, 1951), 32-40, was reprinted first in Howe's *Sherwood Anderson* (New York, 1951), and most recently in Wallace Stegner (ed.), *The American Novel from James Fenimore Cooper to William Faulkner* (New York, 1965). Its title in that collection of essays is "Sherwood Anderson, *Winesburg, Ohio*", pp. 154-165. My quotes are from the last-published version of the essay, p. 162.

23 Howe, p. 160. Howe describes the characters' approach to George Willard as ritualistic choreography. The grotesques approach at night, they approach hesitantly, they take courage because they come to an illuminating moment, the moment passes. Howe says that George is for them "a young priest who will renew the forgotten communal rites by which they may again be bound together". For Dr. Reefy and Dr. Parcival, he is "the lost son returned", whose apparent innocence and capacity for feeling will redeem Winesburg. To Tom Foster and Elmer Cowley, he is a reporter-messenger, bringing news of a dispensation which will allow them to re-enter the world of men.

that "the essential form of Winesburg has been so misunderstood".[24] "Even those who have spoken about a unified structure", he says, "have usually been wrong about the kind of form" (p. 95). The form, he says, "consists of an introduction, three sections, and an epilogue.... Each episode takes its place in the structure of the myth" (p. 104). Schevill's analysis, however, does not convince. The "three sections" are said to consist in (1) the secular portions of the myth, (2) the religious and moral dimensions of the myth, and (3) the extension and amplification of the secular strands of the myth. A brief perusal of the table of contents will suffice to convince one of the inadequacy of Schevill's neatly packaged divisions.[25]

Friedrich Weltz, in an unpublished dissertation in München,[26] examined briefly Winesburg's structure, the independence of each unit in that structure, the general background of the action, and the thematic strand (quest) which runs through all the stories. He shares with Phillips and Cowley the distinction among all the critics of having seen the cyclic character of *Winesburg*. "Worin liegt nun der zyklische Charakter von 'Winesburg, Ohio?'" he asks.

> Die in sich selbstwertigen Geschichten besitzen durch die Ähnlichkeit des Stoffes und der Thematik eine gewisse Parallelität des Ablaufs. Aus diesen parallelen Einzelaussagen ergibt sich das Bild einer Gesamtbewegung: die Suche nach der Schönheit im Leben, dem Versuch Einsamkeit und "frustration" zu überwinden. Dies ist die Mitte des Zyklus, auf sie ist alles bezogen. (p. 31)

Thurston's article in *Accent* (1956) buttressed the growing tendency among Anderson scholars to regard his work as only incidentally realistic. Howe had written that *Winesburg* was fundamentally nonrealistic, and Schevill had located the work within the school of expressionism. Thurston notes:

> What realism there is in *Winesburg* serves symbolic and structural purposes. The constant reference to places and their spatial relationships...serves as one of the

24 James Schevill, *Sherwood Anderson, His Life and Work* (Denver, 1951). Other quotes in the text refer to this edition. See also, Charles C. Walcutt, "Sherwood Anderson: Impressionism and the Buried Life", *Sewanee Review*, LX (Winter, 1952), 28-47.

25 Schevill should at least be given credit for seeing that the collection is more than a mere "casual collection of stories", for opening to others the notion that Winesburg is "intricately constructed". He was also aware that any "misunderstanding of the form of Winesburg" would lead critics to judge "that some of the tales were too fragmentary, unable to stand by themselves".

26 *Vier amerikanische Erzählungszyklen*, 1953.

means of linking the stories together. By setting his twenty protagonists, and numerous minor characters...in a village, Anderson makes of Winesburg a microcosm.[27]

The following year, Roger Asselineau made the same point in his pamphlet *Réalisme, rêve et expressionnisme dans "Winesburg, Ohio"*. "Malgré les apparances", he wrote, "Sherwood Anderson n'était pas un réaliste".[28] Winesburg, he continues, is a revelation of the secret life of the imagination, not a realistic description of small town life; it is "un livre poétique et non point un recueil de contes réalistes". Asselineau's analysis shows a consistency of usage of such symbols as the dream, the dark, and gestures made with the hands.

Malcolm Cowley's introduction to the Viking edition of *Winesburg, Ohio*, gives as the chief unifying factors of the book its single background, its prevailing tone, its central character (George Willard), and its underlying plot (the attempt on the part of the grotesques to establish communication with George Willard). "The structure of the book", he comments, "lies midway between the novel proper and the mere collection of stories.... It is a cycle of stories..."[29] – a form which "ought to be recognized for what it is".[30] Unfortunately, Cowley has never outlined a theory of story cycles nor has he offered a detailed explication of *Winesburg* from that point of view.

Walter Rideout's article in *Shenandoah* (1962), though plagued with several minor inaccuracies,[31] presents, in general, a perceptive analysis of the complex simplicity of *Winesburg*. The unifying elements he most stresses are the setting of all but five of the stories in the evening, the use of recurrent words (like hands), and the growth to maturity of George Willard, with its three aspects of (1) the conflict of the money-making

27 Jarvis A. Thurston, "Anderson and 'Winesburg': Mysticism and Craft", *Accent*, XVI (Spring, 1956), 107-128. Thurston also speaks of "adolescence as a symbol": "the charged atmosphere of adolescence", he says, "*is* the atmosphere of *Winesburg*" (p. 114).

28 No. 2 of *Archives de Lettres Modern* (avril, 1957), p. 5.

29 (New York, 1960), p. 14.

30 Cowley, in a letter to me, June 23, 1966.

31 "The Simplicity of *Winesburg, Ohio*", *Shenandoah*, XIII (Spring, 1962), 20-31. Rideout allowed to enter his final copy such mistakes as calling Ed Handby "Hanby" in one place and "Harby" in another (pp. 29, 30), thus flawing the serious pun, integral to "hand" symbolism in the work. He also calls Belle Carpenter "Belle Carter" (p. 30). One must give Rideout credit, however, for his balanced and perceptive treatment of George Willard's function in the book. He writes: "As for George himself, one can make too much of his role [Howe certainly did] as a character designed to link the tales, unify them, and structure them into a loose sort of *bildungsroman*; on the other hand, one can make too little of it" (pp. 25-26).

world and the world of thoughts and dreams; (2) the growing understanding of his vocation to be a creative writer; and (3) his passage from ignorance to understanding, from a surface-contact with life to an ability to penetrate beneath the surface of lives.

Epifanio San Juan (1963) notes a consistent use of irony which serves Anderson by integrating fact and fancy, balancing reality and dream. Repetitive patterns contribute to the "organic unity of the narrative rendition", he says, so that *Winesburg* "often tends to move in a circular pattern either by force of habit and custom or by force of a sympathetic obedience to the cycle of the seasons, to the life of the instincts and impulses in man".[32] Brom Weber (1964) makes an almost identical remark from a different point of view: "Since the story is an articulation of the narrator's experience, its movement is repetitive and circular".[33] He greatly misunderstands the narrator's handling of his materials, however, calling his angle of vision a "stance of wonder and search".

Rex Burbank (1964) overstresses the centrality of George Willard as "the nascent artist serving his apprenticeship to life".[34] Burbank is one of the few critics to notice any similarity between George Willard and the old writer in the prologue: "like the old writer, he lives many lives, strives to know the many truths of those lives, and grasps the wonder and mystery of life through his receptiveness to all of it" (p. 69). Burbank restates many of Howe's insights about the complex inverse relationship between George and the other grotesques. Willard alone reaches maturity and a certain happiness because he "realizes and accepts loneliness as the essential human condition and understands the value of suffering" (p. 71). Glen Love would disagree with Burbank's stress on George's "apartness" from Winesburg. George, he says, stands "Janus-like between the states of innocence and experience, youth and maturity, agrarian past and city future", and so "is a synecdoche for Winesburg itself".[35]

I acknowledge the serious scholarship which has already been done on *Winesburg* and will try not to duplicate in my own study the previously published findings of intelligent men. Anderson's book has had such an impact on American and European literature, however, that a precise and detailed understanding of its form and its principles of unity is imperative

[32] "Vision and Reality: A Reconsideration of Sherwood Anderson's *Winesburg, Ohio*", *American Literature*, XXXV (1963), 143.
[33] *Sherwood Anderson* (Minneapolis, 1964), p. 39.
[34] *Sherwood Anderson* (New York, 1964), p. 69.
[35] "Sherwood Anderson's American Pastoral", *Dissertation Abstracts*, XXV (1965), 7247.

if the true importance of a theory of short story cycles is to be grasped. Recalling, therefore, Fussell's reminder that "the addition of a single note can change the character of a chord",[36] I will try to offer a fresh perspective on Anderson's book.

I will direct my attention first to an examination of the nature and function of Anderson's narrator; then I will show what associational patterns account for the narrator's telling the stories in the order he chooses; finally, I will discuss the cyclically arranged symbolic patterns which enrich the texture of the cycle.

B. THE NARRATOR

One need not read far into the Winesburg tales to discover that a single narrator is relating all the stories. But one must reread and reflect if he is to appreciate how the narrator maintains a delicate and consistent balance between sympathy and irony in his presentation of the characters of his fancy. No adequate understanding of the stories is possible without a firm grasp of the functions of this fictively realized narrator as he operates at the heart of each of the stories.

In the first place, as a *persona* who yet is the implied author, the narrator fuses the fictional world of the characters in the book with the real world of Anderson the author. He remarks, for instance, in "The Book of the Grotesque" (which is also a prologue to his own book of grotesques), that the old writer also had written a book which he had called "The Book of the Grotesque". "It was never published", the narrator says, "but I saw it once and it made an indellible impression on my mind". The book's central idea, he continues, "has always remained with me. By remembering it I have been able to understand many people and things that I was never able to understand before" (p. 24).

The "I" of the above statements rarely comes to the surface as "I" in the stories that follow "The Book of the Grotesque". After being introduced in this "prologue" he usually calls attention to himself only as storyteller, as controller of the material of his fancy, and not as a participant – slight though his participation in this first episode may be – in the action of the book.

Anderson once wrote, "I have come to think that the true history of

36 Edwin Fussell, "Winesburg, Ohio: Art and Isolation", *Modern Fiction Studies*, VI (Summer, 1960), 107.

life, is but a history of moments".[37] By "true history of life", however, he obviously meant "true history of fictional life". For in *The Modern Writer*, he wrote:

> Consider for a moment the material of the prose writer, the teller of tales. His materials are human lives. To him these figures of his fancy, these people who live in his fancy, should be as real as living people.[38]

In *Winesburg, Ohio*, Anderson's narrator, though not the most impressive, may, for heuristic reasons, be the most important of his fictively realized characters. He assumes the role of an "artist of life" like the old writer. Indeed, the old writer is his first creation.

From this point on, levels of reality and myth intermingle; the real is brother to the imaginary. The old carpenter who "became the nearest thing to what is understandable and lovable of all the grotesques in the writer's book" (p. 25) may be a mere creation of the old writer as the old writer is of the narrator and the narrator is of Anderson. The people whose intimate lives are strung out across the pages of *Winesburg* – are they figures of the old writer's fancy, or of the narrator's fancy, or of Anderson's? Are they, perhaps, George Willard's people?

George himself, of course, is only a fictional character. He, too, however, intends to be a writer, a creator of fancied people. Some of the grotesques of Winesburg pour out their life stories to the young *Eagle* reporter, but most of them do not. If George were to write of them, the majority of his accounts would be invented, though he surely would base his stories on the impressions these people had made on him. George's future mimics the old writer's past. All of the men and women the old writer knew as a younger man have shrunk into a mild and mellow deformity as he aged. As he lies on his bed, the young thing in him drives "a long procession of figures before his eyes" (p. 23). He does not try to paint exact word portraits of the figures, but rather to describe the "deep impression on his mind" that the figures had made.

It is possible, then, that the old writer stands at the head of the work as a later George Willard, a prototype of the George Willard to come. It is possible, too, that the narrator, by summoning to fictional life the figures of the old writer and of George Willard, fictionalized his own initiation into, and projected culmination of his creative career. He stands midway between youth and old age and meditates through his creations both his

37 Quoted in Chase, p. 32.
38 Anderson, *The Modern Writer* (New York, 1925), p. 39.

past and his future as a writer. Finally, I think it probable that Anderson, through these three figures – his narrative *persona*, the old writer, and the young writer George Willard – discovered a suitable form for experimenting with his "new looseness" of structure, with lives flowing past each other, touching and not quite touching, connected and yet not really connected. The people in the stories of *Winesburg, Ohio*, are people many of whom George Willard surely would have known. The old writer knew only the old carpenter and figures of his fancy – probably not the grotesques of Winesburg. The narrator alone could have known all the grotesques of *Winesburg, Ohio*, with that intimacy with which they are revealed, for they all existed in his mind. They were "real" figures of his fancy.

Anderson's narrator often intrudes in the stories to comment on his own presentation of his materials. In the last paragraph of "The Book of the Grotesque" he remarks:

> Concerning the old carpenter...I only mentioned him because he, like many of what are called very common people, became the nearest thing to what is understandable and lovable of all the grotesques in the writer's book. (p. 25)

In "Hands" we find him judging his own formulation of Adolph Meyer's feeling for the boys he taught: "And yet that is but crudely stated. It needs the poet there" (p. 31). And in "The Untold Lie" he asks pardon for the action of the narrative with the excuse that it will "be necessary to talk a little of young Hal so that you will get into the spirit of it" (p. 203).

Throughout the stories, the narrator spins his tales within the traditions of oral storytelling. While treating the figures of his fancy as real people, he consciously addresses his audience: "You see", he tells them in "The Book of the Grotesque", "the interest in all this lies in the figures that went before the eyes of the writer" (p. 23). "You can see for yourself", he adds later, "how the old man...would write hundreds of pages concerning the matter" (p. 25).

The intrusion of "you" and "I" into a narration which otherwise displays the characteristics primarily of a third person onmiscient narrator consciously breaks the illusion of reality and so draws the reader away from over-involvement in the sorrows of the figure who happens for the moment to stand in the spotlight. The narrator also plays with his audience, seems to wink at them, smile at them with a knowing air. He tells them first that the old writer had known people in a peculiarly intimate way, but then adds: "At least that is what the writer thought and the thought pleased him. Why quarrel with an old man concerning his thoughts?" (p. 23). A similar consortment with his audience plays a role in most of the stories. In "Hands", for instance, the narrator invites his audience:

Let us look briefly into the story of the hands. Perhaps our talking of them will arouse the poet who will tell the hidden wonder story of the influence for which the hands were but fluttering pennants of promise. (p. 31)

The narrator refuses, with a metaphoric flourish, his right to be called a poet.

Other phrases which express a type of solidarity between the tale-teller and his audience recur throughout: (my italics) "Long before the time during which *we* will know him..." (p. 36); "In order to understand the man *we* will have to go back to an earlier day" (p. 64); and "Of course something did happen. That is why he went back to live in Winesburg and why *we* know about him" (p. 173). Obviously, the narrator would have known about Enoch Robinson even if Enoch had not gone back to Winesburg. But then he never would have told his story.

Occasionally, the narrator pauses to converse more at length with his audience in a homey, folksy way. At the beginning of the story of Wash Williams, he addresses them:

If you have lived in cities and have walked in the park on a summer afternoon, you have perhaps seen, blinking in a corner of his iron cage, a huge, grotesque kind of monkey....

Had you been in the earlier years of your life a citizen of the village of Winesburg, Ohio, there would have been for you no mystery in regard to the beast in his cage. "It is like Wash Williams", you would have said. (p. 121)

Sometimes he interrupts the flow of narrative to arouse his audience to pay attention to an important, usually symbolic fact. In "Loneliness" he is talking about Enoch's room:

The room in which young Robinson lived in New York faced Washington Square and was long and narrow like a hallway. *It is important to get that fixed in your mind.* The story of Enoch is in fact the story of a room almost more than it is the story of a man. (p. 168, my italics)

Sometimes, too, he interjects comments on his storytelling that allow him to change his pace or to shift his perspective: "I go too fast" (p. 121); or, "That is no part of this story" (p. 97); or, "But this is not the story of Windpeter Winters.... It is Ray's story. It will, however, be necessary to talk a little of young Hal so that you will get into the spirit of it" (p. 203).

Even within the bounds of his customary stance as a third person narrator, the storyteller manages to maintain a delicate balance between a sympathetic presentation of suffering and a certain distance achieved through ironic comment or phraseology. In "The Book of the Grotesque" he describes the past sorrows of the old carpenter whose brother had died of starvation, but saves himself from sentimental involvement in the weeping man: "when he cried he puckered up his lips and the mustache bobbed up and down. The weeping old man with the cigar in his mouth was ludicrous" (pp. 21-22).

A similar kind of refusal to become emotionally enmeshed in his characters controls his presentation of the theatricality of Elizabeth Willard as she determines, at long last, to act – to save her son by driving her scissors, dagger-like, deep into the breast of her husband.

> The scene that was to take place in the office below began to grow in her mind. No ghostly worn-out figure should confront Tom Willard, but something quite unexpected and startling. Tall and with dusky cheeks and hair that fell in a mass from her shoulders, a figure should come striding down the stairway before the startled loungers in the hotel office. The figure would be silent – it would be swift and terrible. (p. 47)

But in the next paragraph, all her imagined strength has flowed suddenly out of her and she stands "weak and trembling in the darkness...clutching at the back of the chair in which she had spent so many long days..." (p. 47).

Similarly, the narrator speaks of Jesse Bentley as "the man who had proclaimed himself the only true servant of God in all the valley of Wine Creek" (p. 79). And in "The Thinker", immediately after Seth Richmond says, with a smirk, that his mother expects him to "stay on here forever just being a boy", the narrator adds, "Seth's voice became charged with boyish earnestness". The narrator arranges word and action in ironic juxtaposition, so that Helen White thinks to herself, "This boy is not a boy at all, but a strong purposeful man"; but when she asks what Seth will do in Cleveland, he replies vaguely, "I'll do something, get into some kind of work where talk don't count.... I don't know. I guess I don't care much" (p. 141). In "'Queer'" too, the narrator allows Elmer Cowley to bring judgment on himself by his deeds – he protests loudly that he will not be queer, but continues to act like a lunatic.

The narrator maintains his ironic distance, finally, by the use of *double-entendre*. He must be winking at his audience as he describes George Willard's walk with Belle Carpenter. George is filled with a new sense of masculine power; Belle is out to catch Ed Handby by one of the oldest of feminine tricks – arousal of jealousy. As she and George pause on a hill near the Fair Grounds, George presses Belle against his body, whispering into the night, incoherently, "lust and night and women".

> Belle Carpenter did not resist. When he kissed her upon the lips she leaned heavily against him and looked over his shoulder into the darkness. In her whole attitude there was a suggestion of waiting. (p. 187)

She does not have long to wait. In an instant George Willard is lying on his back in the bushes and Ed Handby is leading Belle away by the arm.

The narrator of *Winesburg* loves to generalize, universalize, and editorialize. Fortunately, the short story form does not allow the inclusion of extraneous materials to the same extent as does a novel. So *Winesburg* suffers less than Anderson's novels from passages in which Anderson allows his narrator to philosophize. Furthermore, the generalizations one finds in these stories normally have an immediate and close connection with the revelation of a central character or the meaning of a tale. In "The Book of the Grotesque", for instance, we find: "The old writer, *like all of the people of the world*, had got, during his long life, a great many notions in his head" (pp. 22-23; my italics). A similar unobtrusive comment occurs in "Hands". Adolph Meyers, the narrator says, "was meant by nature to be a teacher of youth.... In their feeling for the boys under their charge such men are not unlike the finer sort of women in their love of men" (p. 31).

In the first part of "Godliness" – which, Thurston has argued, is a discarded portion of a novel Anderson had intended to write – the editorial comment expands itself to a distressing degree:

> In the last fifty years a vast change has taken place in the lives of our people. A revolution has in fact taken place. The coming of industrialism, attended by all the roar and rattle of affairs, the shrill cries of millions of new voices that have come among us from overseas, the going and coming of trains, the growth of cities, the building of the interurban car lines that weave in and out of towns and past farmhouses, and now in these later days the coming of the automobiles has worked a tremendous change in the lives and in the habits of thought of our people of Mid-America. (pp. 70-71)

One would expect to find such a passage on the editorial page of a Cleveland newspaper, but not in a short story. (I have quoted only about a third of the passage as it appears in *Winesburg*.)

Two other incidences of editorializing must be mentioned. In "Loneliness", Enoch Robinson inhabits a room to which a large number of artists come to talk of art. The narrator comments:

Everyone knows of the talking artists. Throughout all of the known history of the world they have gathered in rooms and talked. They talk of art and are passionately, almost feverishly, in earnest about it. They think it matters much more than it does. (pp. 168-169)

Comments on art and artists in a work of art also serve the function of blending the levels of the imaginative and the real worlds.

At times the narrator's generalizing comments dive deep beneath the surface of lives into the core emotions of his people. While George and Helen stroll together in "Sophistication", the narrator remarks, "In youth there are always two forces fighting in people. The warm unthinking little animal struggles against the thing that reflects and remembers" (p. 240). While George and Helen pause on the hill above the fair grounds, the narrator continues:

There is something memorable in the experience to be had by going into a fair ground that stands at the edge of a Middle Western town on a night after the annual fair has been held. The sensation is one never to be forgotten. On all sides are ghosts, not of the dead, but of living people.... Farmers with their wives and children and all the people from the hundreds of little farm houses have gathered within these board walls. Young girls have laughed and men with beards have talked of the affairs of their lives. The place has been filled to overflowing with life.... One conceals oneself standing silently behind the trunk of a tree and what there is of a reflective tendency in his nature is intensified. One shudders at the thought of the meaninglessness of life while at the same instant, and if the people of the town are his people, one loves life so intensely that tears come into the eyes. (p. 241)

An important function of the narrator is to "reach beneath the surface of lives", not only in his generalizations, but in the particular insights he offers about the figures of his fancy. Since the people in his story exist only in his imagination, he can penetrate the tissues of their feelings and come to the roots of their existence. But in the tradition of the breezy storyteller, he does not serve his insights in fancy phraseology, but in deceptively simple expressions, the most common of which are "——— had a thought", or "an idea came to ———", or the equivalent.

For instance, after recording the small talk of carpenter and writer in "The Book of the Grotesque", the narrator concentrates on the old writer alone in his bed. "The thing to get at", the narrator remarks, "is what the writer, or the young thing within the writer, was thinking about" (p. 22). Then, with the delicacy of a surgeon of his own fancy, he dissects the layers of the old man's "dream that was not a dream" (p. 23).

The narrator does not merely relate the abstract thoughts of his characters, but often expresses feeling patterns through imagery viewed from within the character. Before she married Dr. Reefy, the tall rich (unnamed) woman had many suitors, one of whom was a jeweler's son who spent long evenings talking earnestly to her of virginity.

At times it seemed to her that as he talked he was holding her body in his hands. She imagined him turning it slowly about in the white hands and staring at it. At night she dreamed that he had bitten into her body and that his jaws were dripping. (pp. 37-38)

An entirely different inner conception of one's role in life is given in the case of Jesse Bentley who, in fancy, "saw himself living in old times and among old peoples. The land that lay stretched out before him became of vast significance, a place peopled by his fancy with a new race of men sprung from himself" (p. 70).

In "The Book of the Grotesque", we read: "The soldier got on the subject of war. The writer in fact, led him to that subject" (p. 21). In the same way, the narrator repeatedly leads his figures to topics most likely to arouse in them intense emotion. Sometimes George Willard fulfills this function for him, though in a significant number of stories, George is either a mere appendage to the epiphany of the story, or does not even appear on the scene.

Quite frequently, the narrator intensifies his protagonist's experience until he is forced to burst out with a character-revelatory emotional utterance.[39] In "Loneliness", Enoch Robinson begins his tale in a calm quiet voice. "He sat on a cot by the window with his head in his hand", and his voice filled George with sadness. After a while, "the old man arose from the cot and moved about the room" – the verbs describing his action still carry an attitude of calm sadness. As his story advances, "the trembling voice of the old man" fills with emotion until he reaches a point painful in the telling. Then: "The old man sprang to his feet and his voice shook with excitement" (p. 176). After a brief outburst, he "dropped into a chair", then again "sprang to his feet and ran to the window". At the peak of his emotional tension, Enoch lets his story gush out, and when the well is empty, he sinks back into his chair in the darkness. A similar process develops in Wash Williams' self-revelation in "Respectability".

[39] See John J. Mahoney, "An Analysis of *Winesburg, Ohio*", *Journal of Aesthetics and Art Criticism*, XV (December, 1956), 246-252.

Finally, the narrator directs his audience's responses by explicitly and implicitly judging the figures of his fancy. The old writer in "The Book of the Grotesque" got so full of his ideas about grotesques that he himself was in danger of becoming one. "He didn't, I suppose", the narrator remarks, "for the same reason he never published the book. It was the young thing inside him that saved the old man" (p. 25). Similarly, the narrator counters with the weight of his privileged opinion the hasty judgments his readers might otherwise form about those grotesques who may be less likable than others on first meeting. One sees this especially in the case of Wash Williams, the misogynist. "Wash Williams was a man of courage", we are told. "A thing had happened that had made him hate life, and he hated it wholeheartedly, with the abandon of a poet". And later: "There was something almost beautiful in the voice of Wash Williams, the hideous, telling his story of hate" (p. 125). Even hatred had made "a poet" of him.

Critics have consistently misunderstood "The Strength of God" because they overlook the narrator's heavy, judgmental voice controlling the text. Curtis Hartman in no way represents the perversion of religion, as Schevill and others continue to suggest. True, he had had little experience with women – a rather common trait among clergymen. He was sexually aroused during one period of his life, by Kate Swift, and sexual awakening in inexperienced men is hardly a rare phenomenon. Like Wash Williams, Curtis Hartman is a brave man. He undergoes intense interior anguish because he has loved his ministry and yet he feels so deeply attracted toward sexual pleasures. The narrator stresses again and again the depth of his commitment: "In reality he was much in earnest", he says. The minister has elected overt sin over what he considers hypocrisy. He is prepared to live openly in lust, to bear the brunt of public scorn, in order to be true to what he feels is deepest in himself at the moment – sexual passion. This passion, he feels, has replaced the passion to "go crying the word of God in the highways and byways of the town" (p. 148). The chip out of the picture window had "just nipped off the bare heel of the boy standing motionless and looking with rapt eyes into the face of Christ". Since the minister symbolically fuses with the boy in the window, the boy's heel represents symbolically his own Achilles heel. Because of the hole in the boy's heel, the minister ceases to look into the face of Christ and begins to peer through the hole in the window at the bare neck and shoulders of Kate Swift. When the minister cries in triumph that "God has manifested himself to me in the body of a woman" he expresses, not a perverted sense of religion, but as deep an insight into incarnational spirituality as one may gather from poems of Donne or Herbert.[40] For those who have experienced the vagaries of spiritual growth, Reverend Curtis Hartman's confusion is certainly comprehensible. When he says: "What I took to be a trial of my soul was only a preparation for a new and more beautiful fervor of the spirit", he is not deluding himself but formulating an insight.[41]

Reverend Curtis Hartman's smashing of the church window stands as one of the few violent acts in all the *Winesburg* stories. It is not the act of a hypocrite or a pervert, but of a sincere, zealous man. It is in some ways symbolic. For once a man has experienced the force of sexual temptations, he can never again return to the days of unknowing innocence. The entire window will have to be replaced and a new, more mature relationship with Christ established. At the same time, hope for such a renewed relationship emerges through the imagery of the window, for the naked woman kneeling by her bed "looked like the figure of the boy in the presence of Christ on the leaded window" (p. 155). Throughout this story, the narrator maintains a tone of serious involvement and respect toward Reverend Hartman. "What he wanted", the narrator stresses, "was to do the work of God quietly and earnestly" (p. 150).

Throughout *Winesburg*, then, one narrative voice controls the tone, mood, direction, and presentation of all the stories. In his role as a fictionalized *persona*, the narrator

(1) draws together the real and the imaginary, fuses the fictional world with the real;

(2) presents in depth, from a privileged point of view and without restrictions of chronology or limitations of space, the psychologically related "figures of his fancy";

(3) comments on his own art of presentation;

(4) cultivates the oral storyteller's familiarity and solidarity with his audience;

(5) balances a sympathetic presentation with the objectivity of ironic distance;

(6) generalizes the meaning of the lives which he presents; philosophizes

[40] In the previous story, the narrator had remarked that Tom Hard, the agnostic, had never seen "God manifesting himself in the little child" (p. 143), his daughter.

[41] Perhaps Christ's remark to Peter is relevant here. He knew that Peter would deny him and turn away from his vocation. At the Supper, He told Peter: "Simon, Satan had desired to have you so that he could sift you like wheat. But I have prayed for you...so that when you have been converted, you can strengthen your brethren" (Luke 22 : 31ff.). The sequel of that story was, in a sense, God manifesting himself in the crow of a cock.

on youth and old age, on city and country life, and on other matters connected with his stories;

(7) so penetrates beneath the surface of lives that his audience may know what his protagonist thinks, feels, and imagines;

(8) brings his grotesques into such a peak of excitement that self-revelation floods from their trembling lips; and

(9) directs his audience's response by explicitly and implicitly judging his characters as he tells their stories.

The narrator, then, by controlling the feeling and form of his work, is the chief source of unity in the cycle. The lives that flow past one another in story after story all live in his fancy. They touch one another and hardly touch one another at all. In Winesburg itself, they seem hardly to know one another; in the narrator's mind they are brothers. As citizens of Winesburg, they mumble, jerk their arms, hide themselves from view, struggle to express themselves, and fail. Only as citizens of the narrator's fancy do they succeed in communicating their inner selves to his listeners.

C. THE ASSOCIATIONAL TECHNIQUE

Does any further structural principle lie behind the order of the stories in the *Winesburg* volume? What function do such stories as the four parts of "Godliness" serve in the collection? What motivation lay behind Anderson's decision to relocate such stories as "The Philosopher" and "Drink"? Besides the halting development of George Willard as he grows through adolescence to maturity, do other thematic patterns or motif-rhythms thread through the stories to shape the collection into a cycle?

1. *Central Character?*

Some critics have called George Willard the central character of Anderson's book. Irving Howe, as was pointed out above (see footnote 23), called him "priest", "lost son", and mythic "reporter-messenger". But George is certainly not the "hero" of *Winesburg*. Although his name appears in all but six of the twenty-five stories,[42] he plays a major role in only seven.[43] In some stories he functions as a mild catalyst to someone

[42] "The Book of the Grotesque", "Paper Pills", and the four stories of the "Godliness" group.

[43] "Mother", "Nobody Knows", "The Teacher", "An Awakening", "Death", "Sophistication", and "Departure".

else's insight into himself,[44] and in others merely listens to someone's self-revelation.[45] In "The Strength of God" and "The Teacher", he unwittingly stimulates Kate Swift's self-revelatory insight, which in turn has an effect on Curtis Hartman's flash of discovery; he also listens, without comprehending, to the earnest words of his teacher and to the jubilant cries of the exultant minister. In several stories ("Adventure", "The Untold Lie") George's name appears, but George himself plays no role in the dynamics of the action.

George cannot, then, sustain such a title as "central character of *Winesburg*". Only the final story in the volume professes to be "concerning George Willard". He does share center stage, however, with other Winesburgers in about 64 out of 216 pages. At the same time, he does not even appear in stories that occupy 66 pages, and operates as catalyst or listener within 122 pages; finally, he appears, but in a minor role, in stories that fill about 90 pages.

Several characters feel that George embodies the spirit of Winesburg. Seth Richmonds thinks to himself, "George belongs to this town...but I'm going to get out of here" (p. 137). In the light of the final story Seth's remark turns ironically on its maker. In "'Queer'", too, Elmer Cowley sensed that George "belonged to the town, typified the town, represented in his person the spirit of the town" (p. 194). In an unorthodox, unheralded way, Elmer leaves that town – striking out both symbolically and actually at George Willard, who for him is a synecdoche for Winesburg, but who himself leaves the town he was thought to typify, and follows Elmer Cowley into the world.

2. *Departure*

The mythic departure of George Willard from the fictive village of Winesburg provides a clear thematic pattern which links stories together, and so will serve as a convenient example for the way in which the associational technique operates in the cycle. George's determination to leave Winesburg is played off against the opposing attitudes of his parents. Tom Willard wants his son to "wake up" and become a successful businessman like himself. Elizabeth Willard wants him to "dream". George does not opt for either attitude as an exclusive way of life. In the

[44] "Hands", "Respectability", "The Strength of God", "The Teacher", and "'Queer'".

[45] "The Philosopher", "Loneliness", "Drink".

final story of the cycle, "Departure", he first counts his money, and then is "carried away by his growing passion for dreams" (p. 247).

In "Mother", George tells Elizabeth Willard at a climactic moment of the story that he wants to leave Winesburg.[46] "I don't know where I shall go or what I shall do but I am going away" (p. 47). "I don't suppose it will be for a year or two", he adds, "but I've been thinking about it" (p. 48). If Phillips' chronology is accurate,[47] George's departure takes place about two and a half years after he makes this statement.

The Winesburg stories, however, occur in mythic time. They do not follow a predominantly chronological sequence. The central actions of "Paper Pills", "Adventure", and "Godliness (Parts I-IV)" do not seem to fit into the two and a half year span which prepares George Willard for departure. The final scene of "The Strength of God" and its sequel, "The Teacher", occur in January, as do the events of "An Awakening". But "Loneliness", though it is situated between "The Teacher" and "An Awakening", is set in October. "'Queer'" moves forward to November, but "The Untold Lie" brings the action back to October.

Anderson does not concern himself so much with logical or chronological sequence as with the psychologically proper season and setting. He even shrugs his shoulders, it seems, at the inconsistencies of age he assigns to his central figures. For him, the designations "old", "young", "seemed older than he was", or "seemed younger than she was" carry greater weight than exact specification of age. In "Death", for instance, Dr. Reefy encounters Elizabeth when she is "a tired gaunt old woman at forty-one", but when he embraces her and warms her with his love, he feels that "he held in his arms not the tired-out woman of forty-one but a lovely and innocent girl" (pp. 227-228). We are led to believe that Elizabeth died a "few months" (p. 228) after this scene. In the earlier story, "Mother", Elizabeth is forty-five! (see p. 39).

The same kinds of inconsistencies plague the age-specification of George Willard. In "The Thinker", when Seth Richmond is already eighteen (see p. 130), George is said to be older than Seth (see p. 134), but

[46] Also in this story, the unreality of Elizabeth Willard's dream of going away to the city to become an actress is played off against the comments of members of theatrical companies who would be passing through Winesburg. "'It's not like that', they said. 'It's as dull and uninteresting as this here. Nothing comes of it'" (p. 46).

[47] Phillips says the stories follow a roughly chronological order, beginning in June ("Hands") in 1895 or 1896 and ending in April about two and a half years later ("Departure"). He acknowledges that "Paper Pills", "Adventure", and the four parts of "Godliness" do not fit into this time span, and that the chronology is not strict. See "Sherwood Anderson's *Winesburg, Ohio*", p. 168.

in "Death", which supposedly takes place about a year after the events of "The Thinker", we are told that "one day in March in a year when her son George became eighteen" (p. 229), Elizabeth Willard died. Eighteen, for Anderson, seems to be the mythic age for the final year of adolescence. When George walks out with Helen in "Sophistication", he must be nineteen. And though the events to which the narrator flashes back could not have taken place more than a couple of months earlier, he introduces them with the faraway phrase, "once on a summer night when he was eighteen..." (p. 235). That was a time of late adolescence. On the page immediately preceding the above phrase, the narrator mythifies the entire period of youth and adolescence.

> There is a time in the life of every boy when he for the first time takes the backward view of life. Perhaps that is the moment when he crosses the line into manhood.... *The eighteen years he has lived* seem but a moment.... (p. 234; italics mine)

George's eighteen years – his mythic period of maturation – have finally ended. In "The Thinker", the adolescence of Seth Richmond held center stage; and even though the narrator remarked that George is older than Seth, he means essentially that George is closer to manhood than is Seth.

The order of the stories, then, follows no strict chronology. George does not accomplish his journey from Winesburg in the dimensions of time but in those of myth.[48] The motif of departure insinuates itself throughout the cycle, sometimes bulging up to the surface, at other times lying just beneath the surface of the words and actions of the tales.

In the "Godliness" stories, David Hardy (in Part II) tries to run away from home but loses his way and, still too young and inexperienced for such a venture, is brought back to his father's house. In "Terror" (Part IV), however, after he has felled Jesse with a rock from his sling, David suddenly matures: "I will myself be a man", he proclaims, "and go into the world" (p. 102).

In "Adventure", Ned Currie, who "like George Willard, was employed on the *Winesburg Eagle*" (p. 112), leaves town to "take up his new life in the city" (p. 113). Seth Richmond too, in "The Thinker" makes a decision to leave Winesburg; the terms of his decision echo George's remarks to

[48] George's journey to the city, lasting, as it does, over two and a half years, reminds one of the journey motif in St. Luke's Gospel. Throughout his public life, Christ (in St. Luke's account) is constantly "going to Jerusalem", though he arrives only once, as George Willard arrives at maturity only once. (See Luke 9 : 51.)

his mother earlier in the volume. "I'll get out of here", Seth tells himself (p. 136). And to Helen White: "I'm going to get out of town. I don't know what I'll do, but I'm going to get out of here and go to work" (p. 138). Since the narrator brings Seth into later stories ("An Awakening" and "Sophistication"), we may assume that the "tomorrow" of his original intent faded gradually into a "some day", and that the decision itself dissolved into a mere velleity.

"'Queer'" tells of Elmer Cowley's flight from Winesburg to the city where, he hopes, everything will be different. "I will get out of here, run away from home" (p. 199), he tells himself, in accents that recall the first wild dash of the child David Hardy more than the purposeful decision of an adult. In Cleveland, he dreams, he will "get work in some shop and become friends with the other workmen" and so become "indistinguishable" (p. 199). The mode of his departure, however, and his inability to comprehend the nature of his queerness, leave the reader little hope that his venture into the world will be successful. Elmer, one feels, wears on his person the coat of arms of Winesburg grotesquerie.

The last three stories of the volume deepen the mythic dimensions of the departure motif. The money that Elizabeth Willard has hidden in a hole near her bed was given her by her father to allow her to leave Winesburg. Since she had not taken this means of "release", she struggles with fading consciousness, trying to regain enough clarity of mind to tell her son about the hidden money so that he might go away. But the money, unused like Elizabeth herself, remains buried in a hole in the wall near the bed.

After his mother's death, George "definitely decided he would make a change in his life, that he would leave Winesburg. 'I will go to some city. Perhaps I can get a job on some newspaper', he thought" (p. 230). Elizabeth died in March in the year when her son became eighteen – that is, in the final year of George's passage from boyhood into manhood.

"Sophistication" equates, in the clearest terms of any story in the collection, the notions of departure and of maturity. "George Willard... was fast growing into manhood", the narrator tells us with one breath, and in the next, "He was about to leave Winesburg to go away to some city where he hoped to get work on a city newspaper and he felt grown up" (p. 234). In that summer "when he was eighteen" (that is, a last-stage adolescent), George tells Helen White, "I've not yet gone away but I'm growing up" (p. 236); that is, mythically, I am going away, but am not yet gone, or, I am growing up but am not yet grown up. Growing up and going away from Winesburg – the village of fragmented lives frozen in attitudes of adolescence – are identical processes.[49]

References to George as "young man" instead of "boy" increase in the final three stories of the cycle. "Departure" is couched in terms that point up the symbolic significances of earlier stories. George summarizes in his person the heart of Winesburg during its bleak and its green seasons.

> All through his boyhood and young manhood George Willard had been in the habit of walking on Trunion Pike. He had been in the midst of the great open place on winter nights when it was covered with snow and only the moon looked down on him; he had been there in the fall when bleak winds blew and on summer evenings when the air vibrated with the song of insects. On the April morning he wanted to go there again, to walk again in the silence. (p. 245)

Trunion (true + union) Pike had once been the center of Winesburg (see p. 210). George's visiting it again in the springtime of his departure is a signal from the narrator that George does not reject Winesburg, but consciously tries to get in touch again with its center before leaving.

Other significant details flash out at the reader from the text. George now has become taller than his father – has surpassed his father, as Bayard Sartoris in *The Unvanquished* grows to be taller than his father, to perform morally courageous deeds which go beyond his father's heroics. In Winesburg, too, "more than a dozen people waited about" to see George off. A woman who had never paid any attention to George before comes up to shake his hand, and "in two words voiced what everyone felt. 'Good luck'" (p. 246). Tom Little, the train conductor, who "had seen a thousand George Willards go out of their towns to the city" (p. 246) looks on without comment. George counts his money in the train, looks up, and is surprised to see Winesburg stilll outside his window. He lets his mind wander to "little things" – minor characters performing insignificant actions – and closes his eyes, as if Winesburg were only an apparition, a figment of imagination like the town of Oz. When he opens his eyes again, "the town of Winesburg had disappeared" (p. 247).

Though George himself initiates his journey from Winesburg in "Mother" when he intimates that "something father said makes it sure that I shall have to go away" (p. 48), the narrator must already be aware of the necessity of George's journey even in "The Book of the Grotesque". The old writer has escaped being a grotesque because of the "young thing" in him. George, in "Sophistication", escapes becoming a grotesque because of the old thing in him:

49 *Cf.* also the narrator's brief exposé on a boy's crossing the line into manhood, pp. 234-235.

In youth there are always two forces fighting in people. The warm unthinking little animal struggles against the thing that reflects and remembers, and the older, the more sophisticated thing had possession of George Willard. (p. 240)

George and the old writer stand in complementary contrast: the old man must learn (as George must later learn) to preserve the young thing in him; the adolescent must grow out of the mode of existence of a "warm unthinking little animal" by the aid of the "thing that reflects and remembers". Critics have called the "young thing" in the old writer "creative imagination". I would say the young thing is love, the force that surrounds even the distorted figures in the old writer's and the narrator's fancies with a sympathetic warmth. The growth in George of this mature love makes his departure from Winesburg imperative.

George Willard first experiences in "Sophistication" a love which bridges the gap separating two isolated individuals. He and Helen share the same mood as, in the darkness, they climb the hill to the Fair Ground. "In the mind of each was the same thought. 'I have come to this lonely place and here is this other', was the substance of the thing felt" (p. 241).

Anderson does not let pass unnoticed his intention of redirecting the end of his cycle toward its beginning. George's experience of love, of a warm opening up of himself to other human beings, is not limited to his communion with Helen White. In a generalizing passage, the narrator puts a sympathetic perspective on the people of his fictive town of Winesburg:

There is something memorable in the experience to be had by going into a fair ground that stands at the edge of a Middle Western town on a night after the annual fair has been held.... The place has been filled to overflowing with life...and now it is night and the life has all gone away. (p. 240)

One stands silently in the night, reflecting on "the meaninglessness of life". Still, the narrator continues, "if the people of the town are his people, one loves life so intensely that tears come into the eyes" (p. 241).

George and Helen were sitting under the roof of the grandstand. "George began to think of the people in the town where he had always lived with something like reverence. He had reverence for Helen. He wanted to love and to be loved by her..." (p. 241). In "An Awakening", George creates his own community of imaginary people. But here, he loves a community he has not created, but who may become in time "figures of his fancy" – figures similar to those who make the old writer whimper like a small dog; figures similar to those with whom the narrator chose to fill his own book of the grotesque.

And so George's background, even before he leaves Winesburg, compares to that of the old writer. George's "old thing" is the writer's "young thing": reflective love. But the very fact that George will eventually develop a reflective selfless love indicates that he will soon be out of place in a land of fragmented lives and frustrated dreams. From the beginning, he had to leave Winesburg.

3. *Adventure*

Besides the cumulative motif of George Willard's mythic departure, the *Winesburg* stories also develop an adventure motif. It begins with Elizabeth Willard's unsteady movement down the papered halls of the Willard House toward her son's room. She halts to kneel at George's door, hears him mumbling (supposedly) to himself, and then moves weakly back toward her own room. But she overhears Tom's advice to his son to "wake up", and then imagines herself, styled as a Lady Macbeth, descending the stairway to kill her husband with "long wicked scissors in her hand" (p. 47). When George comes to her room, they face one another in embarrassed silence and speak in halting, vague phrases. The entire episode is prefaced with a typically bare Andersonian introductory sentence: "One evening in July...Elizabeth Willard had an adventure" (p. 42).

The term "adventure" serves Anderson in a variety of contexts, most of which share the following characteristics: (1) the situation, most generally, deals with the contact of an isolated Winesburger with one or more members of the town; (2) most often, the action undertaken by the isolated Winesburger is an attempt to transcend the limits of his own self-containment; (3) often, the action undertaken perverts or provides a substitute for the acts of loving and being loved, of understanding and being understood, of communing.

Dr. Parcival's "adventure" centered about this refusal to respond to a call for his medical assistance to aid a small girl who had been run over in Main Street. In "Nobody Knows", George Willard "set forth upon an adventure" – his first sex experience with a girl he does not know well, does not love, and toward whom he does not wish to be responsible. Louise Bentley, during her first winter in Winesburg, "had an adventure that gave a new impulse to her desire to break down the wall that she thought stood between her and John Hardy" (p. 92). She "crept into the hall and down the stairs into a closet-like room that opened off the parlor" (p. 93). There, she witnessed the lovemaking of Mary Hardy and her boyfriend. Her own desire to love and to be loved was excited by what she saw, but it goes unfulfilled.

In "Terror", Louise's son David "had an adventure that changed the whole current of his life and sent him out of his quiet corner into the world" (p. 97). David's adventure provides the basis for a new dimension to the motif. David asserts himself against the overpowering influence of Jesse's broken dream, and by so doing completely inverts the alignment of values which Jesse had established. Jesse's being hit with a stone from David's sling places him instead in the role of Goliath, the felled giant. This adventure sends David out into the world: "now", he says, "I will myself be a man and go into the world" (p. 102). The adventure motif, then, is coupled with departure.

Alice Hindman's story is entitled "Adventure". Alice had experienced deep communion and love with Ned Currie before Ned left for Cleveland. Ned had respected her enough not to drag her along as his mistress. Ned never returned, but the entire experience of loving and being loved seemed to satisfy Alice for nine years, until the remarriage of her mother and her own new involvement in the Winesburg Methodist Church forced her again to think of other people, of love, of communion. She joined the church, the narrator tells us, "because she had become frightened by the loneliness of her position in life" (p. 117).

For the next two years, Alice manages to ward off proximate intimacies with men. Still, she "wanted to be loved, to have something answer the call that was growing louder and louder within her" (p. 119). The call does not summon her to sexual fulfillment, but to love, to communion. "And then one night when it rained Alice had an adventure" (p. 119). She runs through the rain, seeking "to find some other lonely human and embrace him" (p. 118). But her effort is frustrated. The man she is running toward is old and deaf. Even the rain on her body does not have the renewing and creative effect she had hoped. She crawls back to her room, "turning her face to the wall", and letting the fact "that many people must live and die alone, even in Winesburg", (p. 120) soak into her.

Alice's "adventure" best exemplifies the generalities of that motif as it appears in *Winesburg*: the attempt to establish contact with another Winesburger, to transcend one's self-containment and isolation; and, since the act emerges from a soul starved for loving and being loved, the setting up of such an attempt (unconsciously) as a substitute for true communion.

Anderson makes explicit his "adventure" motif in five stories before "Adventure" and in five stories after it. In some of the stories "adventure" refers primarily to sexual encounter of one kind or another. In "Terror", however, the "adventure" motif begins to mingle with the "departure" motif. Seth Richmond, when he was sixteen, went on an adventure (p. 131) with two other boys: they ran away from home for about a week, hopping an empty freight car to a town about forty miles away. Kate Swift in "The Teacher" – a woman who had traveled – "had been very adventurous".[50] Tom Foster's trip out of Cincinnati had been "a great adventure for the boy" (p. 211). In "Death", Elizabeth Willard is described as having tried to be "a real adventurer in life" (p. 224). She tells Dr. Reefy:

> I went out Trunion Pike a mile or more and then turned into a side road.... I wanted to go at a terrible speed, to drive on and on forever. I wanted to get out of town, out of my clothes, out of my marriage, out of my body, out of everything.... I wanted to run away from everything but I wanted to run towards something too. (p. 227)

In the final story, George leaves Winesburg to go "meet the adventure of life" (p. 246). The departure motif fuses into one with the adventure motif. At the same time, the phrase "adventure of life" spreads open its arms to embrace every contact with another human being, every attempt at significant communication, every gesture toward understanding and love.

4. *Dream*

A third motif, connected with both the "adventure" and the "departure" motifs, runs through these stories: the "dream" motif. Anderson places his clues to the importance of dreams in *Winesburg*, at the beginning and at the end of the volume. At the inception of the fictional idea of parading a varied, yet related group of characters before the reading public, Anderson's narrator remarks: "In the bed the writer had a dream that was not a dream. As he grew somewhat sleepy but was still conscious, figures began to appear before his eyes" (p. 23). In the book that follows – imaginative literature, a dream that is not a dream – grotesques similar to those that passed before the eyes of the old writer in his bed do, in fact, parade before the reader. They are all figures who stand in some relationship also to George Willard.

In the final paragraph of the last story of the cycle, the narrator tells us

[50] For Kate, however, "adventure" has the further connotation of passionately desiring to struggle out of oneself.

that George experienced a "growing passion for dreams", and that his life in Winesburg "had become but a background on which to paint the dreams of his manhood" (p. 247). As he sits in the train, George thinks of "little things" – simple actions of simple people. These form the background, a flushed canvas, for the painting of his manhood. He has lived through the half-fulfilled and frustrated dreams of his youth. Now he must take the brush in hand and paint the dreams of his manhood. George vaguely planned to become a writer. The dreams of his manhood, like those of the old writer, will be dreams that are not dreams, figures of fancy not unlike those with which the narrator (and Anderson) have filled their book.

Throughout the book, the people of Winesburg struggle to cultivate or to destroy George's penchant for dreaming. Often enough, they themselves speak "as one lost in a dream" (p. 30). Wing Biddlebaum, even when he was Adolph Meyers, used to sit until dusk, "lost in a kind of dream", talking to his students. The caress of his hands, the narrator informs us, was part of his effort "to carry a dream into the young minds" (p. 32). The boys responded "and they began also to dream". With cruel, even tragic irony, however, the dream itself ensnares Adolph Meyers. For a half-witted boy imagined "unspeakable things" in his bed at night and "went forth to tell his dreams as facts" the next morning. From the beatings that followed that day, Wing Biddlebaum became a grotesque – just one of the broken figures in someone else's dream.

Despite his tragic failure to implement the dreams of his own life, Wing chides George because he is "afraid of dreams". The picture he verbally paints for George of clean-limbed young men, during an imagined pastoral golden age, coming to the old man sitting beneath a tree, emerged "out of a dream". His message, hammered home again and again, remains: "You must begin to dream" (p. 30).

George's mother also wants to encourage him to dream but never learns to speak clearly with him. She feels a "deep unexpressed bond of sympathy" for her son which is "based on a girlhood dream that had long ago died" (p. 40). Her husband's advice directly counters the advice Elizabeth would have given her son. Tom repeats over and over "you've got to wake up...you'll wake up...you'll have to wake up" (p. 44). Tom wants his son to succeed; Elizabeth begs God not to let George "become smart and successful" but to "look at people and think" (p. 48).

The dream motif courses strongly through the four "Godliness" stories, providing in the Bentley family a counterpoint to the Williards. Jesse's dreams live in his conscious fancy, where he pictured himself "living in old times and among old peoples" (p. 70). Jesse saw the rich land near Wine Creek as "a place peopled by his fancy with a new race of men sprung from himself". His dream is a greedy dream: "The greedy thing in him wanted to make money faster than it could be made by tilling the land" (p. 81). As an imaginative child, Jesse was always waiting for God to signal approval from the clouds. Jesse's first semi-tragic episode with David occurs because he let "his dreams take entire possession of him" (p. 84). During this scene, before the climactic moment, David is wandering among the bushes, laughing at the little animals and clapping and yelling "wake up, little animal" (p. 85). But Jesse does not wake from his "dream" until David lies unconscious at the foot of a tree.

In "Respectability", Wash Williams sets himself up as the disillusioner. "Already you may be having dreams in your head", he tells George. "I want to destroy them" (p. 125). Wash has seen George walking out on evenings with Belle Carpenter. Perhaps Wash envisions what George cannot, until after "An Awakening", see: that Belle is merely using him to arouse the jealousy of Ed Handby. So Wash tells him the story of his marriage and the ugly scene which turned him against all women forever.

"Loneliness" and "An Awakening" interact as two presentations of harsh awakenings from a dream world. In his room on Washington Square, Enoch Robinson lives among people of his own making, people put together from pieces of men and women he had seen and who had appealed to him. Enoch's privately peopled world crumbles under the loving concern, the sympathy and understanding, of a girl who visits him. Enoch both wanted her to understand him, and at the same time felt deathly afraid that she would. If she understood, he felt, she would reject him as a lunatic. In his room, Enoch felt immeasurably big, in control. He talked aloud to the two dozen shadow people "with an absurd air of importance...giving instructions, making comments on life" (p. 173). When the woman entered the room, he seemed less important, less big. So he tried to drive her away. In so doing, however, he drove away also the people of his fancy.

In "An Awakening", George Willard also feels big, begins to talk aloud, fancies himself in several roles. "As a soldier he pictured himself as an inspector, passing before a long line of men who stood at attention" (p. 183). He feels of immense importance, as Enoch did. "Everything must be in order", he tells his men. In the night, George "felt unutterably big" (p. 185). George convinces himself, as he walks with Belle, that she is about to surrender to him. But George's dream, which the story of Wash Williams in "Respectability" had been unable to destroy, crumbles under the swift, strong hands of Ed Handby, and the double-dealing of Belle Carpenter. As he sneaks home, utterly humiliated and reduced in size, the neighborhood through which he had passed earlier with magnificent thoughts about brotherly love and universal order, "now seemed to him utterly squalid and commonplace" (p. 189). And, needless to say, the ranked and rowed army of his fancy had vanished.

For Tom Foster in "Drink", intoxication serves as a substitute dream state. "The drunken boy talked of Helen White and said he had been with her on the shore of a sea and had made love to her" (p. 218). George, who should have been able to understand such talk, confuses dream with reality. "You quit that", he keeps telling Tom. "You haven't been with her" (p. 219). Tom feels his experience, however, is valid; he has suffered, experienced, "learned things", but has done so without hurting anyone else, as one can do only in dreams and in solitary drunkenness.

"Death" helps to bind the dream-motif to the adventure motif. In this story, "adventure" is at first equated with passionate love: Elizabeth's thoughts "ran away to her girlhood with its passionate longing for adventure and she remembered the arms of men that had held her when adventure was a possible thing for her" (p. 223). Now, a "tired gaunt old woman at forty-one", her conversations with Dr. Reefy relumed her girlhood desires, her "dream, half-dead", that still burned within her. Her dream was a "dream of release" – release from being walled up inside herself. Her imprisonment in the Willard House in Winesburg only emphasized her struggle to get out of herself. She never gave up "her dream of release", "that release that after all came to her but twice in her life, in the moments when her lovers, Death and Doctor Reefy, held her in their arms" (p. 232).

Just as departure into death comprises the rarest adventure any human being undergoes, so too does departure into the adventure of life present the human being with a truly invigorating challenge. Anderson speaks of both as "dreams of release". In "Departure", George frees himself from the cramping effects of his own home town by projecting himself into the future. His dreams do not turn back to Winesburg; his ideals do not direct him toward the community of adolescents and fragmented persons that mill around on Main Street or sit restlessly by a window in their room looking out on the world. His dreams release him from the small town of adolescence and grotesquerie. They are "dreams of his manhood" (p. 247).[51]

51 Other references to dreams in the cycle can be found on pp. 37, 38, 52, 79, 81, 88, 93, 115, 129, 145, 148, and 165.

5. *Hungering*

Most of the inhabitants of Winesburg, whose buried lives the narrator excavates and displays, have tremendous difficulty communicating with one another. Their inability to communicate shows up in their choice of housing, their gestures, their speech patterns. They live in isolated houses on the edge of ravines, or on some unused road leading off of Trunion Pike; or they sit alone in cramped quarters on the second floors of stores and shops, staring through windows onto the meager life of Main Street.

Their stiffened gestures sometimes relax in the evening when they creep forth to experiment with communication or go on an adventure. They are a hungry lot – not starving for food, but hungry for affection, fulfillment, loving and being loved.

Wing Biddlebaum, for instance, "hungered for the presence of the boy, who was the medium through which he expressed his love of man", and "the hunger became again a part of his loneliness and his waiting" (p. 33). Wing's action at the end of the story, his picking bread crumbs from the floor and carrying them rapidly to his mouth, is a pathetically ironic comment on the meager fulfillment allowed to his great hunger. Critics have often so lost themselves in praise of Anderson's two mixed and inadequate similes ("like a priest engaged in some service of his church", and "might well have been mistaken for the fingers of a devotee going swiftly through decade after decade of his rosary") that they have failed to see the obvious relevance to hungering of eating bread crumbs. Having been denied the joy of sharing the feast of human communion, like the Canaanite woman in St. Mark's Gospel (7:24-30), Wing Biddlebaum must content himself with the crumbs from the banquet table.

Jesse Bentley had a great "indefinable hunger within" which made him "more and more silent before people" (p. 68). Jesse hungered for two things: he wanted to be a man of God and a leader among men of God, and he wanted to make money faster than it could be made by tilling the land (see pp. 80-81). Jesse's daughter Louise wanted to get away from the Bentley farm, to "go forth into the world" (which for her, ironically, is Winesburg itself!). She hungered to live among men and women happily and freely, "giving and taking friendship and affection" (p. 88). In the Hardy household, she is cut off, isolated. She hungers for communion with another human being. John Hardy, however, interprets her approach to him as mere desire for sex. And "so anxious was she to achieve something else that she made no resistance". Even in the arms of her husband, who never seemed to understand his wife's need for communing on a level deeper than physical contact, Louise's "vague and intangible hunger... was still unsatisfied" (p. 96).

The hunger motif receives a new twist in "Death". The lover in that story is Death, personified in Elizabeth's mind sometimes as "a strong black-haired youth running over hills", and sometimes as "a stern quiet man marked and scarred by the business of living" (p. 228), personified, that is, sometimes as that passionate lover of Elisabeth's youth, and sometimes as a Dr. Reefy figure. "The sick woman spent the last few months of her life hungering for death" (p. 228), hungering for the arms of a true lover.

Through Anderson's associational technique, the themes and motifs of departure, adventure, dream, and hungering develop as they recur in different contexts. Varied repetitions of situations, actions, and words turn the narrative back on itself. The telling of a new story seems to recall to the narrator certain similarities with a previously told tale. One character is beset with problems not altogether different from those of other fictive figures of the narrator's fancy. Anderson's patterning of motifs, then, is asymmetrical, non-mathematical. It follows the rhythms of association in the narrator's creative consciousness.

D. THE CYCLIC DEVELOPMENT OF SYMBOLISM

Anderson's associational technique affects not only his cyclic patterning of themes and motifs, but also his arrangement of symbols and other tropes. Realistic objects such as fire, wind, rooms, and hands take on added meanings as they recur in new contexts. They deepen and broaden their poetic function as the cycle progresses. A detailed study of Anderson's cyclic method of handling symbols will help us to understand how the dynamic pattern of recurrent development affects every constituent of a short story cycle.

1. *Fire and Wind*

Throughout the cycle, Anderson employs "fire" and "wind" – often as complements – to indicate human passion, warmth, worth (fire) on the one hand, and on the other the breath of love (wind) which intensifies that worth, draws out the warmth, and leads to fulfillment of the passionately intense desire for communion. Elizabeth Willard's disease "had taken the fire out of her figure" (p. 39) but when she thought of her son "her eyes glowed" (p. 40). When her anxious love for her boy's welfare rises in her, the "feeble blaze of life that remained in her body was blown into a flame" (p. 42). Later, in "Death", Dr. Reefy tells her "Love is like a wind stirring the grass beneath trees on a black night" (p. 223). And when he held her in his arms, something young blew to life within her.

In the "Godliness" stories, Jesse's eagerness to become a second Abraham and his intense greed to possess all the land of Wine Creek Valley is described as the "passionate burning thing in his nature" which "flamed up" within him (p. 68). The trope takes a different turn in Jesse's daughter Louise, who once "deliberately set fire to the house" (p. 74) in her desperate attempt to get out of herself, to burn up her prison walls, to have her passion for life recognized.

Joe Welling, in "A Man of Ideas", offers a further perspective on fire.

> Let's take decay. Now what is decay? It's fire. It burns up wood and other things. You never thought of that? Of course not. This sidewalk here and this feed store, the trees down the street there – they're all on fire. They're burning up. Decay you see is always going on. It don't stop.... The world is on fire. Start your pieces in the paper that way. Just say in big letters "The World Is On Fire". That will make 'em look up. (p. 106)

Joe himself resembles a dancing flame, which the King males try to quench, but they cannot snuff his spark. Joe's brief exposé on fire as decay leads the reader to the heart of the Winesburg mystery: the whole town is on fire in a two-fold sense – the pieces of human beings we meet in the stories show signs, most often, of possessing real worth, of being capable at one time of warm human relations, of possessing a passion for life. On the other hand, most of the Winesburgers are burning out in Joe Welling's sense: either their lives have "fallen into the yellow leaf", or they themselves have set their foot firmly in the pathway of inner decay.

In "The Strength of God", Anderson penetrates deeper into the billowing symbol of fire. Curtis Hartman has always been an earnest minister, but he begins to wonder "if the flame of the spirit really burned in him" (p. 148). In the bell tower of the church, his passion for Kate Swift grows until, determined not to be a hypocrite, he decides to yield openly to his lust. In the cold room of the bell tower that January night, "there was no fire" (p. 153) except the fire coursing through his veins. But the sight of the "woman of sin" praying, relumes the burnt out flame of spirit, and the Reverend Hartman's eyes glowed anew as he proclaimed his deliverance to George Willard.

In "The Teacher", George lights a fire in the woods and leaves it burning as he talks to an absent Kate Swift about his love for her. When he arrives home, he builds "a fire in the stove and [lies] down on top of the bed", where he yields himself to his lustful thoughts about Kate Swift and, intermittently, about Helen White. At the same time, we are told, "Kate Swift's mind was ablaze with thoughts of George Willard", in whom, she reasoned consciously, "she had recognized the spark of genius and wanted to blow on the spark" (p. 163). In the dim light of their encounter "her eyes blazed", but a sudden rigidity halts the process of their lovemaking. George at home again "blew out the lamp by the window". As if to assure the readers that his earlier talk of the fire in the woods and in the stove really had symbolic overtones, the narrator continues: "The fire in the stove had gone out and he had to undress in the cold. When he got into bed the sheets were like blankets of dry snow" (p. 165).

In several tales, George Willard is depicted as "afire with curiosity" about the stories to be told him by Wash Williams and Elmer Cowley. Wash himself possesses a lurid light which burns in his eyes. In "Drink", Tom Foster's love for Helen White emerged in his subconscious as fire. As he walks through the streets he mumbles to himself "that Helen White was a flame dancing in the air..." Then he said that "she was a wind, a strong terrible wind, coming out of the darkness of a stormy sea..." (p. 216). Helen White in "Sophistication", however, is "afire with eagerness" to see George Willard. As they walk in the Fair Ground, they see a fire in the distance. "When the wind blew the little flames of the fire danced crazily about" (p. 242). In the next instance, as the "wind whispered among the dry corn blades", George and Helen, like the little flames blown by the wind of their mutual affection, begin to dance crazily about, playing "like two splendid young things in a young world" (p. 242).

2. *Setting*

Besides the rather submerged symbolism of fire and wind, Anderson makes more consistent use of the symbolism of setting and gesture. Often enough, the room of a Winesburger reinforces by its location and interior arrangement the character of its inhabitant. The chief furnishings of most of the rooms (a window, a chair, and a bed) indicate the only kind of existence open to its inmate. On the bed (or in a chair) by the window, he lies (or sits) and dreams. Occasionally, someone comes in through his door, into the range of his friendship, into a position which makes communication almost a possibility. Usually, however, he stares out of his window, an observer of the life outside. He sits or lies down, caught in a debilitating stasis.

The old writer in "The Book of the Grotesque" has the old carpenter raise his bed so he can look out of the window. All of his most intense activity – his day-dreaming and thinking – takes place on his bed. But the old writer does not become a grotesque, because the door of his room is open, because he listens to the stories and sorrows of other people and sympathizes with them, because he recalls with love those he has known in the past, because he listens to the voices of the figures of his fancy and writes down the impressions they make on him.

Wing Biddlebaum stands on "the half-decayed veranda of a small frame house that stood near the edge of a ravine near the town of Winesburg, Ohio" (p. 27). Dr. Reefy "sat all day in his empty office close by a window that was covered with cobwebs. He never opened the window" (p. 35). Elizabeth Willard "sat by a window" in her room looking out over a small frame building into Main Street (p. 41). Her room, we are told, was "tucked away in a corner of the old Willard House". She spends most of her time either "in her bed" where "the little fears that had visited her had become giants" (p. 43), or in her chair by the window. At the end of her interview with her son, he steps "awkwardly out of the room" (p. 48) and closes the door which, for an instant, had been open for halting communication.

Dr. Parcival lives in a rented room above a shoe repair shop at the end of Main Street. Only George Willard enters this room. Usually, Dr. Parcival huddles there alone in his unreasoning fear that the people of Winesburg are coming to crucify him.

Anderson seems to employ this symbolism of setting to help explain how, in his "new looseness" of form, he can insert four stories about Jesse Bentley into the middle of the *Winesburg* volume. Jesse's farmhouse, he tells us, "was in reality not one house but a cluster of houses joined together in a rather haphazard manner. Inside, the place was full of surprises" (p. 63). Also, by mentioning Jesse's dream of peopling the land with figures of his fancy, he ties the "Godliness" block to the rest of the book – for Winesburg too is a land peopled with figures of the narrator's (and ultimately, of Anderson's) fancy.

The dual personality of Louise Bentley expresses itself also through the narrator's symbolic treatment of houses and rooms. Louise once "delberately set fire to the house, and would see no one". Now, she lives "in a brick house on Elm Street in Winesburg" (p. 87). Her first contact with secret passion comes in the "closet-like room" in which Mary Hardy and her beau laugh and play with one another. In the next story, her son David goes "out of his quiet corner into the world" (p. 97).

The upshot of Alice Hindman's effort to burst out of her self-confinement was that she crawled on hands and knees back into her house. "When she got to her own room she bolted the door and drew her dressing table across the doorway" (p. 120), while "the fact that many people must live and die alone, even in Winesburg" (p. 120) begins to force its truth upon her.

In the context of Seth Richmond's limited importance in Winesburg, Anderson devotes a disproportionate amount of space in "The Thinker" to details of the Richmond house: "at one time the show place of the town, but when young Seth lived there its glory had become somewhat dimmed... The Richmond place was in a little valley far out at the end of Main Street." More important symbolically is the remark that Seth's mother never came into Seth's room after he had reached fifteen – which means, of course, that the door to communication between them had been closed by his silent and secret adolescence.

In "The Strength of God", the narrator says that the Presbyterian Church, physically and socially, "held itself somewhat aloof from the other churches" (p. 147). Curtis Hartman, who also holds himself aloof, goes to "a little room called a study in the bell tower of the church" to pray. The single window made of little leaded panes with a design showing Christ laying his hand upon the head of a child, corresponds to the Reverend Curtis Hartman's single-minded approach to life until that time. He punches a hole in that window through the heel of the little boy, and from his secret corner, peers down on Kate Swift next door. Kate's kneeling form, later in the story, is said to resemble the boy in the window's picture. Probably before that time, Curtis Hartman had considered himself to be that boy whom Christ loved and was leading. In a flash, he sees that he is not unlike Kate Swift, and yet Kate Swift, he thinks, has entered into his "window", has assumed a relation to Christ he once thought exclusively his own, while he was giving himself over to lustful thoughts. His smashing of the window shows he is ready for "a new and more beuatiful fervor of spirit" (p. 155).

In his own room, George Willard in "The Teacher" rolls on his bed during the afternoon hugging his pillow and entertaining lustful thoughts while the fire burns in his stove. At night, the fire now having gone out in the stove, he lies on his bed trying to understand what he missed in his two encounters with Kate Swift.

The most important presentation of room symbolism in the *Winesburg* stories, so striking that it sends one immediately to the other tales in the collection to see how the method applies in other cases, is the room symbolism of "Loneliness". The room in which Enoch Robinson lived in New York "was long and narrow like a hallway". The narrator takes special pains to make his readers notice the details of this room which faced Washington Square: "It is important to get that fixed in your mind. The story of Enoch is in fact the story of a room almost more than it is the story of a man" (p. 168).

Enoch, an artist, begins to invent his own people because he finds great difficulty in communicating satisfactorily with his artist friends who speak about form and technique while he notices only the hidden lives beneath the surface of paintings. A dark spot beside the road in one of his paintings represents for Enoch a clump of elder trees in which a woman is hidden. She has been thrown from a horse; she is hurt and suffering, but utters no sound. Enoch, the "child-man" did not want friends, but "people of his own mind, people with whom he could really talk, people he could harangue and scold by the hour, servants, you see, to his fancy" (p. 171). Among such people, Enoch could be self-confident and bold. "He was like a writer busy among the figures of his brain, a kind of tiny, blue-eyed king he was, in a six-dollar room facing Washington Square in the city of New York" (p. 171).

His people did not satisfy him completely, however. "He began to get lonely and wanted to touch actual flesh-and-bone people with his hands." So he got married. "He was happy and satisfied to go on making his living in the advertising place [a bit of autobiography?] until something happened" (p. 173). He separated from his wife and went back to the room facing Washington Square. For a while he was happy. But "a woman whom Enoch began to half-love came into the room. She was too big for the room" (p. 176). He wanted to touch and kiss her; he wanted her to understand, but at the same time couldn't let her understand. His egotism, however, eventually triumphed over his expansive love. He sent the woman out of the room and locked the door. But his people went with her. Now, in a room in the mythic town of Winesburg, where Enoch has become "an obscure, jerky little figure, bobbing up and down on the streets...at evening when the sun was going down", he sits in his own room in the Heffner block. George Willard has come in and gone out through the door. Enoch whimpers: "It was warm and friendly in my room but now I'm all alone" (p. 178). This is a remark applicable to most Winesburgers. Especially in their youth, many of them are warm and friendly in their rooms. But they harden into jerky little obscure figures in a cold room, while outside the October rain drizzles on the muddy streets.

Elmer Cowley has much in common with Enoch Robinson. He appears before the reader for the first time in a symbolic room setting. He peers through a dirty window from his seat "on a box in the rough board shed that stuck like a burr on the rear of Cowley & Son's store in Winesburg" (p. 190). Ray Pearson's tumble-down marriage is echoed by his "tumble-down frame house beside a creek at the back end of the Wills farm" (p. 202). Yet he has spent some pleasant evenings with his children in the tumble-down house by the creek, and his experience with Hal sends him home a less bitter man than he was when the story began. After his mother's death, George "went into his own room and closed the door", that is, he withdrew into himself, trying to let the notion of death penetrate his consciousness.

In contrast to the scenes of frustrated communion, which often take place in small rooms, Anderson's narrator sets moments of partial communication usually in large open places. Wing Biddlebaum and George talk on a grassy bank in the fields on a summer afternoon; Hal Winter and Ray Pearson face each other for one terrific and intense moment of communication in a "big empty field with the quiet corn stocks standing in rows behind them and the red and yellow hills in the distance" (p. 205). The brief communion between Dr. Reefy and Elizabeth Willard takes place in Dr. Reefy's office which "was as large as a barn" (p. 220). Wash Williams tells his story sitting on the train rails which lead out of town. George and Helen commune on the hill outside of town and near the Fair Ground's grandstand.

3. *Gesture*

The most significant symbolic gesture in *Winesburg*, a gesture repeated frequently and at critical moments of attempted communication,[52] is the gesture of reaching out one's hands to touch or grasp another human being. Hands have a symbolic significance in every one of the *Winesburg* stories. Even when the actual word "hands" does not appear, their movement still expresses a desire to communicate. In "The Book of the Grotesque", for instance, though the word "hands" does not occur, the old writer at his desk pours out his love and sympathy for the people of his imagination through the jerky movements of his hands directing his pencil across the paper.

Wing Biddlebaum's manual gestures obviously carry with them signific-

[52] I have counted about two hundred references to hands, arms, and significant manual gestures in the cycle.

ance beyond mere physical movement. The narrator carefully emphasizes that "the story of Wing Biddlebaum is a story of hands" (p. 28). Wing's hands are an essential part of his self-expression. He "talked much with his hands", as do several other of the characters of Winesburg. His gestures, therefore, should tell us as much about him as do his words. Wing's hands, when he is first introduced to the reader, engage themselves in senseless, objectless motion. They "fiddled about the bare white forehead as though arranging a mass of tangled locks" (p. 27), even though Wing, at forty, has no hair on his head at all. While he waits for George Willard, the hands move nervously about. He rubs them together while he looks up and down the road. When he is with George, he thrusts his hands deep into his pockets to conceal them, but brings them out again to pound home a point he wants to make. Always, the key word Anderson's narrator applies to Wing's fingers and hands is "expressive" (pp. 28, 34).

The reversal connected with Wing Biddlebaum's hands arouses an emotion deeper than that of mere pathos. His story delves into the depths of the truly tragic. When they were the hands of Adolph Meyers, Wing's hands conveyed an inspiring dream into the brains of his eager students. "Under the caress of his hands doubt and disbelief went out of the minds of the boys and they began also to dream" (p. 32). By nature, Adolph Meyers was meant to be a teacher of youth; his disaster merits the term "tragic" because the very qualities which assure him success in the art of teaching also lie at the root of his destruction. His fingers are "expressive"; the narrator calls them the "piston rods of his machinery of expression" (p. 28). But his very art of inciting dreams in youth with his hands turns on him when a half-wit relates as fact his dreams of perverted amorous relationships with the schoolteacher. The other students cannot but confess: "He put his arms about me", and "His fingers were always playing in my hair" (p. 32).

As a result of these hideous accusations, the hands of the townspeople knot into fists. "I'll teach you to put your hands on my boy, you beast", roared the saloon keeper. "Keep your hands to yourself." Others came with lanterns, and one dangled a "rope in his hands". Ever after, Adolph Meyers – who had been (like Baudelaire's albatross) a master of expansive visions, a king of the skies – tries to hide away his once beautifully expressive instruments of communication. Some "poet" had said his movements resembled "the beating of the wings of an imprisoned bird", and so Winesburg called him Wing. His gestures, once powerful to shape the visions of youth, were twisted by the brutal fists of hasty men into frustrated and "fluttering pennants of promise" (p. 31).

Wing's hands, though, found a diminished outlet for the kind of activity to which they had been accustomed. In Winesburg, they became "his distinguishing feature, the source of his fame" (p. 29), not because they expressed that nobility of soul and depth of vision which, by nature, he struggled so ardently to impart to youth, but because Wing's nervous rapidity of movement enabled him to pick more berries in a day than anyone else. On this superficial level, then, "Winesburg was proud of the hands of Wing Biddlebaum in the same spirit in which it was proud of Banker White's new stone house and Wesley Moyer's bay stallion, Tony Tip..." (p. 29).

Only once in Winesburg had Wing Biddlebaum allowed his hands to function naturally, to convey his dream to youth. As he talked with George Willard one day in an open field, "Wing Biddlebaum became wholly inspired. For once he forgot the hands. Slowly they stole forth and lay upon George Willard's shoulders" (p. 30). His message, couched in vague phraseology remained forever the same: "You must begin to dream." Transported by the communion of the moment, Wing raised his hands to caress the boy, but sprang back in horror, thrust his hands deep into his pockets, and with tears welling up in his eyes hurriedly took leave of the boy.

Throughout the time of the story's present action, Wing waits on his decaying veranda for George Willard to come visit him. George never arrives, but Wing continues to walk up and down near the ravine "until the sun had disappeared and the road beyond the field was lost in grey shadows" (p. 33). In the darkness on the veranda, "he could not see the hands and they became quiet". Still, "he hungered for the presence of the boy, who was the medium through which he expressed his love of man..." (p. 33). Having eaten some bread and honey, he notices "a few stray white bread crumbs" which lay on the floor by the table. He kneels and picks them up, carrying them to his mouth with "unbelievable rapidity". Wing has been denied a place at the banquet of life. This evening he has been denied even the possibility of communing with the one person of Winesburg with whom he has been able to talk freely. Bread crumbs serve as poor substitute for the presence of George Willard.

Having been introduced to the symbol of hands through such a poignant and impressive story, the reader gradually becomes aware of how persistently hand-symbolism appears throughout the Winesburg stories. "Paper Pills" opens with the bare sentence: "He was an old man with a white beard and huge nose and hands" (p. 35). Dr. Reefy's "were extraordinarily large hands. When the hands were closed they looked like "clusters of unpainted wooden balls as large as walnuts fastened together by steel rods" (p. 35). Dr. Reefy folds his hands into wooden balls, and his thoughts scribbled on scraps of paper into paper balls which he stuffs into his pockets. He sometimes grabs these thought-fragments up in handfuls and throws them playfully at his friend John Spaniard. As a physician, of course, Dr. Reefy serves Winesburg with his hands. So the narrator penetrates the doctor's intimate feelings through metaphorical associations with those hands.

> On the trees there are only a few gnarled apples that the pickers have rejected. They look like the knuckles of Doctor Reefy's hands. One nibbles at them and they are delicious.... The story of Doctor Reefy...is delicious, like the twisted little apples that grow in the orchards of Winesburg. (p. 36)

Dr. Reefy's hands are rough and gnarled like the left-over apples, and his story has a bittersweet taste. In the course of "Paper Pills" the doctor's rough hands contrast starkly with the smooth white hands of the jeweler's son, who, to Dr. Reefy's future wife, seemed to be holding her body in his hands, "turning it slowly about in the white hands and staring at it" (p. 37). Dr. Reefy's hands, rough and gnarled, are also sweet and "delicious".

Elizabeth Willard, too, has long white hands, but the feeling they evoke differs markedly from that suggested by the jeweler's son. In "Mother", they express three kinds of emotional attitudes: (a) listlessness and despair: "she put her head down on her long white hands and wept" (p. 41), and "her long hands, white and bloodless, could be seen drooping over the ends of the arms of the chairs" (p. 42); (b) (imagined) aggressiveness and vengeance: "She clenched her fist" (p. 40), "she took out a long pair of sewing scissors and held them in her hand like a dagger" (p. 45), she would steal noiselessly along, "holding the long wicked scissors in her hand" (p. 47); and (c) desire for communion with another human being: "in the darkness under the trees, they took hold of her hand and she thought that something unexpressed in herself came forth and became a part of an unexpressed something in them" (p. 46), and "when she sobbed she put her hand upon the face of the man" (p. 46), wondering why he did not sob too.

Throughout the book, manual gestures express primarily these three emotional attitides: listlessness or despair, aggressiveness or vengeance, and (most important of all) the pent-up desire to communicate in depth with another human being. Sometimes, as in "Nobody Knows", the narrator's almost mystic concern with the symbolic dimensions of hands takes a ludicrous or a satiric turn. Louise Trunnion sallies forth from her kitchen to meet George Willard. Her hands are still greasy from recently scrubbing pots, and her nose wears a smudge where she has rubbed it with her finger. Still, George "wanted to touch her with his hand", and imagined that even to touch the folds of her gingham dress would be a pleasure. George's sexual excitement allows him to overlook Louise's crudeness. "He took hold of her hand that was also rough and thought it delightfully small" (p. 61).

The mere act of reaching out to touch another human being achieves, as story builds on story, a mythic dimension quite beyond the reach of a single story (even "Hands") taken by itself. In "Surrender", Louise Bentley longs for intimate human contact: "so vague was her notion of life that it seemed to her just the touch of John Hardy's hand would satisfy" (p. 94). But John misinterpreted her meaning. And "so anxious was she to achieve something else that she made no resistance" (p. 96). Throughout her married life, her hunger for affection and communion, which she conceived at first as a touching of hands, increases rather than abates.

Similarly, when Ned Currie took Alice Hindman into his arms, she experienced (at the age of sixteen) what she considered to be true love and communion of spirits. After Ned's long absence, Alice begins to search for a re-achieval of such a union. She "put out her hand and touched the folds" of Will Hurley's coat (p. 118). In the rain, she wanted "to find some other lonely human and embrace him" (p. 119). But the old man she encounters put "his hand to his mouth" and shouts back, "What? What say?" Alice sinks down on her lawn and crawls back "on her hands and knees through the grass to the house" (p. 120).

The same symbolic structure of touch operates in "Respectability". Wash Williams was a passionate man whose first two years of married life suffered no dearth of passionate embraces. "I loved her", he told George Willard later; "I kissed her shoes and the ankles above her shoes. When the hem of her garment touched my face I trembled" (p. 126). But when he found that his wife had acquired three other lovers, he "didn't want to touch them or her". They separated. Later, her mother sent for him. He again became tender toward his wife. "I thought that if she came in and just touched me with her hand I would perhaps faint away. I ached to forgive and forget" (p. 127). But his wife appeared naked and Wash, in fury, threw a chair at his mother-in-law and sank into irrevocable misogyny.

The ebb and flow of the relationship between Seth Richmond and

Helen White in "The Thinker" begins with a touch of their hands. Seth remains quiet, silent, inactive. Helen puts "her hand boldly into Seth's hand" before his retiring masculinity responds. Seth seems actually afraid of committing himself to another – especially to a girl. "The hand of the girl was warm and a strange, dizzy feeling crept over him." He suddenly decides to tell Helen about George's love for her, trying unconsciously, it seems to escape the demands of a kind of union for which he is not yet ready. In the world of his daydreams, he imagines himself lying in deep grass beneath a tree. "Beside him, in the scene built in his fancy, lay Helen White, her hand lying in his hand" (p. 140). But in reality, he was becoming uneasy under the pressure and presence of Helen White's hand. "Releasing the hand of the girl, he thrust his hands into his trouser pockets" (p. 140). As they prepare to part, Helen puts "her hand upon Seth's shoulder" and begins to "draw his face down toward her own upturned face". But she, too, senses inadequacy of response on Seth's part. She lets "her hand fall heavily to her side" and both take their leave. The same kind of ebb and flow runs through George Willard's relationship with Kate Swift in "The Teacher", and with Belle Carpenter in "An Awakening". Violent hands or fists, however, destroy the attempted embrace in both of these stories.

Enoch Robinson lived in a cramped room full of imaginary people. But "he began to get lonely and to want to touch actual flesh-and-bone people with his hands" (p. 171). His desire becones especially strong when a young woman comes to visit him. "I wanted to touch her with my fingers and to kiss her. Her hands were so strong and her face was so good" (p. 176). During Enoch's story, George listens with growing compassion. "He wanted to put his arms about the little old man" (p. 175). But he does not. And when Enoch's story ends, George rises abruptly and walks out, leaving a dejected Enoch all alone in his empty room.

Elmer Cowley's manual gestures remind one both of Wing Biddlebaum and of Joe Welling. His hands seem almost to operate as disconnected appendages to his person. For the first several pages of "'Queer'" Elmer carries his shoes in his hand. (He has a large hole in the heel of one of his stockings, not unlike the hole in the heel of the boy's picture in Curtis Hartman's church.) As he watches George Willard and later as he views the dexterity with which the traveling man, with one hand, unfastens and refastens his collar, Elmer's hands tremble. His arms "flew about", as he spoke with Mook. "I won't be queer. I don't care what they think." When he tried to talk, "his arms began to pump up and down" (p. 198). Leaving Winesburg, Elmer, in his attempt at communication, bursts into a frustrated rage. His arms begin "to flay the air. Like one struggling for release from hands that held him he struck out, hitting George Willard blow after blow on the breast, the neck, the mouth" (p. 201). In "The Untold Lie", which follows "'Queer'" immediately, Hal Winters and Ray Pearson actually arrive at a moment of communication which the narrator expresses in the language of hands. Hal "came and put his two hands on the older man's shoulders" so that together "they made a picture" (p. 205).

The intensity of hand-symbolism increases during the final three stories of the volume. As in "The Teacher", George Willard had "raised a hand and with it groped about in the darkness" (p. 166) trying to comprehend his experiences that evening, so in "Death", Elizabeth Willard "was forever putting out her hand into the darkness and trying to get hold of some other hand" (p. 244). Elizabeth's relation to Tom Willard seems almost to correspond to George's connection with Louise Trunnion. Tom was "at hand and wanted to marry at the time when the determination to marry came to her" (p. 224) just as Louise was at hand and willing when George itched for his first sexual experience. Like Louise's hands, too, Tom's were always dirty – "There was always paint on his hands and face during those days..." (p. 227). Throughout her life, Elizabeth had been "thrusting her hand into the darkness", but rarely had she found another hand to grasp. Now, however, "in the darkness of her room she put out her hand, thrusting it from under the covers of her bed, and she thought that death like a living thing put out his hand to her" (p. 228). Earlier, Dr. Reefy had taken her into his arms. And so, Elizabeth had experienced release from her self-imprisonment only "twice in her life, in the moments when her lovers, Death and Doctor Reefy, held her in their arms" (p. 232). But when Dr. Reefy extended his hand to greet George after Elizabeth's death, both felt so awkward that the doctor drew it back again. George himself "put out his hand" to touch and half-lift the sheet that covered his mother, "but his courage failed him". Never, not even in death, did George and his mother achieve that communion of souls which both so earnestly desired.

During the short time George spent sitting with the dead body of his mother, he thought of Helen White. Especially after his mother's death, George desired with all his heart "to come close to some other human, touch someone with his hands, be touched by the hand of another" (p. 235), even as his mother had desired. In "An Awakening", George had felt a similar need for companionship, though he expressed it in an adolescent image: "If there were only a woman here I would take hold of her hand and we would run until we were both tired out" (p. 185). In "Sophistication", however, the narrator remarks that George prefers that his "some other human" be a woman only "because he believes that a woman will be gentle, that she will understand. He wants, most of all, understanding" (p. 235). By "understanding", Anderson does not, of course, mean comprehension of specific information, but rather, as in *Ein Hungerkünstler*, openness to another person.

The walk of George and Helen in "Sophistication" proceeded without conversation. George mumbled "come on" and took hold of her hand and that was all they said. On the hill in the darkness, they "held each other tightly" and experienced communion. The narrator expresses it in the generalizing phrase: "I have come to this lonely place and here is this other" (p. 241). In "An Awakening", George had felt himself in control of the order of things. Now as he walked with Helen, he felt that "her woman's hand was assisting him to make some minute readjustment of the machinery of his life" (p. 241). After their brief splurge of energy, the tripping and tumbling down the hill, they regain a quiet communion: Helen "took his arm and walked beside him in dignified silence" (p. 243).

As George stands on the station platform waiting to board his train in "Departure", a small crowd of Winesburgers mill about. Symbolically, they seal a pact of open communication with the young writer, as each of them presses the young man's hand. A woman George had hardly known, "put out her hand", and "in two words she voiced what everyone felt. 'Good luck', she said sharply and then turning went on her way" (p. 246). Winesburgers are more adept at the handshake of farewell than at the handshake of welcome. The psychology of the insecure makes an open-handed welcome almost an impossibility. Friendship, openness to love, depth of communication – each of them involves a risk, a risk which most of the Winesburgers are either unable or unwilling (because of their past pattern of experiences) to make. And so their hands, normally, either plunge deep into their pockets, or wave wildly about, flailing the air, or strike out in rage and frustration, or commune only with one another in the nervous act of rubbing or wringing.

E. CONCLUSION

Anderson's short story cycle does not depend for its unity primarily on its realistic setting in a small midwestern town, nor on the centrality of a chief protagonist (George Willard), nor even on its development of a central theme (loneliness). Howe's comment that the unity of *Winesburg* consists, in the last analysis, in a "unity of feeling", has significance only when the sources of that unity of feeling are adequately understood. My analysis has shown, I trust, that Anderson's creation of a privileged, first-person omniscient narrator in the oral storytelling tradition, and his cyclical use of the associational technique on the levels of theme, motif, and symbol form together the chief unifying forces of his book.

The community which emerges gradually, as story follows story, does not occupy a realistic village in Ohio. Rather, it inhabits a landscape in the narrator's imagination. George Willard listens to the life-story of only three of the *Winesburg* grotesques (Dr. Parcival, Wash Williams, and Enoch Robinson)[53]; he himself is a leading protagonist in relatively few of the tales ("Nobody Knows", "An Awakening", "Sophistication", and "Departure") and a minor participant in several others ("Mother", "The Thinker", "The Strength of God", "The Teacher", "'Queer'", "Drink", and "Death"). Yet his position is central to the cycle because of the mythic dimensions accorded to his departure from Winesburg and his initiation into "the adventure of life" as he grows through the timeless period of adolescence to the mythic age of manhood. In the community, he functions, too, as a link (through his dream of becoming a creative writer) with the world beyond his own land of Oz.

The realistic details of *Winesburg*, as Thurston and others have adequately pointed out, often serve symbolic ends. Manual gestures, the setting of one's house, the furnishing of one's room (all controlled by the narrator's voice) also help to form the book's unity of feeling.

The rhythms of the cycle draw together episodes more by the psychological principles of association than by the demands of logic or chronology. "The Book of the Grotesque" introduces the notion of creating, from the fragments of people one has known, figures of one's own fancy – a motif which operates on various levels in "Mother", "Godliness", "Loneliness", "An Awakening", and which serves as a fictional construct for the entire volume. The dream-motif begins in this opening story also and, as I have already shown, continues throughout the book. "Hands" emphasizes at the outset of the cycle the central symbolic significance of manual gesture in delineating character and in expressing the themes of

[53] Tom Foster relates the experience of an evening, but not his life story. The Reverend Curtis Hartman shouts jubilantly that he has been rescued from perdition, but does not fill George in on the details. Wing Biddlebaum's story emerges in a flashback sequence occasioned in the narrator's psyche by his telling of Wing's meeting in an open field with George but Wing never tells his story to George.

isolation and estrangement. "Paper Pills" and "Mother" introduce sensitive and sympathetic characters who are to appear in a balanced corresponding position at the end of the cycle. "Papers Pills" proves that love and communion are possible, even in Winesburg. "Mother" introduces the departure-motif and delineates in the persons of Tom and Elizabeth Willard the conflict between two basic attitudes toward life: desire for "practical success" versus that of "dream-release". In this story, too, George's intention of becoming a creative writer is first mentioned.

In "The Philosopher" George's intention of becoming a writer assumes great importance in the eyes of Dr. Parcival, the first of the Winesburgers cryptically to tell George the story of his life. In "Nobody Knows", George Willard, appearing for the first time as a central protagonist, reveals his inexperience and his adolescent fear of responsibility when he accepts mere sexual pleasure as a substitute for interpersonal communion. From this embryonic level, George must develop into that healthy maturity he will possess in "Sophistication".

The themes and motifs of the "Godliness" stories are perfectly consonant with those coursing through the rest of the cycle. As a group, these stories balance the group from "The Strength of God" through "An Awakening" in the second half of the cycle. The individual stories in "Godliness, Parts I and II" and "The Strength of God" / "The Teacher" cannot stand alone as independent entities, but require each other for the completion not only of their meaning but also of their ironic action. Both groups treat earnestly religious figures, the one tempted by greed of land, the other by lust for sexual pleasure. Both involve a sexually deprived woman and a confused boy. Both concern God's supposed manifestation of himself, through the boy in "Godliness I and II" and through the woman (who is likened to the figure of the boy in the window) in "The Strength of God" and "The Teacher". "Surrender" treats a woman who sought true union in love but could not find it; "Loneliness" treats a man to whom true union in love was open, but who rejected it. "Terror" shows David Hardy's awakening into manhood through a sudden but responsible decision to leave Winesburg; "An Awakening" pictures the disillusionment of George Willard in a moment when his adolescent dreams of sexual conquest burn brightly in his mind. In the four stories of the "Godliness" block are presented the motifs of departure, of the dream, and of adventure; the symbolism of setting, room, and gesture; and the themes of loneliness and hunger for human communion. All are developed in the same spirit and under the control of the same sympathetically ironic voice which presents the other stories of the *Winesburg* cycle.

Joe Welling's manual gestures recall those of Wing Biddlebaum's. But Joe escapes tragedy by his volubility; further, "A Man of Ideas" introduces humor into the cycle. Alice Hindman's story highlights the characteristics of the adventure-motif in *Winesburg;* "Adventure" also portrays a good and sensitive human being, isolated from life by the vagaries of fate. Alice's efforts to communicate with another human being are dashed and she, like so many other Winesburgers, is forced to learn that "many people must live and die alone, even in Winesburg" (p. 120). "Adventure", finally, brings to consciousness for the first time in the cycle, the figure of a naked woman – a figure which reappears for different purposes in "Respectability" and "The Strength of God".

"Respectability" stands as the mathematical center of the cycle. Again, a sensitive figure ("something sensitive and shapely in the hand", p. 121) lives an isolated life in Winesburg. Ironically, Wash is a telegraph operator – a man with his hand on the mainline of midwestern communication. But "he did not associate with the men in the town in which he lived" (p. 122). He is only the second person in the cycle to tell his story to George, and the first to go into the reasons why he left his previous place of residence to come to Winesburg. With the reappearance of a naked woman figure, a cumulative notion of sex begins to emerge. Wash's reaction to his mother-in-law's ruse argues that mere sex without love (such as George had experienced with Louise Trunnion) is of little value. Wash's self-revelation attempts to disillusion George about Belle Carpenter, but George does not heed his admonition. Only later, in "An Awakening", does he find, through bitter and humiliating experience, that Wash's warning had been well founded.

The two stories which follow "Respectability" balance, in a way, the two stories which precede it. "A Man of Ideas" and "Adventure" treat of male and female adults respectively;"The Thinker" and "Tandy" deal with male and female children respectively. Joe Welling's verbosity contrasts sharply with Seth Richmond's self-imposed silence. Joe is called a "man of ideas" and Seth "the thinker". But though Joe has many schemes, he should rather be tabbed a man of words than a man of ideas; and Seth's silence, as the narrator explicitly points out, has nothing to do with depth of insight. In "The Thinker", the departure motif couples with the growth-to-maturity theme as Seth haltingly converses with Helen White. George appears here in a new light as "an excited dog" who scurries about, sniffing out bits of information for the *Eagle.* His job forces him to deal with trivialities, though one day he will be a creative writer and record his planned love experiences with Helen White. Seth's remark that "George belongs to this town", prepares the reader for George's greater immersion in the life of the town, while at the same time it modifies our ideas about George's departure.

Tandy wants above all else to be "strong to be loved" (p. 145). Yet, as the case of Alice Hindman proves, by contrast, strength and fidelity in a woman, though admirable, will not assure enduring happiness. In "Tandy" one of the central themes of *Winesburg* spills from the melancholy mouth of an unnamed stranger: "I am a lover and have not yet found my thing to love" (p. 144). Finally, "Tandy" prepares for "The Strength of God" through its opening paragraph in which Tom Hard, the agnostic, speaks often about religion but "never saw God manifesting himself in the little child..." (p. 143).

Curtis Hartman in "The Strength of God" saw God manifesting himself in the body of a woman who, the narrator comments, looked like the child in the leaded window (see p. 155). In "The Teacher", Kate tried to influence George Willard, but fell in love with him instead. Angry with herself, she kneels and pounds the pillow on her bed. The Reverend Curtis Hartman, watching her from his tower retreat, receives a flash of self-discernment. So Kate actually taught Reverend Hartman more than she had taught the groping George.

In "Loneliness" Enoch Robinson, the third character in the cycle to relate his life's story to George Willard, continues the line of sensitive creatures crushed by fortune. Enoch by deliberately prolonging his own adolescence, is partially responsible for his own isolating egotism. "He never grew up and of course he couldn't understand people and he couldn't make people understand him" (p. 178). Room symbolism here reaches its peak of importance and spreads its significance in both directions toward the earlier and later stories in the cycle. "Loneliness" recalls "The Book of the Grotesque", for Enoch among his imaginary people "was like a writer busy among the figures of his brain..." (p. 171). Enoch's people also number about "two dozen" (p. 173) – the approximate number of leading characters in *Winesburg, Ohio*. George Willard is said to be "like Enoch Robinson", and so we are not surprised, in the next story, to see him creating his own band of imaginary people.

In "An Awakening", George first expresses his desire to get into contact with something huge and ordered, something like the smoothly operating machinery of the stars. Like Enoch Robinson in the preceding story, George feels immense among his imaginary people. The world transforms itself under his enthusiastic response to the ordinary drab streets. Big as he feels, George sinks into insignificance in the presence of the wily Belle Carpenter. They, "the woman and the boy" (p. 187), walk out on the hill near the Fair Grounds. After George's humiliation, that voice in the night which earlier had spoken to him of the order and perfection of the universe, falls silent. The disillusionment of which Wash Williams had warned him, has taken its painful course.

Elmer Cowley in "'Queer'" considers George Willard to be an embodiment of everything that makes Winesburg. He "typified the town, represented in his person the spirit of the town" (p. 194). Ironically, Elmer himself (as many Anderson critics have remarked) comes closer than any other character in the book to typifying Winesburg grotesquerie. Further, in this central story of the second half of the cycle, all the major themes, motifs, and symbols converge in an integrated unity. Elmer, too, is the only Winesburger, other than George Willard, actually to leave the town for good.

The technique of reversal of insight employed by Anderson in earlier stories such as "Nobody Knows", "The Teacher", and "An Awakening", recurs in "The Untold Lie". Hal Winters asks Ray Pearson's advice, but actually Ray himself readjusts his thinking because of his contact with Hal. As he leaves Hal and turns back across the field, he begins to recall the "pleasant evenings spent with thinlegged children" (p. 209) – the recollection of his family earlier in the story had evoked in Ray the feeling of being harnessed in marriage to his wife and a wagonload of children.

Tom Foster in "Drink", stood in the "shadow of the wall of life" (p. 185). None of the violent, lustful, brutal, heinous human acts he had seen seemed to affect him. His drunkenness allows him to break momentarily through the wall of life without hurting other people. His experience, while he is intoxicated, in some ways parallels that of George with his imaginary soldiers and Enoch Robinson with the figures of his brain. Under the influence of alcohol, Tom (like the stranger in "Tandy") found his "thing to love". He found Helen White in the mythic garments of fire and wind.

The final three stories of the volume reach back through the cycle and gather together in a compact and emphatic form all previous motifs, themes, and symbols. Adventure-as-love merges in "Death"[54] with adventure-as-death, just as the adventure of departure becomes one, in

[54] "Death" also continues the submerged Christian symbolism of the volume. Elizabeth Willard dies in March, on Friday, at 3:00 P.M. This forces us to recall, too, that Anderson placed his late story, "The Philosopher", next to "Mother" in the early portion of the cycle. "The Philosopher" ends ominously with Dr. Parcival's conviction that "everyone in the world is Christ and they are all crucified" (p. 57).

the final story, with "the adventure of life" itself. "Sophistication" completes George's process of maturation and prepares him to assume a mature role in the cycle of life. In "Death", Dr. Reefy of "Paper Pills"[55] embraces Elizabeth Willard of "Mother". Elizabeth's body beneath the sheets has a form so young and graceful that George questions whether it is his mother there after all. His thoughts, in fact, fly to Helen White. At the same time, George "definitely decided he would... leave Winesburg" (p. 230).

Both "Death" and "Sophistication" begin with a view of the stairway leading to Dr. Reefy's office. In "Sophistication", George Willard stands beneath it. His mother died in March. Now, the season is autumn, and George "was about to leave Winesburg to go away to some city" (p. 234). George and Helen, during their brief experience together, grow into a new-found maturity while at the same time they retain their youthfulness. The theme of communion reaches its climax in the feeling of George and Helen, which the narrator sums up in the phrase: "I have come to this lonely place and here is this other" (p. 241). George finally seems to understand the relationship of sexuality to love. He experiences with Helen a communion which he had never experienced before, and so "had taken hold of the thing that makes the mature life of men and women in the modern world possible" (p. 243).

With such an insight, George is prepared to face the adventure of life. The time is April – a year and a month after his mother's death. The wind blowing in the first paragraph of "Departure" recalls the wind that had accompanied George and Helen in their walk to the Fair Grounds. In the passage describing George's early morning walk down Trunion Pike, Anderson makes sure that his readers accept George now as a carrier of Winesburg's substance, as a man who has experienced this mythic village in a fictive Ohio town during all of its seasons and in all of its moods. George had communed with its people in the great open places. In doing so, he had passed from mere "boyhood" to "manhood". George had "been in the habit of walking on Trunion Pike", which is "a great open place". Now, on this April morning, "he wanted to go there again, to walk again in the silence" (p. 245) as he had "on winter nights... in the fall... and on summer evenings" (p. 245). Mention of berry pickers recalls the great open fields of "Hands". The long process of George Willard's mythic departure from Winesburg finally completes its course. George opens his eyes and "the town of Winesburg had disappeared".

[55] The events of "Death" must occur, actually, before those of "Paper Pills". See p. 221.

As Anderson had said, then, *Winesburg* presents characters not in a tightly plotted novel, but within a new loose form which he himself described as "lives flowing past one another". Not all of these characters impinge directly on the consciousness of George Willard, their emerging representative and prognosticated ideal, though his hopefully successful venture into the world beyond the confines of Winesburg, Ohio, gives them an earnest of successful liberation from their own narrow world. Neither do the characters of Winesburg affect one another directly as real people, but only as real figures of fancy in the symbolic territory of the narrator's brain and as real dream figures in the mythic background kingdom of George Willard's manhood.

VI

CONCLUSION

A genre, Wellek and Warren say,[1] should be conceived as a grouping of literary works based, theoretically, upon both "outer form" and "inner form". In my analyses of *Ein Hungerkünstler*, *The Unvanquished*, and *Winesburg, Ohio*, I have centered my attention on what I have called static structures (outer form) and dynamic structures (inner form).

Short story cycles can be highly complex works of art. Their overall structure emerges from the complexus of static and dynamic patterns of their self-contained, relatively independent components. Each short story has its own static and dynamic structures. At the same time, connective patterns on all levels draw these together to form a cycle.

The patterns which unify a cycle of stories may be patterns of setting, action, theme, character, tone, symbol, subject matter, style, or (to borrow Friedrich Weltz's term)[2] "conception". Usually, more than one such pattern rivets story to story. In some cycles, theme-patterns or motif-patterns predominate (*Ein Hungerkünstler*, *L'Exil et le royaume*); in others, some character or group of characters undergo a change from one condition to another (*Red Cavalry*, *The Unvanquished*); in still others, a unity of conception, tone, or subject links the stories to one another more strongly than any other pattern (*Winesburg, Ohio*, *The Pastures of Heaven*); in others still, a setting or locale (usually treated symbolically) serves as a dominant unifying backdrop to the thematic actions of each story (*Dubliners*, *The Martian Chronicles*).

The most pervasive unifying pattern of short story cycles is the dynamic pattern of recurrent development. It operates on every level. It affects an author's presentation of settings, themes, motifs, gestures, characters, symbols, and style. It affects structures, narrative devices, chronology, and rhetoric. It consists, most simply, in the repetition of a previously used element (motif, phrase, character, etc.) in a modified form or context, in such a way that the original usage takes on added dimensions in the later context. Also, the original usage is itself affected (in retrospect) by its new relationship to an expanded context.

1 *Theory of Literature* (New York, 1956), p. 221.
2 *Vier amerikanische Erzählungszyklen*. See pp. 101ff.

This typically cyclic pattern often amplifies and deepens the significance of the repeated element to such an extent that it becomes a symbol. One need only think of the oft-repeated gesture in *Winesburg* of stretching out one's hand to another human being, or the varied appearances of sacramental or pseudo-sacramental objects in *Dubliners*, or the repeated occasions of evil fortune befalling associates of the Munroes in *The Pastures of Heaven*.

Besides this typically cyclic pattern of recurrent development, one finds such devices as symmetrical and asymmetrical structures, ironic contrasts, framing stories, and so forth. Traditionally, the term STRUCTURE has been applied primarily to the "planned framework of a piece of literature",[3] – what I have called "static" structure. The static structure of a short story cycle reveals how the author intended his stories to form a group. The chief divisions of his book probably point out the stages of progression in the cycle. They hint at the broad outline of the cycle's movement, direction, and development.

My aim in this study has been to analyze[4] three twentieth-century short story cycles which I judged to be representative of the range, versatility, and scope of the genre. Centering my discussion first and last in the texts themselves, I have tried to discover what characteristics are essential to the genre and which ones recur with sufficient consistency to warrant systematization. Then, drawing both from my own reading and from the studies of other scholars, I have tried to outline a general theory of short story cycles and to propose a methodology for their investigation.

Though I have tentatively suggested an historical perspective on the genre, I have nowhere concerned myself centrally with the question of genesis and historical development. My chief interest has been a detailed description of the aesthetic patterns one finds in three representative twentieth-century short story cycles. A comparison of shared characteristics led me to pinpoint in what precise ways the form of a short story cycle differs fundamentally from that of a "mere" collection of stories and from that of a traditional novel.

The spectrum of short story cycles include, at one pole, collections whose strands of unity are hidden. Diversity of narrators, settings, central

[3] C. Hugh Holman, *A Handbook of Literature* (New York, 1960), p. 473. I have used PATTERN to mean recognizable design, whether static or dynamic.

[4] Michel Dassonville, *L'Analyse de texte* (Québec, 1957): "Analyser un texte c'est le décomposer methodiquement en ses éléments constitutifs.... Analyser un texte, c'est essayer de le comprendre parfaitement afin de l'apprécier et de le faire apprécier.... Critiquer un texte c'est juger clairement de distinctement la part de vrai et de faux, de beau et de laid, de bien et de mal qui s'y trouve." pp. xxii-xxiii.

characters, or techniques have misled critics of these books to treat them as collections of unrelated stories. Some of these stories, removed from their proper place in their cycle and transplanted into the foreign soil of an anthology, are bound to baffle the experts. *Ein Hungerkünstler* – whose title story has run the gamut of possible interpretations – has served well as a representative of this pole. Other cycles which cluster at this end of the spectrum are: *L'Exil et le royaume*, *Dubliners*, *Knight's Gambit*, and *The Red Pony*.

At the other end of the spectrum, we find cycles whose strands of unity are so apparent that critics have welcomed them with open arms into the crowded kingdom of the novel. A single narrator, setting, central character or set of characters, theme, and so forth makes critics overlook the structure of the parts and the ways in which those parts are molded into a whole. I have pointed out distinguishing differences between novel-structure and the patterns of a short story cycle by comparing Faulkner's *The Unvanquished* to his *Sartoris*. *The Unvanquished* is joined at this end of the spectrum of cycles by such works as *Tortilla Flat*, *The Story of Gösta Berling*, *Georgia Boy*, and possibly *The Hamlet*.

I have chosen *Winesburg, Ohio*, to exemplify the central area of the spectrum. A sufficient number of unifying strands show above surface in *Winesburg* to prevent critics from discarding it as a disconnected series of discrete stories. At the same time, no obvious external action controls the patterning of the stories, so critics balk at calling it a novel. In my analysis of the associational technique in *Winesburg* I have tried to show the dynamics of the "cyclical habit of mind" at work. By pointing up the various patterns of recurrent development in *Winesburg*, I hope to have made other scholars more aware of these patterns in other story cycles. Hovering somewhere near the center of the short story cycle spectrum with *Winesburg* are such books as *In Our Time*, *Red Cavalry*, *The Pastures of Heaven*, *My Name Is Aram*, and *The Martian Chronicles*.

A short story cycle, I have said, is a book of short stories so linked to each other by their author that the reader's successive experience on various levels of the pattern of the whole significantly modifies his experience of each of its component parts. The kinds of short story cycles, like the kinds of novels, are numerous. One may choose any relevant criterion – subject matter, century, narrative devices, method of composition, theme – and establish a new subdivision of short story cycles. If I ask how did the author put his stories together to form a cycle, I would arrive at the divisions: composed cycles, arranged cycles, and completed cycles. If I ask what is the strongest unifying link in any particular set of cycles, I would discover such divisions as: theme-cycles, character-cycles, mood-cycles, cycles on some particular subject (marriage, war, death), cycles set in one locale, cycles narrated in the first person, and so forth.[5]

Still, in every kind of twentieth-century short story cycle, one characteristic remains constant – the dynamic pattern of recurrent development. In the books I have treated in detail, this cyclic pattern clearly appears as a publicly recognizable aesthetic design which differs markedly from the design of a novel and which is totally absent from the "mere" collection of stories. On the basis of this persistent formal distinction, which I have adequately demonstrated in the three major chapters of my study, I propose that the ever-increasing body of short story cycles be recognized for what it is: a unique literary genre.

I do not make this proposal merely for the sake of academic argument. I do not love categories in themselves and have no desire to procreate "baby genres" in the pastures of criticism as Bert Munroe spawned "baby curses" in *The Pastures of Heaven.* Rather, I am convinced that the appreciation of any literary work is largely dependent upon one's understanding of its intrinsic aesthetic designs. Many of the cycles mentioned in this study, though written by some of our century's finest writers (Kafka, Hemingway, Anderson, Babel, Faulkner, Steinbeck, Camus), have nevertheless been frequently misunderstood, misjudged, and therefore undervalued.

Public recognition of the short story cycle as a unique genre will be only a first step to increased understanding and appreciation of such unjustly neglected works. I trust that the first step will not be the last.

5 The German language sometimes seems better adapted for naming such categories. Weltz proposes three divisions: *Stoffzyklen, Beispielszyklen,* and *Kompositionszyklen.* See p. 101.

BIBLIOGRAPHY

Chapter I

BOOKS

Alexandrova, Vera, *A History of Soviet Literature, 1917-1964, from Gorky to Solzhenitsyn* (Garden City, New York: Doubleday Anchor Books, 1964).
Bates, H. E., *The Modern Short Story: A Critical Survey* (London: Nelson and Sons, 1941).
Beach, Joseph Warren, *The Twentieth Century Novel* (New York: Century, 1932).
Bennett, E. K., *A History of the German Novelle*, 2nd ed., revised and continued by H. M. Waidson (Cambridge: University of Cambridge Press, 1961).
Booth, Wayne C., *The Rhetoric of Fiction* (Chicago: University of Chicago Press, 1961).
Brooks, Cleanth, and Robert Penn Warren, *Understanding Fiction*, 2nd ed. (New York: Appleton-Century-Crofts, 1959).
Brown, Edward J., *Russian Literature Since the Revolution* (New York: Collier, 1963).
Chekhov, Anton, *Letters on the Short Story, the Drama, and Other Literary Topics*, selected and edited by S. Friedland (London: Vision, 1965).
Crane, Ronald S. (ed.), *Critics and Criticism: Ancient and Modern* (Chicago: Regnery, 1952).
Daiches, David, *The Novel and the Modern World*, rev. ed. (Chicago: University of Chicago Press, 1960).
Dassonville, Michel, *L'Analyse de texte* (Québec: Les Presses Universitaires Laval, 1957).
Forster, Edward Morgan, *Aspects of the Novel* (New York: Harcourt, Brace, 1927).
Frye, Northrop, L. C. Knight *et al.*, *Myth and Symbol: Critical Approaches and Applications* (Lincoln: University of Nebraska Press, 1963).
Goodman, Paul, *The Structure of Literature* (Chicago: University of Chicago Press, 1954).
Grabo, Carl H., *The Technique of the Novel* (New York: Scribner's, 1928).
Hale, Nancy, *The Realities of Fiction* (Boston: Little, Brown, 1961).
Hardy, Barbara, *The Appropriate Form: An Essay on the Novel* (London: Athlone, 1964).
Hugo, Howard E., *Aspects of Fiction: A Handbook* (Boston and Toronto: Little, Brown, 1962).
Kazin, Alfred, *On Native Grounds: An Interpretation of Modern American Prose Literature* (New York: Reynal and Hitchcock, 1942).
Kramer, Priscilla M., *The Cyclical Method of Composition in Gottfried Keller's Sinngedicht* (New York: Lancaster, 1939).
Langer, Susanne K., *Philosophy in a New Key: A Study in the Symbolism of Reason, Rite, and Art* (New York: New American Library [Mentor Paperback], 1951).
Lubbock, Percy, *The Craft of Fiction* (New York: Cape, 1931).
Ludwig, Jack, *Recent American Novelists* (Minneapolis: University of Minnesota Press, 1962 [UMPAW]).
Miller, James E., Jr. (ed.), *Myth and Method: Modern Theories of Fiction* (Lincoln: University of Nebraska Press, 1960).
Muir, Edward, *The Structure of the Novel* (New York: Harcourt, Brace, 1929).

Mustard, Helen M., *The Lyric Cycle in German Literature* (Morningside Heights, New York: King's Crown Press, 1946).

O'Connor, Frank (pseud., Michael O'Donovan), *The Lonely Voice: A Study of the Short Story* (Cleveland and New York: World Book Co., 1963).

—, *The Mirror in the Roadway: A Study of the Novel* (New York: Knopf, 1956).

O'Connor, William Van (ed.), *Forms of Modern Fiction* (Minneapolis: University of Minnesota Press, 1948).

O'Faolain, Sean, *The Short Story* (London: Collins, 1948).

Perrine, Laurence, *Story and Structure* (New York: Harcourt, Brace, and World, 1959).

Rohrberger, Mary, *Hawthorne and the Modern Literary Short Story: A Study in Genre* (New Orleans: Tulane University Press, 1961).

Ross, Danforth, *The American Short Story* (Minneapolis: University of Minnesota Press, 1961 [UMPAW]).

Sebeok, Thomas A., *Myth: A Symposium* (Bloomington: Indiana University Press, 1965 [first published, 1955]).

Stegner, Wallace (ed.), *The American Novel from James Fenimore Cooper to William Faulkner* (New York and London: Basic Books, 1965).

Straumann, Heinrich, *American Literature in the Twentieth Century*, 3rd ed. rev. (New York: Harper and Row, 1965).

Tate, Allen (ed.), *The Language of Poetry* (Princeton: University Press, 1942).

Trask, Georgianne, and Charles Burkhart (eds.), *Storytellers and Their Art* (Garden City, New York: Doubleday Anchor Books, 1963).

Wellek, René, and Austin Warren, *Theory of Literature* (New York: Harcourt, Brace, 1956).

Weltz, Friedrich, *Vier amerikanische Erzählungszyklen* – J. London: "Tales of the Fishpatrol"; Sh. Anderson: "Winesburg, Ohio": J. Steinbeck: "The Pastures of Heaven"; E. Hemingway: "In Our Time" (Dissertation: Universität München, 1953).

West, Ray B., and Robert B. Stallman (eds.), *The Art of Modern Fiction* (New York: Rinehart, 1949).

Wheelwright, Phillip, *Metaphor and Reality* (Bloomington: Indiana University Press, 1962).

Wiese, Benno von, *Die deutsche Novelle von Goethe bis Kafka: Interpretationen*, 2 vols. (Düsseldorf: August Gabel, 1960).

ARTICLES

Brooks, Cleanth, "The Formalist Critic", *Kenyon Review*, XIII (1951), 1-6.

Friedman, Norman, "What Makes A Short Story Short?", *Modern Fiction Studies*, IV (Summer, 1958), 103-117.

Hinkley, H. B., "The Framing Tale", *Modern Language Notes*, XLIX (February, 1934), 69-80.

Müller, Joachim, "Das zyklische Prinzip in der Lyrik", *Germanisch-Romanische Monatsschrift*, XX (1932), 1-20.

Olson, Elder, "An Outline of Poetic Theory", in *Critics and Criticism: Ancient and Modern*, ed. Ronald S. Crane (Chicago: Regnery, 1952), 546-566.

Ortega y Gasset, José, "The Nature of the Novel", *Hudson Review*, X (Spring, 1957), 11-42, translated by Evelyn Rugg and Diego Marin.

Stegner, Wallace, "Teaching the Short Story", Davis Publications in English No. 2, University of California Department of English (Fall, 1965).

Von Abele, Rudolph, "*Ulysses*: The Myth of Myth", *PMLA*, LXIX (June, 1954), 358-364.

Wheelwright, Philip, "Poetry, Myth, and Reality", in *The Language of Poetry*, ed. Allen Tate (Princeton: University Press, 1942), 3-33.

Chapter II

ANDERSON See bibliography of Chapter V.

BABEL

Alexandrova, Vera, *A History of Soviet Literature*, 143-155.

Brown, Edward J., *Russian Literature Since the Revolution*, 115-124.

Terras, Victor, "Line and Color: The Structure of I. Babel's Short Stories in *Red Cavalry*," *Studies in Short Fiction*, III (1966) 141-156.

Trilling, Lionel, "Introduction" to *Isaac Babel: The Collected Stories*, ed. and trans. by Walter Morison (Cleveland and New York: World [Meridian], 1955), 9-37.

CAMUS

"Albert Camus Special Number", *Modern Fiction Studies*, Vol. X (Autumn, 1964), articles by M. M. Madison, Richard Lehan, Glen Sandstrom, Marilyn G. Rose, J. H. Matthews, Naomi C. Jackson, Brian T. Fitch, Ben Stoltzfus, and Maurice Beebe.

Benyon, John S., "Image and Symbol in the Work of Albert Camus", *Yale French Studies*, IX (January, 1955), 42-53.

Brée, Germaine (ed.), *Camus: A Collection of Critical Essays* (Englewood Cliffs, New Jersey: Prentice-Hall, 1962).

—, *Camus* (New Brunswick, New Jersey: Rutgers University Press, 1959).

Crépin, Simone, *Albert Camus* (Bruxelles: Commission belge de bibliographie, 1960).

Gadourek, Carina, *Les Innocents et les coupables. Essai d'exégese de l'oeuvre d'Albert Camus* (The Hague: Mouton, 1963).

Hanna, Thomas, *The Thought and Art of Albert Camus* (Chicago: Regnery, 1958).

King, Adele, *Albert Camus* (New York: Grove Press [Evergreen], 1964; originally Edinburg: Oliver and Boyd, 1964).

Nicolas, André, *Une Philosphie de l'existence: Albert Camus* (Paris: Presses Universitaires de France, 1964).

Picon, Gaëtan, Review of *L'Exil et le royaume* in *Le Mercure de France* (May, 1957), 127-131. English translation in *Camus: A Collection of Critical Essays*, ed.Germaine Brée (Englewood Cliffs, New Jersey: Prentice-Hall, 1962).

"Special Camus Issue", *Yale French Studies*, Vol. XXV (Spring, 1960).

Thody Philip, *Albert Camus* (London: Hamish Hamilton, 1961).

Vigée, Claude, "L'Errance entre l'exil et le royaume", in *La Table ronde*, No. 146 (1960), 120-126.

Weinburg, Kurt, "The Theme of Exile", *Yale French Studies*, XXV (Spring, 1960), 33-40.

Wetherill, Frank Doster, "Albert Camus and the Kingdom of Nature", unpublished dissertation (University of Southern California, 1964).

FAULKNER See bibliography of Chapter IV.

HEMINGWAY

Baker, Carlos, *Hemingway: The Writer As Artist* (Princeton: University Press, 1952).

Hale, Nancy, *The Realities of Fiction*, 95-101.

Hart, Robert Charles, "Writers on Writing", unpublished dissertation (Northwestern University, 1954); 52-53 on *In Our Time*.

Weeks, Robert P., *Hemingway: A Collection of Critical Essays* (Englewood Cliffs, New Jersey: Prentice-Hall, 1962), Twentieth Century Views.

Weltz, Friedrich, *Vier amerikanische Erzählungszyklen*, 68-87.

Young, Philip, *Ernest Hemingway* (Minneapolis: University of Minnesota Press, 1964 [UMPAW]).

JOYCE

Baker, James R., "Ibsen, Joyce, and the Living-Dead", in William T. Moynihan (ed.), *Joyce's The Dead* (Boston: Allyn and Bacon, 1965), 64-70; reprinted from *A James Joyce Miscellany: Third Series*, ed. Marvin Magalaner (Carbondale: Southern Illinois University Press, 1962).

Brandebur, James (ed.), *Quest and Flight: A Study of Fact and Symbol in Dubliners* (Cincinnati: University of Cincinnati Press, 1961).

Carrier Warren, "*Dubliners*: Joyce's Dantean Vision", *Renascence*, XVII (1965), 211-215.

Colum, Padraic, "Introduction" to *Dubliners* (New York: Modern Library, 1926), v-xiii.

Deming, Robert H., *A Bibliography of Joyce Studies* (Lawrence: University of Kansas Libraries, 1964).

Ellmann, Richard, *James Joyce* (New York: Oxford University Press, 1959).

Friedrich, Gerhard, "The Gnomonic Clue to James Joyce's *Dubliners*", *Modern Language Notes*, LXXII (June, 1957), 421-424.

—, "Joyce's Pattern of Paralysis in Dubliners", *College English*, XXII (April, 1961), 519-520.

—, "The Perspective of Joyce's *Dubliners*", *College English*, XXVI (1965), 421-426.

Ghiselin, Brewster, "The Unity of Joyce's *Dubliners*", *Accent*, XVI (Spring, 1956), 75-87; and (Summer, 1956), 196-213.

Gibbons, T. H., "*Dubliners* and the Critics", *Critical Quarterly*, IX (1967), 179-187.

Gilbert, Stuart (ed.) *Letters of James Joyce* (New York: Viking, 1957); for *Dubliners*, see letters 55, 60-64.

Givens, Seon (ed.) *James Joyce: Two Decades of Criticism* (New York: Vanguard, 1963).

Golding, Louis, *James Joyce* (London: Thornton Butterworth, 1933).

Goldman, Arnold, *The Joyce Paradox: Form and Freedom in His Fiction* (Evanston, Illinois: Northwestern University Press, 1966).

Gould, Gerald, Review of *Dubliners* in *The New Statesman*, III (June 27, 1914), 374-375; reprinted in Moynihan (ed.), *Joyce's The Dead* (see below).

Gray, Paul Edward, "James Joyce's *Dubliners*: A Study of the Narrator's Role in Modern Fiction", *Dissertation Abstracts*. XXVI (1966), 6042.

Hart, Clive (ed.) *James Joyce's Dubliners: Critical Essays* (London: Faber and Faber, 1969).

"James Joyce Special Number", *Modern Fiction Studies*, IX (Spring, 1958); articles by Walton Litz, Grant H. Redford, Julian B. Kaye, D. J. F. Aitken, H. K. Russell, Robert Bierman, and Maurice Beebe and Walton Litz.

Jones, William Powell, *James Joyce and the Common Reader* (Norman: University of Oklahoma Press, 1955.)

Joyce, Stanislaus, "The Background to 'Dubliners'", *The Listener*, LI (March 25, 1954), 526-527.

Kenner, Hugh, *Dublin's Joyce* (Bloomington: Indiana University Press, 1956).

Levin, Harry, *James Joyce: A Critical Introduction*, rev. augmented ed. (Norfolk, Connecticut: New Directions Paperback, 1960).

Levin, Richard, and Charles Shattack, "First Flight to Ithaca – A New Reading of Joyce's 'Dubliners'", *Accent*, IV (Winter, 1944), 75-99, reprinted in Givens (ed.), *James Joyce: Two Decades of Criticism*, 47-94.

Litz, A. Walton, *James Joyce* (New York: Twayne, 1966).

Ludwig, Jack Barry, "James Joyce's *Dubliners*", in *Stories: British and American*, ed. J. B. Ludwig and W. Richard Poirier (Boston: Houghton Mifflin, 1953), 384-391.

Magalaner, Marvin, "James Joyce's *Dubliners*", *Dissertation Abstracts*, XI (1951), 1037-38.

—, *Time of Apprenticeship. The Fiction of the Young James Joyce* (London: Abelard-Schuman, 1959).

—, and Richard M. Kain, *Joyce: the Man, the Work, the Reputation* (New York: New York University Press, 1956). For Dubliners, see pages 53-101.

Moynihan, William T., *Joyce's The Dead* (Boston: Allyn and Bacon, 1965 [Allyn and Bacon Casebook Series]).

Ryf, Robert S., *A New Approach to Joyce: A Portrait of the Artist as a Guide Book* (Berkeley: University of California Press, 1962).

Scholes, Robert E., "Further Observations on the Text of *Dubliners*", *Virginia University Bibliographical Society: Studies in Bibliography*, XVII (1954), 107-122.

—, "Some Observations on the Text of *Dubliners*: 'The Dead'", *Virginia University Bibliographical Society: Studies in Bibliography*, XV (1962), 191-205.

Slocum, John J., and Herbert Cahoon, *A Bibliography of James Joyce* (New Haven: Yale University Press, 1953).

Smidt, Kristian, *James Joyce and the Cultic Use of Fiction* (Oslo: Akadenisk forlag, 1955).

Strong, Leonard A. G., *The Sacred River: An Approach to James Joyce* (London: Methuen, 1949).

Tindall, William York, *A Reader's Guide to James Joyce* (New York: Noonday, 1959).

Walzl, Florence L., "Pattern of Paralysis in Joyce's *Dubliners*", *College English*, XXII (January, 1961), 221-228.

KAFKA See bibliography, Chapter III.

O'CONNOR

Burke, John J., Jr., S. J. "Convergence of Flannery O'Connor and Chardin", *Renascence*, XIX (1966), 41-47, 52.

Drake, Robert, *Flannery O'Connor* (Grand Rapids, Michigan: Eerdmans, 1966).

Hyman, Stanley E., *Flannery O'Connor* (Minneapolis: University of Minnesota Press, 1966).

Kaan, Jean Marie, O.S.F. "Everything That Rises Must Converge", *Catholic World*, CCIV (1966), 154-159.

Sullivan, Walter, "Flannery O'Connor, Sin, and Grace: *Everything That Rises Must Convenge*", *The Hollins Critc*, II (1965), 1-8, 10.

STEINBECK

Beebe, Maurice, and Jackson R. Bryer, "Criticism of John Steinbeck: A Selected Checklist", *Modern Fiction Studies*, XI (Spring, 1965), 90-103.

Boynton, Percy, *America in Contemporary Fiction* (Chicago: University of Chicago Press, 1940); Steinbeck: 241-257.

Fontenrose, Joseph, *John Steinbeck: An Introduction and Interpretation* (New York: Barnes and Noble, 1963)[American Authors and Critics Series]).

French, Warren, *John Steinbeck* (New York: Twayne, 1961 [Twayne's United States Authors Series]).

Gannett, Lewis, *John Steinbeck: Personal and Bibliographical Notes* (New York: Viking, 1939 [Pamphlet]).

Gierasch, Walter, "Steinbeck's *The Red Pony* – II: 'The Great Mountains'", *Explicator*, IV (1946), item 39.

Goldsmith, Arnold L., "Thematic Rhythm in *The Red Pony*", *College English*, XXVI (February, 1965), 391-395.

"John Steinbeck Special Number", *Modern Fiction Studies*, Vol. XI (Spring, 1965); articles by Peter Lisca, Arthur F. Kinney, Howard Levant, Jules Chametzky, John Antico, Mordecai Marcus, Donna Gerstenberger, Warren French, Curtis L. Johnson, James W. Tuttleton, and Maurice Beebe and J. R. Bryer.

Kinney, Arthur F., "The Arthurian Cycle in *Tortilla Flat*", *Modern Fiction Studies*, XI (Spring, 1965), 11-20.

Lisca, Peter, *The Wide World of John Steinbeck* (New Brunswick, N. J.: Rutgers University Press, 1958).

Moore, Harry T., *The Novels of John Steinbeck: A First Critical Study* (Chicago: Normandie House, 1939).

Schumann, Hildegard, *Zum Problem des kritischen Realismus bei John Steinbeck* (Halle: Niemeyer Verlag, 1958).

Tedlock, E. W., Jr., and C. V. Wicker (eds.), *Steinbeck and His Critics: A Record of Twenty-Five Years* (Albuquerque: University of New Mexico Press, 1957).

Watt, F. W., *John Steinbeck* (New York: Grove [Evergreen Pilot], 1962).

Weltz, Friedrich, *Vier amerikanische Erzählungszyklen*, 46-67.

WELTY

Appel, A., *A Season of Dreams: The Fiction of Eudora Welty* (Baton Rouge: Louisiana State University Press, 1965).

Harris, Wendell V., "The Thematic Unity of Welty's *The Golden Apples*", *Texas Studies in Literature and Language*, VI (Spring, 1964), 92-95.

Vande Kieft, Ruth M., *Eudora Welty* (New York: Twayne, 1962).

Chapter III

PRIMARY

Kafka, Franz, *Amerika*, Hrsg. Max Brod, dritte Ausgabe (New York: Schocken Books, 1946).

—, *Beschreibung eines Kampfes*, Hrsg. Max Brod, zweite Ausgabe (New York: Schocken Books, 1946).

—, *Briefe* 1902-1924, Hrsg. Max Brod (New York: Schocken Books, 1958).

—, *Briefe an Milena*, Hrsg. Willy Haas (New York: Schocken Books, 1952).

—, *Ein Hungerkünstler. Vier Geschichten* (Berlin: "Die Schmiede", 1924).

—, *Erzählungen und kleine Prosa*, Hrsg. Max Brod, dritte Ausgabe (New York: Schocken Books, 1946 [my edition, 1963 c., 1965 imprint]).

—, *Hochzeitsvorbereitungen auf dem Lande*, Hrsg. Max Brod (New York: Schocken Books, 1953).

—, *Der Prozeß*, Hrsg. Max Brod (New York: Schocken Books, 1946).

—, *Das Scholß*, Hrsg. Max Brod (New York: Schocken Books, 1946).

—, *Tagebücher*, 2 vols, Hrsg. Max Brod (New York: Schocken Books, 1949).

SECONDARY

Books

Anders, Günther, *Kafka, Pro und Contra* (München: C. H. Beck, 1951 [Preface, 1946]); English translation by A. Steer and A. K. Thorlby, as *Franz Kafka* (London: Bowes and Bowes, 1960).

Baumer, Franz, *Franz Kafka* (Berlin: Colloquium Verlag, 1960.

Beißner, Friedrich, *Der Erzähler Franz Kafka* (Stuttgart: W. Kohlhammer, 1952).

—, *Kafka der Dichter* (Stuttgart: W. Kohlhammer, 1958).

Bense, Max, *Die Theorie Kafkas* (Köln/Berlin: Kiepenheuer und Witsch, 1952).

Bezzel, Christoph, *Natur bei Kafka: Studien zur Ästhetik des poetischen Zeichens* (Nürnberg: Verlag Hans Carl, 1964 [Erlanger Beiträge zur Sprach- und Kunstwissenschaft, 15]).

Binder, Hartmut, *Motiv und Gestaltung bei Franz Kafka* (Bonn: Bouvier, 1966).

Born, Jürgen, Ludwig Dietz, et al. *Kafka Symposium* (Berlin: Wagenbach, 1965).

Brod, Max, *Franz Kafka. Eine Biographie*, 3d ed. (Berlin: S. Fischer, 1954); English translation (New York: Schocken, 1947); original edition (Prague: Heinrich Mercy Sohn, 1935).

—, *Verzweiflung und Erlösung im Werke Kafkas* (Frankfurt am Main: S. Fischer Verlag, 1959).

Camus, Albert, *The Myth of Sisyphus and Other Essays*, trans. Justin O'Brien (New York: Random House, 1955); orginally: *Le Mythe de Sisyphe* (Paris: Gallimard, 1942).

Collins, Hildegard Platzer, "A Study of the Relationships between Technique and Theme in the Shorter Works of Kafka", unpublished dissertation (University of Southern California, 1962).

Dentan, Michel, *Humour et création littéraire dans l'oeuvre de Kafka* (Paris: Minard, 1961 [also, Genève: Droz, 1961]).

Emrich, Wilhelm, *Franz Kafka* (Bonn: Athenäum, 1958).

Flores, Angel, *Franz Kafka. A Chronology and Bibliography* (Houlton, Maine: Bern Porter, 1944).

Flores, Angel, and Homer Swander (eds.), *Franz Kafka Today* (Madison: University of Wisconsin Press, 1958 [Paperback editions: 1962, 1964]).

Flores, Angel (ed.), *The Kafka Problem* (New York: New Directions, 1946, 1963).

Furst, Norbert, *Die offenen Geheimtüren Franz Kafka* (Heidelberg: W. Rothe, 1956).

Goodman, Paul, *Kafka's Prayer* (New York: Vanguard, 1947).

Goth, Maja, *Franz Kafka et les lettres françaises (1928-1955)* (Paris: José Corti, 1956).

Gray, Ronald (ed.), *Kafka: A Collection of Critical Essays* (Englewood Cliffs, New Jersey: Prentice Hall, 1962).

Hasselblatt, Dieter, *Zauber und Logik. Eine Kafka-Studie* (Köln: Verlag für Wissenschaft und Politik, 1964).

Hemmerle, Rudolf, *Franz Kafka: Eine Bibliographie* (München: Robert Lerche, 1958).

Heselhaus, Clems, "Franz Kafkas Erzählenformen", *Deutsche Vierteljahrschrift*, XXVI (1952), 353-376.

Hillmann, Heinz, *Franz Kafka: Dichtungstheorie und Dichtungsgestalt* (Bonn: H. Bouvier und Companie, 1964 [Bonner Arbeiten zur deutschen Literatur, Bd. 9]).

Janouch, Gustav, *Franz Kafka und seine Welt. Eine Bildbiographie* (Wien: Deutsch, 1964).

—, *Gespräche mit Kafka: Erinnerungen und Aufzeichnungen* (Frankfurt am Main: S. Fischer, 1951); trans. as *Conversations with Kafka*, by Goronwy Rees (London: Derek Verschoyle, 1953).

Järv, Harry, *Die Kafka-Literatur: Ein Bibliographie* (Malmö-Lund: Bo Cavefors, 1961).

König, Gerd, "Franz Kafkas Erzählungen und kleine Prosa", unpublished dissertation (University of Tübingen, 1954).

Kowal, Michael, "Franz Kafka. Problems in Interpretation", unpublished dissertation (Yale University, 1962).

Morrison, Jean A., "Kafka as Hungerkünstler", unpublished dissertation (Tulane University, 1963).

Muschg, Walter, *Tragische Literaturgeschichte* (Bern: Francke, 1953).

Neider, Charles, *The Frozen Sea: A Study of Franz Kafka* (New York: Oxford University Press, 1948).

Nemeth, André, *Kafka ou le mystère juif* (Paris: Jean Vigneau, 1947).

Pascal, Roy, *The German Novel* (London: Meuthen and Company, 1956 [University Paperbacks, 1965]).

Politzer, Heinz, *Franz Kafka: Parable and Paradox* (Ithaca, New York: Cornell University Press, 1962); German edition, *Franz Kafka der Künstler* (Berlin: S. Fischer Verlag, 1965). The later edition completes the Järv bibliography in its appendix, 512-526, bringing it up to December, 1964.

Pongs, Hermann, *Franz Kafka, Dichter des Labyrinths* (Heidelberg: Wolfgang Rothe, 1960).

Rattner, J., *Kafka und das Vaterproblem* (München: Reinhardt, 1964).

Reiss, Hans Siegbert, *Franz Kafka: Eine Betrachtung seines Werkes* (Heidelberg: L. Schneider, 1952).

Rhein, Phillip H., *The Urge To Live: A Comparative Study of Franz Kafka's Der Prozeß and Albert Camus' L'Étranger* (Chapel Hill: University of North Carolina Press, 1964 [Studies in Germanic Languages and Literatures, No. 45]).

Robert, Marthe, *Kafka* (Paris: Gallimard, 1960 [La Bibliotheque Idéal]).

Rochefort, Robert, *Kafka, oder die unzerstörbare Hoffnung* (Wein/München: Herold, 1955), übersetzt von Hubert Greifeneder; originally in French: *Kafka, ou l'Irréductible Espoir* (Paris: René Julliard, 1947).

Sarraute, Nathalie, *L'Ère du soupçon. Essais sur le roman* (Paris: Gallimard, 1956).

Sokel, Walter H., *Franz Kafka. Tragik und Ironie* (München: Langen-Müller, 1964). Eng. trans. *Franz Kafka* (New York: Columbia University Press, 1966).

Steiner, Heiri and Jean Gebser, *Anxiety: A Condition of Modern Man* (New York: Dell, 1962 [Visual No. 2]), trans. from German by Peter Heller.

Steinhauer, Harry, *Die Deutsche Novelle, 1880-1933* (New York: W. W. Norton, 1936).

Struc, Roman S., "Food, Air, and Ground. A Study of Basic Symbols in Kafka's Short Stories", unpublished dissertation (University of Washington, 1963).

Tauber, Herbert, *Franz Kafka, Eine Deutung seiner Werke* (Zürich: Oprecht, 1941); English translation, *Franz Kafka, An Interpretation of His Work* (New Haven, Connecticut: Yale University Press, 1948).

Wagenbach, Klaus, *Franz Kafka, Die Erzählungen* (Frankfort: Fischer, 1961).

—, *Franz Kafka 1883-1924: Manuskripte, Erstdrucke, Dokumente, Photographien* (Berlin: Akademie der Künste, 1966).

Walser, Martin Johannes, *Beschreibung einer Form. Versuch über die epische Dichtung Franz Kafkas* (München: Franke, 1961); originally, disseration, (University of Tübingen, 1952).

Weinberg, Kurt, *Kafkas Dichtungen. Die Travestien des Mythos* (Bern/München: Francke, 1963).

Weltsch, Felix, *Religion und Humor im Leben und Werk Franz Kafkas* (Berlin: Herbig, 1957).

von Wiese, Benno, *Die Deutsche Novelle von Goethe bis Kafka: Interpretationen*, 2 Bände (Düsseldorf: August Gabel, 1960).

Wilson, Colin, *The Outsider* (Boston: Houghton Mifflin, 1956).

Articles

Ackermann, Paul Kurt, "A History of Critical Works on Franz Kafka", *German Quarterly*, XXIII (March, 1950), 104-113.

Adeane, Louis, "The Hero Myth in Kafka's Writing", in *Focus One* (1945), 48-56.

Asher, J. A., "Turning Points in Kafka's Stories", *Modern Language Review*, LVII (January, 1962), 47-52.

Auden, W. H., "K.'s Quest", in *The Kafka Problem*, ed. Angel Flores (New York: New Directions, 1946, 1963), 47-52.

Baum, Oskar, "Recollections", in *The Kafka Problem*, ed. Angel Flores (New York: New Directions, 1946, 1963).

Beebe, Maurice and Naomi Christensen, "Criticism of Franz Kafka: A Selected Checklist", *Modern Fiction Studies*, VIII (1962), 80-100.

Beissner, Friedrich, "Kafka the Artist", in *Kafka: A Collection of Critical Essays*, ed. Ronald Gray (Englewood Cliffs, New Jersey: Prentice Hall, 1962); trans. of *Kafka der Dichter* (Stuttgart: Kohlhammer, 1958).

Benson, Ann Thornton, "Franz Kafka: An American Bibliography", *Bulletin of Bibliography*, XXII (1958), 112-114.

Bergel, Lienhard, "'Blumfeld, an Elderly Bachelor'", in *The Kafka Problem*, ed. Angel Flores (New York: New Directions, 1946, 1963), 172-178.

Brod, Max, "Franz Kafkas Nachlaß", *Weltbühne*, Jahrg. 20 (July 17, 1924), No. 29, 106-109.

Burgum, Edwin Berry, "Kafka and the Bankruptcy of Faith", *Accent* (Spring, 1943), 154-167; reprinted in *The Kafka Problem*, ed. Angel Flores.

Carrive, Jean, Untitled note attached to his translation of "Die [*sic*] kleine Frau", entitled "Un petit bout de femme", *Le Cheval de Troie* (Paris, 1948), No. 6, 808-809.

Caspel, P. P. J. van, "Josefine und Jeremias", *Neophilologus*, XXXVII (1953), No. 4, 241-245.

Cohn, Dorrit Claire, Review of Sokel's *Franz Kafka*, in *German Quarterly*, XXXIX (January, 1966), 115-117.

Edel, Edmund, "Zum Problem des Künstlers bei Kafka", *Deutschunterricht*, XV (1963), 9-31.

Flores, Kate, "Biographical Note", in *The Kafka Problem*, ed. Angel Flores.

Gibian, George, "Dichtung und Wahrheit: Three Versions of Reality in Franz Kafka", *German Quarterly*, XXX (January, 1957), 20-31.

Goldschmidt, H. L., "Key to Kafka", *Commentary*, VIII (August, 1949), 129-138.

Gray, Ronald, "Introduction", in *Kafka*, ed. Ronald Gray (Englewood Cliffs, New Jersey: Prentice Hall, 1962).

—, "Kafka the Writer", in *Kafka*, ed. Ronald Gray (Englewood Cliffs, New Jersey: Prentice Hall, 1962), 61-73.

Heller, Erich, "The World of Franz Kafka", in *Kafka*, ed. Ronald Gray (Englewood Cliffs, New Jersey: Prentice Hall, 1962), 99-122; reprinted from Heller's *The Disinherited Mind* (London: Bowes and Bowes, 1952).

Hesse, Hermann, "Franz Kafkas Nachlaß", *Berliner Tageblatt* (September 9, 1925).

Henel, Ingeborg C., "Ein Hungerkünstler", *Deutsche Vierteljahrsschrift*, XXXVIII (1964), 230-247.

—, Review of Weinberg's *Kafkas Dichtungen*, in *Germanic Review*, XL (November, 1965), 311-314.

Hermsdorf, Klaus, "Künstler und Kunst bei Franz Kafka", *Weimarer Beiträge* (1964), 404-412; reprinted in *Franz Kafka aus Prager sich 1963*, ed. Paul Reimann (Präg: Verlag der Tschechoclowakischen Akademie der Wissenschafter, 1965), 95-107.

Heselhaus, Clems, "Franz Kafkas Erzählenformen", *Deutsche Vierteljahrsschrift für Literaturwissenschaft und Geistesgeschichte*, XXVI (1952), Heft 3, 353-76.

Jolas, Eugene, "Franz Kafka's Stories and Ascending Romanticism", *Vertical Yearbook* (New York: Gotham Book Mart, 1941), 169-172.

Lerner, Max, "The Human Voyage", in *The Kafka Problem*, ed. Angel Flores (New York: New Directions, 1946, 1963).

Magny, Claude-Edmonde, "The Objective Depiction of Absurdity", *Quarterly Review of Literature*, II (1945), No. 3, 211-227; reprinted in *The Kafka Problem*, 75-96.

Mann, Thomas, "Homage", in *The Castle*, by Franz Kafka, translated by Willa and Edwin Muir, definitive edition (New York: Alfred A. Knopf, 1954), ix-xvii.

Muir, Edwin, "Franz Kafka", in *Kafka*, ed. Ronald Gray (Englewood Cliffs, New Jersey: Prentice Hall, 1962), 33-44; reprinted from *Life and Letters* (London, June, 1934).

Pasley, J. M. S., "Franz Kafka's MSS: Description and Select Inedita", *Modern Language Review*, LVII (January, 1962), 53-59.

Pasley, Malcolm, and Klaus Wagenbach, "Versuch einer Datierung sämtlicher Texte Franz Kafkas", *Deutsche Vierteljahrsschrift*, XXXVIII (Juli 1964), 149-167.

Pfeiffer, Johannes, "The Metamorphosis", in *Kafka*, ed. Ronald Gray (Englewood Cliffs, New Jersey: Prentice Hall, 1962), 53-59; taken from Pfeiffer's *Die Dichterische Wirklichkeit*. (Göttingen: Richard Meiner, 1962).

—, "Franz Kafka: 'Eine kleine Frau'", in *Wege zur Erzählkunst* (Hamburg: Wittig, 1953), 108-116.

Politzer, Heinz, "Problematik und Probleme der Kafka-Forschung", *Monatshefte für deutschen Unterricht, deutsche Sprache und Literatur* (Madison, Wisconsin: 1950), 273-280.

Rahv, Philip, "The Hero as Lonely Man", *Kenyon Review* (Winter, 1939), 60-74.

Reiss, H. S., "Recent Kafka Criticism (1944-1955) – A Survey", in *Kafka*, ed. Ronald Gray (Englewood Cliffs, New Jersey: Prentice Hall, 1962), 163-180.

Richter, Helmut, "Zu einigen neueren Publikationen über Franz Kafka", *Weimarer Beiträge*, IV (1959), 568-578; reviews of books by von Wiese, Beißner, König, Emrich, Reimann, Elsberg, Siebenschein, Wieskopf, Fischer, Maritini, and Wagenbach.

Rubinstein, William C., "A Hunger Artist", *Monatshefte*, XLIV (January, 1952), 13-19.

Schillemiet, Jost, "Welt im Werk Franz Kafkas", *Deutsche-Vierteljahrsschrift*, XXXVIII (July, 1964), 168-191.

Seyppel, Joachim H., "The Animal Theme and Totemism in Franz Kafka", *Literature and Psychology*, IV (September, 1954), No. 4, 49-63; newsletter of the Conference in Literature and Psychology.

Slochower, Harry, "Franz Kafka – Pre-Fascist Exile", in *A Franz Kafka Miscellany* (New York: Twice a Year Press, 1940), 7-24.

Spann, Meno, "Die beiden Zettel Kafkas", *Monatshefte*, XLVII (1955), No. 6, 321-328.

—, "Franz Kafka's Leopard", *The Germanic Review*, XXXIV (April, 1959), 85-104.

Stallman, Robert W., "Kafka's Cage", *Accent* (Winter, 1948), No. 8, 117-125; reprinted in Ray B. West and R. W. Stallman (eds.), *The Art of Modern Fiction* (New York: Rinehart, 1949), 366-372; also in *Franz Kafka Today*, ed. Angel Flores and Homer Swander (revised version of the article, entitled: "A Hunger Artist"), 61-70.

Steinhauer, Harry, "Hungering Artist or Artist in Hungering. Kafka's 'A Hunger Artist'", *Criticism*, IV (1962), 28-43.

Vigée, Claude, "Les artistes de la faim", *Table Ronde* (Avril, 1957), 43-64.

Vivas, Eliseo, "Kafka's Distorted Mask", in *Kafka*, ed. Ronald Gray (Englewood Cliffs, New Jersey: Prentice Hall, 1962); reprinted from *Creation and Discovery* (New York: Noonday Press, 1955); first in *Kenyon Review* (Winter, 1948), 51-69.

Waidson, H. M., "The Starvation-Artist and the Leopard", *The Germanic Review*, IV (1960), 262-269.

Walker, Augusta, "Allegory, A Light Conceit", *Partisan Review*, XXII (Fall, 1955), No. 4, 480-490.

Warren, Austin, "Franz Kafka", in *Kafka*, ed. Ronald Gray (Englewood Cliffs, New Jersey: Prentice Hall, 1962); reprinted from *Rage for Order* (Ann Arbor: University of Michigan Press, 1948).

—, "Kosmos Kafka", in *The Kafka Problem*, ed. Angel Flores (New York: New Directions, 1946, 1963).

Waterman, Arthur E., "Kafka's 'The [*sic!*] Hunger Artist'", *C*[ollege] *E*[nglish] *A*[ssociation] *Critic*, XXIII (1961), 9.

Wiese, Benno von, "Der Künstler und die moderne Gesellschaft", *Akzente*, V (1958), 112-123.

Wilson, Edmund, "A Dissenting Opinion on Kafka", in *Kafka*, ed. Ronald Gray (Englewood Cliffs, New Jersey: Prentice Hall, 1962).

Winkler, R. O. C., "The Novels", in *Kafka*, ed. Ronald Gray (Englewood Cliffs, New Jersey: Prentice Hall, 1962); reprinted from *Scrutiny*, VII (1938), No. 3.

Woodring, Carl R., "Josephine the Singer, or the Mouse Folk", in *Franz Kafka Today*, ed. Angel Flores and Homer Swander (Madison: University of Wisconsin Press, 1958).

Chapter IV

PRIMARY

Faulkner, William, *Sartoris* (New York: Harcourt, Brace, 1929; also, London: Chatto and Windus, 1932).

—, *The Sound and the Fury* (New York: Cape and Smith, 1929).

—, *As I Lay Dying* (New York: Cape and Smith, 1929).

—, *Light in August* (New York: Smith and Haas, 1932).

—, *Absalom, Absalom!* (New York: Random House, 1936).

—, *The Unvanquished* (New York: Random House, 1938).

—, *The Hamlet* (New York: Random House, 1940).

—, *Go Down, Moses* (New York: Random House, 1942; Modern Library, 1955), earlier edition read: *Go Down, Moses and Other Stories*.

—, *Intruder in the Dust* (New York: Random House, 1948).

—, *Knight's Gambit* (New York: Random House, 1948).

—, *New Orleans Sketches*, ed. Carvel Collins (New Brunswick: Rutgers University Press, 1958; Evergreen Edition. New York: Grove Press, 1961).

—, *Essays, Speeches and Public Letters*, ed. James B. Meriwether (New York: Random House, 1965).

SECONDARY

Bibliographies

Vickery, Olga W., "A Selective Bibliography", in *William Faulkner: Three Decades of Criticism*, ed. Frederick J. Hoffman and Olga W. Vickery (East Lansing: Michigan State University Press, 1960), 383-428.

Sleeth, Irene Lynn, "William Faulkner: A Bibliography of Criticism", *Twentieth Century Literature*, VIII (April, 1962), 18-43.

Volpe, Edmond L., *A Reader's Guide to William Faulkner* (New York: Noonday, 1964), 413-422.

Reviews of The Unvanquished

Anonymous, Review in *Lettres Françaises* (25 août 1949), 3.

Birney, Earle, "The Two William Faulkners", *The Canadian Forum*, XVIII (June, 1938), 84-85.

Blanzat, J., Review in *Figaro Littéraire* (6 août 1949), 5.

Boutang, Pierre, "L'Invaincu", in *Aspects de la France* (21 juillet 1949), 3.

Boyle, Kay, "Tattered Banners", *The New Republic*, XCIV (March 9, 1938), 136-137.

Braspart, M., Review in *Réforme* (13 août 1949), 7.
Carrouges, Michel, Review in *Monde nouveau-Paru* (mars 1950), 43.
Chaufeteau, J., Review in *Arts et Lettres* (No. 16, 1949), 58.
De Voto, Bernard, "Faulkner's South", *Saturday Review of Literature*, XVII (February 19, 1938), 5.
Kazin, Alfred, "In the Shadow of the South's Last Stand", *New York Herald Tribune* (Books), February 20, 1938, 5.
Kronenberger, Louis, "Faulkner's Dismal Swamp", *The Nation*, CXLVI (February 19, 1938), 212, 214.
Lalou, René, Review in *Nouvelles Littéraires* (1 septembre 1949), 3.
Lebesque, Morvan, Review in *Climats* (5 août 1949), 8.
Le Breton, M., (édition anglaise), review in *Études anglaises* (juillet-septembre 1939), 313.
Neville, Helen, "The Sound and the Fury", *Partisan Review*, V (June, 1938), 53-55.
Sigaux, J., Review in *Gazette des Lettres* (1 octobre 1949), 7.
Vallette, J., Review in *Mercure de France* (novembre, 1949), 532.

Interviews and Special Issues of Periodicals

Faulkner at West Point, ed. Joseph L. Fant III and Robert Ashley (New York: Random House, 1964).
Faulkner in the University, Class Conferences at the University of Virginia, 1957-1958, ed. Frederick L. Gwynn and Joseph L. Blotner (New York: Vintage, 1965).
Faulkner Studies I-III (Spring 1952-Winter, 1954); later this magazine became *Critique: Studies in Modern Fiction.*
Faulkner: Three Studies, XI, No. 1 (September, 1962) of *The Emporia State Research Studies*, essays by Robert Dorsch, Dorothy D. Greer, and Sherland N. Dirksen.
The Mississippi Quarterly: Special Faulkner Issue, Vol. XI (Fall, 1958); essays by David Applewhite, Raymond Bernberg, William Doster, Scott Greer, Elmo Howell, Bruce McElderry, Hallet Smith, T. D. Young, and Floyd Watkins; mainly a symposium on *Light in August.*
Modern Fiction Studies. Special Faulkner Number, Vol. II (Autumn, 1956); essays by Melvin Backman, Robert Flyn, David L. Frazier, Roma A. King, W. R. Noses and Karl E. Zink. The bibliography lists no works devoted solely to *The Unvanquished.*
Perspective. Faulkner Number 1, Vol. II (Summer, 1949); essays by Ruel E. Foster, Phyllis Hirsheleifer, Sumner C. Powell, Russell Roth, and Ray B. West.
Perspective. Faulkner Number 2, Vol. III (Autumn, 1950); essays by Harry M. Campbell, Romy Hudson, Olga W. Vickery and Edgar W. Whan.
The Princeton University Library Chronicle. Special Faulkner Issue, Vol. XVIII (Spring, 1957); essays by Hodding Carter, Maurice E. Coindreau, Carvel Collins, George P. Garret; James B. Meriwther's "William Faulkner: A Checklist", 136-158.
La Revue des Lettres Modernes, Vol. V (Winter, 1958-1959); essays by Cyrille Arnavon, Roger Asselineau, Melvin J. Friedman, Maurice Le Breton, Stanley D. Woodworth; reprinted essays by Warren Beck, Robert Penn Warren.
Studies in Faulkner, No. 6 of *Carnegie Series in English* (Pittsburgh: Carnegie Institute of Technology, 1961); essays by Ann L. Hayes, John A. Hart, Ralph A. Ciacio, Beekman W. Cottrell and Neal Woodruff, Jr.

Other Critical Works Consulted

Books

Backmann, Melvin, *Faulkner, the Major Years: A Critical Study* (Bloomington, Indiana: Indiana University Press, 1966).

Beck, Warren, *Man in Motion: Faulkner's Trilogy* (Madison: University of Wisconsin Press, 1961).

Brooks, Cleanth, *William Faulkner: The Yoknapatawpha Country* (New Haven: Yale University Press, 1963).

Campbell, Harry Modean and Ruel E. Foster, *William Faulkner: A Critical Appraisal* (Norman: University of Oklahoma Press, 1951).

Cowley, Malcolm, *The Faulkner-Cowley File: Letters and Memories, 1942-1962* (New York: Viking, 1966).

Emerson, O. B., "William Faulkner's Literary Reputation in America", unpublished dissertation (Vanderbilt University, 1962).

Hoffman, Frederick J., *William Faulkner* (New York: Twayne, 1961, 1966).

Hoffman, Frederick J. and Olga W. Vickery (eds.), *William Faulkner: Three Decades of Criticism* (East Lansing: Michigan State University Press, 1960).

Holmes, Edward M., *Faulkner's Twice-Told Tales* (The Hague: Mouton, 1966).

Howe, Irving, *William Faulkner: A Critical Study* (New York: Random House, 1952); rev. and expanded 2nd ed. (Vintage Books, 1962).

Kirk, Robert W. and Marvin Klotz, *Faulkner's People: A Complete Guide and Index to Characters in the Fiction of William Faulkner* (Berkeley and Los Angeles: University of California Press, 1963).

Longley, John Lewis, Jr., *The Tragic Mask: A Study of Faulkner's Heroes* (Chapel Hill: University of North Carolina Press, 1963).

Loughrey, Rev. Thomas Francis, "Values and Love in the Fiction of William Faulkner", unpublished dissertation (University of Notre Dame, 1962).

Malin, Irving, *William Faulkner: An Interpretation* (Stanford: University Press, 1957).

Meriwether, James B., "The Place of *The Unvanquished* in William Faulkner's Yoknapatawpha Series", unpublished Ph. D. dissertation (Princeton University, 1958).

Millgate, Michael, *William Faulkner* (New York: Grove Press, 1961).

—, *The Achievement of William Faulkner* (London: Constable, 1966).

Miner, Ward L., *The World of William Faulkner* (Durham: Duke University Press, 1952).

Nathan, Monique, *Faulkner par lui même* (Bourges: Tardy, 1963 [Écrivaines de toujours]).

O'Connor, William Van, *The Tangled Fire of William Faulkner* (Minneapolis: University of Minnesota Press, 1954).

—, *William Faulkner* (Minneapolis: University of Minnesota Press, 1954; rev. ed., 1965 [Minnesota Pamphlets on American Writers, No. 3]).

Robb, Mary Cooper, *William Faulkner: An Estimate of His Contribution to the American Novel* (Pittsburgh: University of Pittsburgh Press, 1957).

Simpson, Hassell A., "The Short Stories of William Faulkner", unpublished dissertation (Florida State University, 1962).

Slatoff, Walter J., *Quest for Failure: A Study of William Faulkner* (Ithaca: Cornell University Press, 1960).

Swiggart, Peter, *The Art of Faulkner's Novels* (Austin: University of Texas Press, 1962).

Thompson, Lawrence, *William Faulkner: An Introduction and Interpretation* (New York: Barnes and Noble, 1963).

Tuck, Dorothy, *A Handbook of Faulkner* (London: Chatto and Windus, 1965).

Vickery, Olga W., *The Novels of William Faulkner: A Critical Interpretation* (Baton Rouge: Louisiana State University Press, 1959, 1964).
Volpe, Edmond L., *A Reader's Guide to William Faulkner* (New York: Noonday, 1964).
Waggoner, Hyatt H., *William Faulkner: From Jefferson to the World* (Lexington: University of Kentucky Press, 1959).
Warren, Robert Penn (ed.) *Faulkner: A Collection of Critical Essays* (Englewood Cliffs, New Jersey: Prentice-Hall, 1966).
Woodworth, Stanley D., *William Faulkner en France (1931-1952)* (Paris: M. J. Minard, 1959 [Lettres Modernes]).

Articles

Brumm, Ursula, "Wilderness and Civilization: A Note on William Faulkner", *Partisan Review*, XXII (Summer, 1955), 340-350; reprinted in *Three Decades*, 125-134. On *Go Down, Moses*.
Cowley, Malcolm, "Introduction", *The Portable Faulkner*, (New York: Viking, 1946) 1-24; reprinted in *Three Decades*, 94-108.
Greet, Thomas Y., "The Theme and Structure of Faulkner's *The Hamlet*", *PMLA*, LXXII (September, 1957), 775-790; reprinted in *Three Decades*, 330-347.
Knoll, Robert E., "'The Unvanquished' for a Start", *College English*, XIX (May, 1958), 338-343.
Leaver, Florence, "Faulkner: The Word as Principle and Power", *South Atlantic Quarterly*, LVII (Autumn, 1958), 464-476; reprinted in *Three Decades*, 199-209.
—, "The Structure of 'The Hamlet': A Study in Meaning and Form", *Accent*, XV (Spring, 1955), 125-144.
Lisca, Peter, "'The Hamlet' Genesis and Revisions", *Faulkner Studies*, III (Spring, 1954), 5-13.
Lytle, Andrew, "The Son of Man: He Will Prevail", *Sewanee Review*, LXII (Winter, 1955), 114-137.
Mayoux, Jean-Jacques, "The Creation of the Real in William Faulkner", *Études anglaises*, (February, 1952) 25-39; translated and reprinted in *Three Decades*, 156-173.
O'Donnell, George Marion, "Faulkner's Mythology", *Kenyon Review*, I (Summer, 1939), 285-299.
Roth, Russell, "The Brennan Papers: Faulkner in Manuscript", *Perspective* (Summer, 1949), 219-224.
—, "William Faulkner: The Pattern of Pilgrimage", *Perspective*, II (Summer, 1949), 246-254.
Tick, Stanley, "The Unity of *Go Down, Moses*", *Twentieth Century Literature*, VIII (July, 1962), 67-73.
Warren, Robert Penn, "William Faulkner", *New Republic*, CXV (August 12, 1946), 176-180, continued (August 26, 1946), pp. 234-237; reprinted in *Three Decades*, 109-124. Original title: "Cowley's Faulkner".

Chapter V

PRIMARY

Anderson, Sherwood, *Winesburg, Ohio* (New York: B. W. Huebsch, 1919); reprints by Modern Library and Penguin: 1922, 1946 respectively; new edition: New York: Viking, 1960; English edition, London: Cape, 1922.
—, *The Triumph of the Egg* (New York: B. W. Huebsch, 1921).

—, *Horses and Men* (New York: B. W. Huebsch, 1923).
—, *A Story Teller's Story* (New York: B. W. Huebsch, 1924).
—, *The Modern Writer* (New York: Gelber, Lilienthal, 1925).
—, *Sherwood Anderson's Notebook* (New York: Boni and Liveright, 1926).
—, *Death in the Woods* (New York: Liveright, 1933).
—, *Plays: Winesburg and Others* (New York: Scribner's Sons, 1935).
—, *Sherwood Anderson's Memoirs* (New York: Harcourt, Brace, 1942).
—, *The Sherwood Anderson Reader* (New York: Houghton, Mifflin, 1947).
—, *The Portable Sherwood Anderson* (New York: Viking, 1949).
—, *Letters of Sherwood Anderson*, ed. Howard Mumford Jones with Walter B. Rideout (Boston: Little, Brown, 1953).

Bibliographies

Gozzi, Raymond Dante, "A Bibliography of Sherwood Anderson's Contributions to Periodicals, 1914-1946", *Newberry Library Bulletin*, Ser. 2, No. 2 (December, 1948), 71-82. This is a condensation of Gozzi's unpublished Master's thesis: "A Descriptive Bibliography of Sherwood Anderson's Contributions to Periodicals", Columbia University, 1947.
Sheehy, Eugene P., and Kenneth A. Lohf, *Sherwood Anderson: A Bibliography* (Los Gatos, California: Talisman, 1960).

SECONDARY

Books

Allen, Walter, *The Modern Novel in Britain and the United States* (New York: Dutton, 1964).
Asselineau, Roger, *Réalisme, rêve et expressionnisme dans "Winesburg, Ohio"*, No. 2 of *Archives de Lettres Modern* (avril, 1957) [Études de critique et d'histoire littéraire, Paris].
Boynton, Percy H., *Literature and American Life* (Boston: Ginn, 1936).
Burbank, Rex, *Sherwood Anderson* (New York: Twayne, 1964).
Calverton, V. F., *The Liberation of American Literature* (New York: Scribner's, 1932).
Chase, Cleveland B., *Sherwood Anderson* (New York: McBride, 1927).
"Configuration critique de Sherwood Anderson, Textes réunis et presentés par Roger Asselineau", *La Revue des lettres modernes* (1963), Nos. 78-80, 1-158; articles by Asselineau, John T. Flanagan, Robert M. Lovett, Caesare Parvese, William L. Phillips, Lionel Trilling, Charles C. Walcutt – in every case, a translation of previous article, except in the case of Asselineau's article.
Dahlberg, Edward, *Alms for Oblivion* (Minneapolis: University of Minnesota Press, 1964).
Fagin, Nathan Bryllion, *The Phenomenon of Sherwood Anderson* (Baltimore: Rossi-Bryn, 1927).
Gold, Michael, *The Hollow Men* (New York: International Publishers, 1941).
Hartwick, Harry, *The Foreground of American Fiction* (New York: American Book Company, 1934).
Hatcher, Harlan, *Creating the Modern American Novel* (New York: Farrar and Rinehart, 1935).
Hoffman, Frederick J., *Freudianism and the Literary Mind* (Baton Rouge: Louisiana State University Press, 1945).
Howe, Irving, *Sherwood Anderson* (New York: Sloane, 1951, 1962).
Kazin, Alfred, *On Native Grounds* (New York: Reynal and Hitchcock, 1942).

Lewisohn, Ludwig, *Expressionism in America* (New York: Harper and Bros., 1932).
Manly, John M., and Edith Rickert, *Contemporary American Literature* (New York: Harcourt, Brace, 1929).
McIntyre, Ralph E., "The Short Stories of Sherwood Anderson", unpublished Master's thesis (Columbia University, June 1949).
Michaud, Régis, *The American Novel Today* (Boston: Little, Brown, 1928).
Newman, Frances, *The Short Story's Mutations* (New York: Huebsch, 1925).
O'Brien, Edward J., *The Advance of the American Short Story* (New York: Dodd, Mead, 1923).
Pattee, Fred L., *The New American Literature, 1890-1930* (New York: Century, 1930).
Phillips, William Louis, "Sherwood Anderson's *Winesburg, Ohio:* Its Origins, Composition, Technique, and Reception", unpublished Ph. D. dissertation (University of Chicago, 1950); not available through University Microfilms, but only through the University of Chicago Library.
Quinn, Arthur H., *American Fiction* (New York: D. Appleton-Century, 1936).
Rosenfeld, Paul, *Port of New York* (New York: Harcourt, Brace, 1924).
Schevill, James, *Sherwood Anderson, His Life and Work* ([Denver]: University of Denver Press, 1951).
"Sherwood Anderson Memorial Number", *Newberry Library Bulletin*, Second Series, No. 2 (December, 1948); articles by Stanley Pargellis, George Daugherty, Waldo Frank, Roger Sergel, Norman Holmes Pearson, and Raymond Gozzi.
"Sherwood Anderson Number", *Shenandoah*, XIII (Spring, 1962); articles by Frederick J. Hoffman, Walter B. Rideout, James K. Feibleman, Jon S. Lawry and Cratis D. Williams.
"Sherwood Anderson, Homage to", *Story*, XIX (September-October, 1941); major articles by Waldo Frank, Lewis Galantiere, Julius W. Friend, William Saroyan, Harry Hansen and Paul Rosenfeld; shorter comments by Theodore Dreiser, Van Wyck Brooks, Gertrude Stein, Thomas Wolfe, Jesse Stuart, Ben Hecht and Manuel Komroff.
Stegner, Wallace (ed.), *The American Novel* (New York: Basic Books, 1965).
Thurston, Jarvis Aydelotte, "Sherwood Anderson: A Critical Study", unpublished Ph. D. dissertation (State University of Iowa, 1946); abstract in Iowa University, *Doctoral Dissertations and Abstract References*, VI (1942-1948), 474-475.
Trilling, Lionel, *The Liberal Imagination* (New York: Viking, 1950).
Van Doren, Carl, *The American Novel, 1789-1939* (New York: Macmillan, 1940).
—, *Contemporary American Novelists, 1900-1920* (New York: Macmillan, 1922).
Wagenknecht, Edward Charles, *Calvalcade of the American Novel* (New York: Holt, 1952).
Weber, Brom, *Sherwood Anderson* (Minneapolis: University of Minnesota Press, 1964).
Weltz, Friedrich, *Vier amerikanische Erzählungszyklen*: J. London: "Tales of the Fish Patrol", Sherwood Anderson: "Winesburg, Ohio", J. Steinbeck: "The Pastures of Heaven", E. Hemingway: "In Our Time", unpublished Ph. D. dissertation (Universität München, 1953); available through microfilm from the University of Munich's library, or through interlibrary loan from the Library of Congress.
Whipple, T. K., *Spokesman: Modern Writers and American Life* (New York: Appleton, 1928).
White, Ray L. (ed.) *The Achievement of Sherwood Anderson: Essays in Criticism* (Chapel Hill, North Carolina: University of North Carolina Press, 1966).

Articles

A. Reviews of *Winesburg, Ohio*. American.

[Anon.], "A Gutter Would Be Spoon River", *New York Sun*, June 1, 1919, 3.

[Anon.], "Winesburg, Ohio", *Dial*, LXVI (June 28, 1919), 666.
[Anon,], "Winesburg, Ohio", *Nation*, CVIII (June 28, 1919), 1017.
[M.A.], "A Country Town", *New Republic*, XIX (June 25, 1919), 257.
[W.S.B.], "Ohio Small Town Life", *Boston Evening Transcript* (June 11, 1919), 3.
Beffel, John N., "Small Towns and Broken Lives", *New York Call* (September 1, 1919), 10.
Boynton, H. W., "All Over the Lot", *Bookman*, XLIX (August, 1919), 728-733.
Crane, Hart, "Sherwood Anderson", *Pagan* (September, 1919), 60.
D[ell], F[loyd], "American Fiction", *Liberator*, II (September, 1919), 47.
Jones, Idweal, "Winesburg, Ohio", *San Francisco Chronicle*, (August 31, 1919).
Jones, Llewellyn, "The Unroofing of Winesburg", *Chicago Evening Post* (June 20, 1919), 9.
Mencken, H. L., "Anderson Great Novelist, Says Mencken", *Chicago American* (1919); undated clipping in Newberry Library Collection.
Rascoe, Burton, "Winesburg, Ohio", *Chicago Tribune* (June 7, 1919), 13.
Weaver, J. V. A., "Sherwood Anderson", *Chicago Daily News* (June 11, 1919), 12.

B. Reviews of *Winesburg, Ohio*. Foreign.

[Anon.] "Sherwood Anderson", *London Observer* (June 4, 1922).
[Anon.] "The Unequal Story-Teller", *Times Literary Supplement* (July 13, 1922).
[Anon.] "The Candid Critic", *London Evening Standard*, (July 26, 1922).
[Anon.] "Winesburg, Ohio", *Glasgow Herald* (August 6, 1922).
Lalou, René, "Winesburg, Ohio", *Europe*, XV (September 15, 1927), 114-116.
O'Sullivan, Vincent, "Precisions sur la littérature americaine", *Mercure de France*, CXXXVI (December 1, 1919), 535.

C. Articles on *Winesburg, Ohio*.

Berland, Alwyn, "Sherwood Anderson and the Pathetic Grotesque", *Western Review*, XV (Winter, 1951), 135-138.
Bishop, John Peal, "The Distrust of Ideas", in *The Collected Essays of John Peal Bishop* (New York: Scribner's, 1948), 233-240; originally in *Vanity Fair*, XX (December, 1921), 10-12.
Boyd, Ernest, "Introduction" to *Winesburg, Ohio: A Group of Tales of Ohio Small-Town Life* (New York: Modern Library [1922]).
Budd, Louis J., "The Grotesques of Anderson and Wolfe", *Modern Fiction Studies*, V (Winter, 1959-1960), 304-310.
Cestre, C., "A Story Teller's Story", *Revue angloamericaine*, III (October, 1925), 175.
Ciancio, Ralph Armando, "The Grotesque in Modern American Fiction: An Existential Theory", *Dissertation Abstracts*, XXVI (July, 1965), 365-366.
Cowley, Malcolm, "Anderson's Lost Days of Innocence", *New Republic*, CXLII (February 15, 1960), 16-18.
—, "Introduction", to *Winesburg, Ohio* (New York: Viking, 1960), 1-15.
Crane, Hart, "Sherwood Anderson", *Double Dealer*, II (July, 1921), 42-45.
Crawford, Nelson A., "Sherwood Anderson, the Wistfully Faithful", *Midland*, VIII (November, 1922), 297-308.
Daugherty, George H., "Anderson, Advertising Man", *Newberry Library Bulletin*, Second Series, No. 2 (December, 1948), 30-38.
Fadiman, Clifton, "Sherwood Anderson: the Search for Salvation", *Nation*, CXXXV (November 9, 1932), 454-456.
Fagin, Nathan B., "Sherwood Anderson: The Liberator of Our Short Story", *English Journal*, XVI (April, 1927), 271-279.

Ferres, John H., "The Right Place and the Right People: Sherwood Anderson's Search for Salvation", *Dissertation Abstracts*, XIX (1959), 3302-3303.

Fitzgerald, F. Scott, "Echoes of the Jazz Age", *Scribner's* XC (November 1931), 461.

Frank, Waldo, "Sherwood Anderson: A Personal Note", *Newberry Library Bulletin*, Second Series, No. 2 (December, 1948), 39-43.

—, "*Winesburg, Ohio* After Twenty Years", *Story*, XIX (September-October, 1941), 29-33.

[Fredenthal, David], "Winesburg, Ohio", *Life*, XX (June 10, 1946), 74-79.

Fussell, Edwin, "*Winesburg, Ohio*: Art and Isolation", *Modern Fiction Studies*, VI (Summer, 1960), 106-114.

Geismar, Maxwell David, "Anderson's *Winesburg*", *New York Times Book Review* (July 18, 1943), 4.

Gochberg, Donald, "Stagnation and Growth: The Emergence of George Willard", *Expression* (University of Maryland), IV (1960), 29-35.

Gold, Herbert, "The Purity and Cunning of Sherwood Anderson", *Hudson Review*, X (Winter, 1957-1958), 548-557; reprinted in Charles Shapiro (ed.), *Twelve Original Essays on Great American Novels* (Detroit: Wayne State University Press, 1958), 196-209.

Gregory, Alyse, "Sherwood Anderson", *Dial*, LXXV (September, 1923), 243-246.

Gregory, Horace, "Introduction" to *The Portable Sherwood Anderson* (New York: Viking, 1949), 1-31.

Hartwick, Harry, "Broken Face Gargoyles", in his *The Foreground of American Fiction* (New York: American Book, 1934), 111-150.

Hoffman, Frederick J., "The Voices of Sherwood Anderson", *Shenandoah*, XIII (Spring, 1962), 5-19.

Howe, Irving, "The Book of the Grotesque", *Partisan Review*, XVIII (January-February, 1951), 32-40; reprinted in his *Sherwood Anderson* (New York: Sloane, 1951, 1962).

—, "Sherwood Anderson, *Winesburg, Ohio*", in Wallace Stegner (ed.) *The American Novel from James Fenimore Cooper to William Faulkner* (New York: Basic Books, 1965), 154-165; reprint of the above.

Jones, Howard Mumford, "Introduction" to *Letters of Sherwood Anderson*, ed. Jones and Walter B. Rideout (Boston: Little, Brown, 1953), vii-xxii.

Kazin, Alfred, "The New Realism – Sherwood Anderson and Sinclair Lewis", in his *On Native Grounds: An Interpretation of Modern American Prose Literature* (New York: Reynal and Hitchcok, 1942) 205-226.

Kintner, Evelyn, "Sherwood Anderson: Small Town Man", unpublished Master's thesis (Bowling Green State University, 1942).

Laughlin, Rosemary M., "'Godliness' and the American Dream in *Winesburg, Ohio*", *Twentieth-Century Literature*, XIII (1967), 97-103.

Love, Glen Allen, "Sherwood Anderson's American Pastoral", *Dissertation Abstracts*, XXV (1965), 7247.

Lovett, Robert Morss, "The Promise of Sherwood Anderson", *Dial*, LXXII (January, 1921), 79-83.

—, "Sherwood Anderson", *New Republic*, LXXXIX (November 25, 1936), 103-105.

Macy, John, "The Short Story", *Saturday Review of Literature*, IV (January 14, 1928), 517.

Mahoney, John J., "An Analysis of *Winesburg, Ohio*", *Journal of Aesthetics and Art Criticism*, XV (December, 1956), 246-252.

Maresca, Carol J., "Gestures and Meaning in Sherwood Anderson's *Winesburg, Ohio*", *College Language Association Journal*, IX (1966), 279-283.

McCole, Camille, "Sherwood Anderson – Congenital Freudian", *Catholic World*, CXXX (November, 1929), 129-133.

Moore, Paul Elmer, "The Modern Current in American Literature", *Forum*, LXXIX (January, 1928), 127-136.

Morris, Lawrence S., "Sherwood Anderson: Sick of Words", *New Republic*, LI (August 3, 1927), 277-279.

Murphy, George D., "The Theme of Sublimation in Sherwood Anderson's *Winesburg, Ohio*", Modern Fiction Studies, XIII (1967), 237-246.

Pearson, Norman Holmes, "Anderson and the New Puritanism", *Newberry Library Bulletin*, Second Series, No. 2 (December, 1948), 52-63.

Phillips, William Louis, "The First Printing of Sherwood Anderson's *Winesburg, Ohio*", *Studies in Bibliography*, IV (1951-1952), 211-213.

—, "How Sherwood Anderson Wrote *Winesburg, Ohio*", *American Literature*, XXIII (March, 1951), 7-30.

Picht, Douglas R. "Anderson's Use of Tactile Imagery in *Winesburg, Ohio*", *Research Studies*, XXXV (1967), 176-178.

Rosenfeld, Paul, "Introduction" to *The Sherwood Anderson Reader* (New York: Houghton, Mifflin, 1947), i-xxx.

Rideout, Walter B., "The Simplicity of *Winesburg, Ohio*", Shenandoah, XIII (Spring, 1962), 20-31.

San Juan, Epifanio, Jr., "Vision and Reality: A Reconsideration of Sherwood Anderson's *Winesburg, Ohio*", *American Literature*, XXXV (1963), 137-155.

Sergel, Roger, "The Man and the Memory", *Newberry Library Bulletin*, Second Series, No. 2 (December, 1948), 44-51.

Smith, Rachel, "Sherwood Anderson: Some Entirely Arbitrary Reactions", *Sewanee Review* (April, 1929), 159-163.

Sullivan, John H., "Winesburg Revisited", *Antioch Review*, XX (Summer, 1960), 213-221.

Tanselle, G. Thomas, "Additional Reviews of Sherwood Anderson's Work", *Papers of the Bibliographical Society of America*, LVI (1962), 358-365.

Thurston, Jarvis Aydelotte, "Anderson and 'Winesburg': Mysticism and Craft", *Accent*, XVI (Spring, 1956), 107-128.

Trilling, Lionel, "Sherwood Anderson", *Kenyon Review*, III (Summer, 1941), 293-302; reprinted with revisions in *The Liberal Imagination*. New York: Viking, 1950.

Wagenknecht, Edward Charles, "Sherwood Anderson: the 'cri de coeur' as Novel", in his *Cavalcade of the American Novel* (New York: Holt, 1952), 311-318.

Walcutt, Charles C., "Sherwood Anderson: Impressionism and the Buried Life", *Sewanee Review*, LX (Winter, 1952), 28-47.

Weber, Brom, "Anderson and 'the Essence of Things'", *Sewanee Review*, LIX (Autumn, 1951), 678-692.

Whipple, Thomas King, "Sherwood Anderson", in his *Spokesman* (New York: Appleton, 1928), 115-138.

Winther, S. K., "The Aura of Loneliness in Sherwood Anderson", *Modern Fiction Studies*, V (Summer, 1959), 145-152.

INDEX

DE PROPRIETATIBUS LITTERARUM

edited by

C. H. VAN SCHOONEVELD

Series Maior

1. Marcus B. Hester, *The Meaning of Poetic Metaphor: An Analysis in the Light of Wittgenstein's Claim that Meaning is Use*. 1967
2. Rodney Delasanta, *The Epic Voice*. 1967.
3. Bennison Gray, *Style: The Problem and its Solution*. 1969.
5. Raimund Belgardt, *Romantische Poesie: Begriff und Bedeutung bei Friedrich Schlegel*. 1970.
7. Theodore B. Wood, *The Word 'Sublime' and its Context*. 1971.
8. Ewa M. Thompson, *Russian Formalism and Anglo-American New Criticism: A Comparative Study*. 1971.
9. David G. Hale, *The Body Politic*. 1971.
10. Ernest A. Gallo, *The "Poetria Nova" and its Sources in Early Rhetorical Doctrine*. 1971.
11. David M. Miller, *The Net of Hephaestus: A Study of Modern Criticism and Metaphysical Metaphor*. 1971.
12. William W. Ryding, *Structural Patterns in Medieval Narrative*. 1971.
14. Burton Raffel, *The Forked Tongue: A Study of the Translation Process*. 1971.
15. Paul M. Levitt, *A Structural Approach to the Analysis of Drama*. 1971.
17. John T. Braun, *The Apostrophic Gesture*. 1971.
19. Forrest L. Ingram, *Representative Short Story Cycles of the Twentieth Century: Studies in a Literary Genre*. 1971.
20. Frances K. Barasch, *The Grotesque: A Study in Meanings*. 1971.
22. James W. Nichols, *Insinuation: The Tactics of English Satire*. 1971.

MOUTON · PUBLISHERS · THE HAGUE